RULES FOR REACTIONARIES

RULES FOR REACTIONARIES

HOW TO MAINTAIN INEQUALITY AND STOP SOCIAL JUSTICE

LEE BEBOUT

NEW YORK UNIVERSITY PRESS New York

NEW YORK UNIVERSITY PRESS
New York
www.nyupress.org

© 2025 by New York University
All rights reserved

Please contact the Library of Congress for Cataloging-in-Publication data.

ISBN: 9781479829545 (hardback)
ISBN: 9781479829514 (paperback)
ISBN: 9781479829538 (library ebook)
ISBN: 9781479829521 (consumer ebook)

This book is printed on acid-free paper, and its binding materials are chosen for strength and durability. We strive to use environmentally responsible suppliers and materials to the greatest extent possible in publishing our books.

The manufacturer's authorized representative in the EU for product safety is Mare Nostrum Group B.V., Mauritskade 21D, 1091 GC Amsterdam, The Netherlands.
Email: gpsr@mare-nostrum.co.uk.

Manufactured in the United States of America

10 9 8 7 6 5 4 3 2 1

Also available as an ebook

To the reactionaries of all parties.

For Jayden Michael Bebout-Vega

We actively struggle for a
more just world because the other
alternatives are simply not acceptable.

Preface: Outside Agitators and the Office Door **xi**

Introduction: The Underside of Our National Conversations on Race, Gender, and Justice **1**

RULE #1: Define and Disavow **29**

RULE #2: Weaponize Victimhood **58**

RULE #3: Build Reactionary Utopias **87**

RULE #4: Label Your Opponents Extreme (so that You Can Appear Reasonable) **115**

RULE #5: Misdirect by Blaming a Convenient Cause **144**

Conclusion: On Faith in Dialogue: Cruel Optimism, World-Making, and Reimagining Conversation **173**

Coda **201**

Acknowledgments **205**

Notes **209**

Bibliography **239**

Index **259**

About the Author **265**

PREFACE

Outside Agitators and the Office Door

Language is commitment. —Drew Lopenzina

In late spring 2024, student activists established encampments at universities across the United States and other countries. After attacks by Hamas seven months prior, Israel had invaded and bombed population centers in Gaza, killing tens of thousands of civilians, displacing nearly two million Palestinians, and decimating the critical infrastructure of hospitals, schools, and roads. Following years of advocating for their universities to disclose investments in and divest from companies tied to the state of Israel, students set up tents on campus commons and occasionally overtook buildings like student activists of years past. They dubbed these encampments "People's Universities" and hosted teach-ins, seder meals, and other communal activities to build solidarity and press their cause. In response, many university administrations called in campus, local, and state police to disband the encampments and arrest the protestors. At various institutions, police forces beat, tear-gassed, shot with rubber bullets, tased, and assaulted in other ways students, faculty, and community members.

These university escalations and their popular support were made possible by a set of rhetorical choices that cast student protestors as illegitimate. University administrators and spokespeople, police departments, and local and national political figures claimed that the protests were the work of "outside agitators," argued that the protests were violent and disruptive, and asserted that protestors were extremists who must be punished for breaking the law. Mainstream news sources quickly adopted and amplified this framing, and it spread through social media. Students protesting the killing of Palestinian civilians and the wholesale destruction of Gaza were rendered illegitimate and dangerous.

Of course, casting those who advocate for social justice as violent, disruptive, extremist, and law-breaking outside agitators is nothing new. Rather it embodies a coalescence of tried-and-true reactionary rhetorical strategies. For example, during the Civil Rights movement, segregationists deployed this framing against activists who sought to end Jim Crow practices. In his "Letter from a Birmingham Jail," Martin Luther King Jr. addressed many of these claims directly. When called outside agitators, King noted, he and others were invited in by the local community members. He argued that the violence was not at the hands of the protestors, but rather their committed nonviolence exposed the violence of the system needed to keep white supremacy in place. To the charge of extremism, he advocated the necessity and tradition of extremism for justice. Responding to claims that Civil Rights activists broke laws, he pointed to a higher form of justice and identified just and unjust laws.

Looking back sixty years, few would dispute King's forceful refutation. Today, a broad-reaching popular consensus has emerged that has sanitized and sanctified the memory of King and the Civil Rights movement. Yet like an eternal return, the rhetorical strategies deployed against social transformation efforts of the past exist and thrive today. Why is it that these and other reactionary rhetorical strategies continue to work to obstruct social change? Is it simply because they are effective or because we truly do not learn from the past? Yes and yes. But at the heart of *Rules for Reactionaries* is another, more powerful answer.

My friend and former colleague Drew Lopenzina has a small sign on his office door. It reads: "Language is commitment." It's a simple sign, really a thin strip of white paper with small black lettering. I remember when we worked together at Sam Houston State University and our offices were in the same short hallway. I would read that sign and wonder what he meant by it. One day I asked. Drew explained the phrase encapsulated the idea that "the language we use, whether we are conscious of it or not, is a reflection of our thought and the concepts to which we have committed ourselves, whether passively or through deliberate agency."[1] In other words, at one level, when used with care and consideration, language is a critical tool for forwarding the values we wish to uphold in the world. Whether one demands "disclosure and divestment" from Israel's war on Palestine, pauses before uttering the correct pronoun or name of someone they are speaking to or about, or takes the time to ask sincere questions of their conversation partners, each of these examples and countless others illustrate ways that we commit to our values through language.

Yet we do not always use language with care and consideration. Sometimes—and more often than not—we adopt the language we hear, uncritically accepting commitments to the status quo and injustice. While politicians, campus administrators, and police agencies may have tarred antiwar, antigenocide encampments as the work of "outside agitators" to delegitimize the protests, as the narrative spread through news and social media and beyond, those who accepted and repeated the "outside agitators" claim committed themselves to the values of the status quo and injustice. Would so many support violent arrest of "community members," a term that may be easily applied to nonstudent protestors?

Because language is commitment, the uncritical embrace of language leads to a seeming eternal return. We find ourselves unable to escape the discursive ruts and patterns of injustice, incapable of striking out in new directions. We read the news or listen to the radio, we talk to loved ones or strangers, we hear from politicians and celebrities, and through many of these exchanges, we encounter similar conversations to those we have faced before. Ultimately, however, if we are to commit to building a better world, we must be aware of the language that has fashioned the world as it is.

INTRODUCTION

The Underside of Our National Conversations on Race, Gender, and Justice

In early June 2020, protests roiled the United States, sparked by the murder of George Floyd by a Minneapolis police officer who knelt on the Black man's neck for nine minutes and twenty-nine seconds. Protestors marched in the country's largest cities but also in suburban, exurban, and, occasionally, more rural locations. While driving one day, I heard a radio host explaining that this time felt different, after the killing of Floyd on video for all the world to see and the protests that followed. It seemed, he thought, that real police reform and meaningful confrontation with white supremacy could happen—America would finally have its national conversation on race and we would build a better world. Hearing this, I tried to be hopeful. I had heard this optimism from well-intentioned white people before: when Barack Obama invited Henry Louis Gates Jr. and Sgt. James Crowely to the White House for a "Beer Summit," after the acquittal of George Zimmerman for killing Trayvon Martin and the protests of the killing of Mike Brown in St. Louis, and when self-proclaimed white nationalists marched on Charlottesville, Virginia. After each of these flashpoints and so many others, the hope for a national conversation on race and the social transformation it would surely bring about always fell from the mind of politicians, the news media, and white America. The national conversation on race is a "cruel optimism," always a "dream deferred."[1]

For many, the idea of a "national conversation on race"—one that will heal America's wounds—is heavily associated with President Bill Clinton. But the origins of this call for a healing conversation are more complex. In June 1993, President Clinton withdrew his nomination of Lani Guinier for assistant attorney general for Civil Rights. When he nominated her barely one month prior, conservative politicians and pundits almost immediately attacked the legal scholar whose writings had shaped the discourse surrounding democracy and racial justice. Ronald Regan–era Justice Department official Clint Bolick evoked the "welfare queen" trope when he dubbed Guinier the "quota queen," a label that stuck.[2] George Will charged that Guinier believed that only other Black people could legitimately represent the interests of Black citizens and claimed that she was an extremist, a racially polarizing figure aiming to dilute democracy in order to promote "progressive" social outcomes.[3] The resistance to Guinier was so swift and vociferous and Clinton's resolve so weak that he withdrew the nomination before Guinier was able to have a confirmation hearing and defend her work on racial justice.

In July 1993, Guinier emerged strong from the ordeal and with a powerful vision, she called for a "national conversation on race."[4] She recognized that her scuttled nomination and the nonproductive tension surrounding flashpoints of race and inequality could not lead to racial justice if Americans could not engage one another in open and honest conversation.[5]

Three years after withdrawing Guinier's nomination, on June 13, 1997, Clinton took up Guinier's call for a national conversation on race and, like other presidents before him, established a President's Advisory Board on Race.[6] Indeed, today, when racial flashpoints erupt and politicians and pundits call for a national conversation on race or ask if now is the time that the United States will finally have a national conversation on race, they often allude to or explicitly credit Clinton with initiating this call in 1997.

Clinton's call for a national conversation on race must be contextualized through the contemporaneous racial flashpoints of the 1990s and the racial impact of centrist policies. With the end of the Cold War, US domestic strife was more readily apparent in the national media. Prior to Clinton's election, the Rodney King beating and the subsequent LA uprisings captured the national imagination. In 1994, Clinton signed the centrist-oriented crime bill. During 1995, the O. J. Simpson murder trial and Louis Farrakhan's Million Man March coupled with reports that shifting demographics would reduce or even replace the white majority stoked white racial anxieties. The next year, Clinton signed the welfare reform act that, along with his previous crime bill, was rooted in anti-Black discourse and would have a racially disparate impact for years to come. In June 1997, Clinton's call for a national conversation on race seemed to be an answer to these flashpoints and tensions. The purpose of the panel was to create a study that would be the foundation for presidential and legislative action. Healing America's racial divide would be the hallmark of the Clinton presidency.

Clinton's Advisory Board on Race was chaired by eminent historian of Black life John Hope Franklin and included members with experience in politics, policy advising, business, and community relations. In its year and few months of existence, the committee fostered "dialogues on race ... in thirty-nine states and eighty-nine cities, attracting some seventeen thousand participants.... Clinton backed his 'Initiative on Race' with three televised presidential assemblies and dispatched administration officials to speak at hundreds of gatherings nationwide."[7] As its culminating act, the committee submitted its report, "One America in the 21st Century," along with ancillary materials that could be used to develop cross-racial dialogue. Notably, the report's analysis of the United States' racial dynamics and the recommendation of building cross-racial dialogue were mild, reformist, and in no way aligned with radical racial politics of the time or today.[8]

Unsurprisingly, throughout its existence, the committee endured sustained attack. Conservatives complained that John Hope Franklin and other members were not qualified to lead a national conversation on race.[9] Others complained that conservative voices, like Ward Connerly, an outspoken critic of affirmative action, were not included on the committee.[10] News media reported turmoil and a lack of progress within the committee.[11] Indigenous activists expressed concern that the panel lacked Indigenous representation.[12] In the end, while the report recommended specific, concrete actions that the US political leadership could take, the report languished. Preoccupied by the Monica Lewinski scandal as well as an impeachment inquiry and proceedings, Clinton failed to act on what could have been the foundational document of his presidential legacy. Indeed, in his autobiography, Clinton only gave sparse, passing references to the committee.[13] In essence, his call for a national conversation on race and the committee's guidance for how such conversations should take place died on the vine.

Since the withering away of Clinton's announcement of careful study and bold action, calls for a national conversation on race have recurred quite often across the political and media landscape. When a flashpoint arises, declarations of dialogue and hope for change soon follow. In truth, however, these calls for a transformative national conversation on race are too narrowly framed, limited by their own utopian imaginings, calling forth the promise of absolving us of our national sin in exchange for the right words. However, while Clinton called for a national conversation led by his advisory board, a more organic conversation thrived outside of and responding to the committee's work. For example, Charles Krauthammer noted that a national conversation on race was already in existence: "It is nonsense . . . to think that America suffers from a dearth of conversation about race. We can't stop talking about race. Prop. 209, O.J. Piscataway, the gerrymandering cases. . . . Is there an issue under the American sun that has not been given a racial cast?"[14] For Krauthammer and others, the national conversation did not begin with how to heal wounds of injustice but with other questions: Should we continue to address race? And might race-neutral policies focused on individual merit be more in line with American and Enlightenment ideals? In essence, their conversation on race focused less on questions of race and justice and more on whether a conversation on race should be had at all.

While I disagree vehemently with the notions that we should stop addressing race and adopt purely race-neutral strategies, this broader reframing of the national conversation on race is critical because it illustrates that some of the active participants in the conversation embraced a posture of what I term *reactionary entrenchment*, a position from which one seeks to obstruct social justice efforts and works to maintain a status quo of inequality. This type of entrenchment is not limited to reactions to the One America initiative. Rather than prescribing a national conversation on race, I am describing a discordant conversation that has long been ongoing. For example, when Guinier advocated a national conversation, there was already a conversation on race, one which deemed the conversation unnecessary and declared her a "quota queen." Indeed, long before and well after Clinton's executive order creating his advisory committee, US racial discourse has been shaped not just by those seeking justice but also those seeking the cessation or derailment of meaningful dialogue. To be fair, this entrenchment may not be the intent behind these interlocutors, but, as this book seeks to explore, it is certainly the impact.

Although we may hear utopian calls for a national conversation on race arise in response to contemporary flashpoints and tensions, it is necessary to recognize that there has been a national conversation on race going on for centuries. When focused on racial liberation and justice, this conversation has been led often but not exclusively by people of color. Frederick Douglass, William Apess, Sojourner Truth, Ida B. Wells, W. E. B. DuBois, James Baldwin, Vine Deloria, and others have been openly engaged in conversation, identifying the US racial pathology of white supremacy and seeking to root it out. Despite the breadth and acumen of this ongoing dialogue, it has not taken the shape of Guinier's—then Clinton's—longed-for, transformative, and utopian national conversation on race. Why? Because those invested in whiteness and the contemporary racial status quo have long actively worked to disrupt conversations on racial justice. That is, white supremacy, in its extreme and everyday manifestations, has shaped an underside to the United States' national conversation on race, an underside that is often ignored as part of the racial dialogue but that has tremendous power in shaping the country's racial dynamics.

There is a growing body of impactful scholarship exploring how meaningful communication about racism can be accomplished. *Rules for Reactionaries* turns its attention to another type of discourse, the rhetorical maneuvers deployed to forestall meaningful conversation and change. Here I assert that the longed-for, idealized national conversation on race has yet to come not simply because of media inattention, although that is surely part of the social equation. Rather, meaningful dialogue and social transformation have been hindered by common rhetorical practices that obscure and deflect from engaging racial and other forms of injustice.

The Other Intersectionality

Of course, the national conversation on race is but one—although central—long-enduring and often-derailed discourse surrounding justice, equity, and social transformation in the United States. The national conversation on race as an outgrowth and expression of racial justice struggles can be placed beside and against often less formally labeled national conversations on gender equality, LBGTQ rights, and other critical issues. Although these struggles have not been approached the same way in public discourse, they have all occupied central positioning in the US political, cultural, and social imagination for sporadic yet sustained stretches of time. However, they are often not framed as "national conversations." Moreover, because these justice struggles are adjacent and often intersect, they regularly draw on common rhetorical strategies. Likewise, the oppositional forces that seek to squelch these efforts deploy common discursive maneuvers to derail the conversation and efface the struggle for change.

Consider and pair the social media emergent hashtags-cum-social movements #BlackLivesMatter and #MeToo. #BlackLivesMatter emerged in 2013 as a response to the acquittal of George Zimmerman for the killing of Trayvon Martin. While #MeToo was initially coined by Tarana Burke in 2006, the phrase rose to prominence in 2017 when media attention turned to the sexual assault allegations against Harvey Weinstein and other well-known public figures. Both "Black Lives Matter" and "#MeToo" are part of longer historical struggles, and both seek to publicly identify a problem of inequality: one contends that Black lives have been treated without value and dignity resulting in disproportionate state-sanctioned violence, and the other underscores how sexual harassment and assault of women is pervasive. These phrases marshal attention to the everyday nature of systems of oppression—they name the often-unnamed and seek to imagine and mobilize community through articulation.

Unsurprisingly both slogans-turned-movements were countered with negating discursive maneuvers. "All Lives Matter" and "#NotAllMen" were political, rhetorical rejoinders used to quell calls for social transformation. These phrases did not exist in the US popular and political lexicon until "Black Lives Matter" and "#MeToo" did. "All Lives Matter" and "#NotAllMen" arose as responses only, nullifications of cries for justice. These slogans of reactionary entrenchment did not call into being a better world but rather sought to halt a new world from emerging.

This book is concerned with how justice struggles and their attendant "conversations" are actively restrained by a rhetoric of entrenchment. In order to expose these reactionary rhetorical maneuvers, we must recognize the adjacent and intersecting relationships between these "conversations." Although talking about race is not the same as discussing sex, gender, sexual orientation, or other social factors—and vice versa—there are critical commonalities that allow for discursive alignments to arise in reactionary movements. I opened this book with race because since the 1990s, it has been explicitly framed as a "national conversation," while other movements' status as national conversations have been largely implicit. But I am interested in *both* how various justice struggles may share a common repertoire *and* how those who oppose the efforts may too share strategies of entrenchment. Arguably this is rooted in the shared historical coalescence of these efforts.

During the mid- to late twentieth century, the United States and the world experienced what Howard Winant has described as "the racial break."[15] Antiracist, antifascist, and anticolonial struggles produced a dramatic rupture in the global order of white supremacy. Governments and other institutions shifted from explicitly supporting racial hierarchy to openly affirming diversity and equality. This does not mean that white supremacy ended. Rather, these institutions, in order to maintain their hegemonic standing, adopted and modified the aims of aggrieved communities as a means of maintaining a new status quo of racial inequality.[16] Critically, however, Winant's racial break provides a model for understanding justice struggles more broadly.

While antiracist, antifascist, and anticolonial efforts transformed the global racial terrain, other freedom struggles forged their own realignments. Women gained greater access to higher education and the workforce. LBGTQ folk achieved legal protections and greater social and cultural acceptance. These efforts happened within and apart from the struggle against white supremacy. And as with the racial break, the institutions that relied on broad structures of inequality did not simply give way. Rather, they realigned, adopting some strategies activists advocated, allowing patriarchy and heterosexism and other systemic inequalities to maintain a less explicit standing in this "reorder of things."[17]

The racial break provides a model for thinking of the realignment of white supremacy, patriarchy, and heterosexism. Gene Wise describes shifts in intellectual history as earthquakes wherein the tectonic plates shift, find new alignment, and pressure builds anew.[18] Winant's concept of the racial break dovetails with this earthquake metaphor. In the mid- to late twentieth century, the United States and large portions of the world saw a *multifocal* rupture and global realignment of white supremacy, patriarchy, and heterosexism wherein these systems of power were maintained by incorporating select social justice reforms.[19] As these freedom struggles coalesced through the twentieth and early twenty-first centuries, so too did efforts to retain the old world. Conceptualizing this cultural, social, and political realignment along the axes of race, sex, and sexual orientation allows us to recognize why the discursive strategies deployed against one aggrieved community may be similar to those wielded against others. For example, not only do "All Lives Matter" and "#NotAllMen" emerge as nullifying rejoinders to calls of social transformation, but white people and men may claim that they have been victimized by programs to address the inequalities faced by people of color and women. Troping on the foundational work of Kimberlé Crenshaw in naming intersecting systems of power, these discursive moments embody another form of intersectionality where white supremacy, patriarchy, and heterosexism draw on and reinforce one another, wherein power and those invested in it seek to cede little and resist a transforming world through a shared set of rhetorical strategies.[20]

Drawing on Winant's and Wise's imaginings of tectonic realignment, I imagine white supremacy and other systems of oppression as a vast, sprawling, ideological terrain—mapped topographically—that gives shape to individual acts, state policies, symbolic representations, and other forms of inequality.[21] This terrain of inequality stretches beyond a linear spectrum and continuously unfolds beyond the "horizon of expectations" awaiting future discovery.[22] Reimagining white supremacy and other systems of inequality through the metaphor of terrain requires a recognition that varied forms of inequality are all parts of a larger whole. That is, engaging in entertaining and soothing fantasies of racial or gendered violence may be quite different from discriminatory housing policies or healthcare access. However, they arise like mountains and prairies out of a shared land mass. Discourse, the language we use, forges the routes that connect diverse coordinates of this ideological terrain. Some language strategies, like those I try to highlight in this book, are more used than others. For those committed to social justice, these well-worn discursive routes and their ability to connect and maintain a terrain of inequality need to be acknowledged and mapped.

Treating systems of inequality as a discursive, ideological terrain allows us to not rigidly categorize and map people into fixed identity coordinates. Rather, like Earth, the terrain in which we all live, everyone inhabits systems of injustice. Some folks clearly have more power to alter and find comfort in this terrain, but we are all inhabitants and shaped by these systems of power, moving along, occupying varied coordinates, navigating others, and falling into the ruts of our repeated over and over again routes.

For me, "reactionary" is not as a fixed, stable political category; rather, "reactionary" names those invested in systems of inequality, those who fall prey to the impulses and tendencies to hold onto the status quo (ante).[23] As such, I use "reactionary" to name the efforts to retain the old hierarchies or maintain inequality in new systems. "Reactionary" is useful in the way it names the discrete and overlapping projects of inequality. For scholars, "reactionary" is often used in opposition to "progressive" in the way that "conservative" is used in contrast to "liberal." For example, Albert Hirschman's *The Rhetoric of Reaction*, sets up a bipolar system wherein the history of Western democracy and political economy are shaped by the shifting tensions between progressive and reactionary forces.[24] I do not use "reactionary" in this way. Rather, I contend that the reactionary rhetoric Hirschman located in right-oriented thought can also be found in the work of liberals. Drawing on Richard Shorten, I recognize that reactionism may comprise "a seam that runs right through the right's history, and down into the present."[25] However, there is danger in conflating reactionary politics and the right, for doing so obscures how disparate political projects, including progressive ones, may fall prey to or embrace reactionary tendencies.[26] Thus, my use of "reactionary" both recognizes its place within the right *and* acknowledges that these practices exist throughout the political landscape.

In part, my use of "reactionary" stems from studying these rhetorical strategies after the aforementioned multifocal rupture and global realignment of systemic inequality. Just as W. E. B. DuBois suggested that whiteness paid public (i.e., social) and psychological wages, so too do other systems of inequality like heteropatriarchy and Christian nationalism.[27] It should go without saying that men, straight folk, and Christians have long experienced sociopolitical privilege in the United States. However, despite the maintenance of systemic inequality, many people across the political landscape may feel that they have lost their social and psychological wages. When I deploy "reactionary," I am not simply trying to signal a conservative thread throughout history. Rather, I am naming the multifocal *reaction* to a shifting yet still unequal society and the loss of social and psychological wages to those still invested in these systems.[28]

Why Study Reactionary Entrenchment?

Reactionism must be understood as a long-enduring, broad-reaching social force in the United States.[29] Often we recognize reactionary efforts when they break the assumed tranquility at the surface of our social and political lives. In these ruptures, reactionism is confused with extremism. Consider two recent examples. In 2017 a crowd of khaki- and polo-shirt-clad white nationalists gathered with tiki torches on the campus of a major US university and chanted "Jews will not replace us." In 2022, the US Supreme Court overturned nearly fifty years of legal precedent to deny women the right to bodily autonomy and allowing states to render abortion—at any time and without exception—illegal. In these cases and others, many responded with shock, and often with horror. But these moments did not arise out of nowhere. Responses of surprise, however, indicate that too often we confuse reactionism with extremism. We would do well to remember, though, that even when water appears calm at the surface, it does not reveal what is happening below.

Reactionary impulses and commitments exist in everyday and extreme manifestations. Language carries and imparts ideology. Therefore, studying reactionary rhetoric allows us to map how both the mainstream and extreme deploy specific maneuvers to obstruct social transformation and maintain inequality. One does not need to join an organization of white supremacists in order to vote for those who will protect Jim Crow–era monuments to the Confederacy—they only need to feel that the possibility of a more just, multiracial society threatens their place in the world. One does not need to seek a *Handmaid's Tale* future in order to privilege the potential life of a fetus over the bodily autonomy of women—they simply need to believe that life begins at conception and that abortion victimizes the unborn. In these instances, a shared discursive repertoire forges an alignment between the extreme and the mainstream. In these cases, reactionism mobilizes through a logic of weaponized victimhood wherein whiteness or the unborn are targeted and must be protected. Ultimately, turning attention directly to reactionary rhetorical strategies allows us to understand these efforts not as discrete undertakings and isolated incidents but as the powerful social force they are.

Moreover, this shared discursive repertoire does not simply unite the extreme and the mainstream. It also fosters coalition between potentially divergent reactionary causes and communities. Sometimes it is difficult to remember, but the constituent ideologies of reactionism—white supremacy, antifeminism, heterosexism, Christian nationalism, and extractive capitalism, to name a few—are not bounded together through some metaphysical connection across space and time. They emerge from and propel movements of retaliation between entities whose interests may not otherwise overlap. What allows these efforts to establish solidarity and mobilize coalitions? I contend that shared rhetorical strategies facilitate coalescence by making diverse concerns legible, uniting reactionary forces into a stronger obstructive front. As I explore in later chapters, Christian nationalism, white supremacy, and men's rights antifeminism may each point to different problems in the United States today (i.e., secular humanism, diversity, and feminism, respectively); they all imagine a utopian future through the recuperation of a static, mythic past and position themselves as aggrieved victims of the contemporary social order. Although any one of these reactionary movements may have limited political power, particularly at the national level, when they mobilize together because their shared discursive repertoire makes them legible across difference *and* unites the mainstream and the extreme factions, they are forces of entrenchment to be reckoned with.

These reactionary rhetorical strategies are not simply efforts to defeat "the left" through engagement and deliberation. Rather they also function to solidify and mobilize identities invested in the status quo (ante). Consider, for example those who see themselves as centrist or even left leaning who also believe that racism, sexism, and other systemic inequalities are aberrant because they do not see how these systems impact them. Or consider those who feel that white men are at a distinct disadvantage in today's society. While significant bodies of scholarship challenge these perspectives, reactionary rhetorical strategies can recruit people into mobilizing against their professed beliefs in antiracism, feminism, or other commitments to social transformation.

On the Limits of Language

There are likely two ready critiques to a project focusing on rhetorical strategies and their relationship to social transformation. The first critique may be described as arising from a materialist position: *We should spend less emphasis on the language and ideologies that underwrite white supremacy and other systems of oppression when material goals must be achieved.* In other words, hearts and minds will be won as a result of addressing wealth inequality and the opportunity gap. At times, this critique foregrounds class over race or gender. David Roediger notes that Marxist scholars like Adolph Reed and Walter Benn Michaels "discern in activism and education around racism the diversionary initiatives of a 'class' of academics, middle managers, and political hired hands who, consciously or otherwise, divert attention from the hard facts of economic inequality and keep us preoccupied instead with obsessing about identity. This 'antiracism/industrial complex' ... allegedly expresses the interests of a professional/managerial class serving capital."[30] In these critiques, antiracism, and arguably feminism, become a means for stabilizing the class hierarchy. According to this critique, anticapitalist solutions must be foregrounded over purportedly identitarian issues. In contrast, Roediger recognizes that while antiracist workshops and conversations are not a panacea, there is value in "what feminists called 'consciousness raising' ... where whiteness is concerned."[31] But for those aligned with Reed and Benn

Michaels's critique, facilitating conversations on racism and whiteness becomes a means of distracting from addressing economic inequality. Ibram X. Kendi advances a similar yet distinct materialist position by contending that racist ideas and language emerged as a result of policies. Kendi's logic contends that if we uproot and replace racist policies, then antiracist ideas will follow.[32] Kendi's emphasis on policy over ideology suggests a critique of an exploration of the rhetorics of reactionary entrenchment. One may hear Kendi say that we do not need to change the way we think or communicate; we must change our policies and actions. Once our policies have changed, our ideas and language will change as well.

The second critique of examining how rhetorical strategies may be deployed to forestall social transformation rejects the liberal faith in a marketplace of ideas wherein deliberation will result in greater equality and social progress. Proponents of this critique may point out that there is no guarantee that civil dialogue will bring about social change. Many advocates of civil dialogue will point to great orators of years past—Frederick Douglass and Martin Luther King Jr. are common examples—as evidence of the power of words to change minds. While such a move obscures the tremendous violence required to usher in changes in policy, those who refuse to romanticize liberal deliberation merely point to the ongoing, entrenched inequality today that has pervaded after centuries of national conversations.

This totalizing faith in civil dialogue is epitomized in a July 2020 public letter published in *Harper's Magazine* titled "A Letter on Justice and Open Debate" and signed by a breadth of political and cultural workers including Thomas Chatterton Williams, Noam Chomsky, David Brooks, Francis Fukuyama, J. K. Rowling, and numerous others. The letter embraces calls for police reform and "greater equality and inclusion across our society."[33] Yet the thrust of the letter critiques the rise of so-called cancel culture wherein "editors are fired for running controversial pieces; books are withdrawn for alleged inauthenticity; journalists are barred from writing on certain topics; professors are investigated for quoting works of literature in class; a researcher is fired for circulating a peer-reviewed academic study; and the heads of organizations are ousted for what are sometimes just clumsy mistakes."[34] Through this oversimplified recitation of controversies, the letter positions social justice critiques as aligned with the illiberalism of the Donald Trump administration. From there, the letter embraces civil dialogue in a manner that is all too familiar for those fighting for social justice: "The way to defeat bad ideas is by exposure, argument, and persuasion, not by trying to silence or wish them away."[35] In this move, the *Harper's* letter promotes the concept of the marketplace of ideas and paired it with an unyielding faith in the progress narrative of history.

The letter was immediately met with criticism for the hypocrisy of its signatories and its sloppy conflation of historical events.[36] But the letter's unquestioned faith in civil dialogue must also be interrogated. If civil dialogue and the marketplace of ideas are the key ingredients of social justice, then how do the signatories—all members of the cultural and political elite—explain the endurance of inequality and the rise of fascist populism at the time? Those finding fault with the *Harper's* letter may also offer a critique of this book: *Isn't taxonomizing rhetorical maneuvers of sociopolitical entrenchment just a step toward advocating a more liberal marketplace of ideas?*

In truth, just as calls for dialogue have been viewed as foundational for democratic society, these calls have also long been deployed to quell critiques by aggrieved communities. That is, civil dialogue, listening, and organizational committees may be as much strategies for perpetual inaction as they are strategies for social transformation.[37] Calls for civil dialogue are predicated on the notion that all participants are afforded equal rights even when we know that in the real world some are more equal than others. What does it mean to ask for "civility" of those whose loved ones have been murdered by state actors? Does this request not echo the calls for "patience" directed at Martin Luther King Jr.? Not only are civility and patience laudable virtues, but in the rhetorics of entrenchment—in response to calls for justice—they "almost always [mean] . . . never."[38]

As a scholar committed to social transformation, I take these critiques to heart. We must not merely change hearts and minds but policies and conditions. Our interrogation must not simply focus on race or gender, but on the sociopolitical conditions—white supremacy, heteropatriarchy, and capitalism—that produce these identities. We must not let a blind faith in civil dialogue get in the way of mobilizing people to build a better world. Yet these critiques are not necessarily at odds with the type of scholarship that seeks to explore how rhetorical practices can be used to hone or hinder deliberative democracy.

Regarding the first critique, I do not see the emphasis on the discursive and the ideological to be at odds with the material and structural, nor do I find addressing racial and gender inequality to be in contradiction with addressing class inequality. These manifestations of inequality are dialectical, and while the material and structural may be the originating force for the discourse and ideology of white supremacy, as many have illustrated, this does not mean that focusing on changing policies will result in changing ideas. Indeed, changing policies—effecting material and social transformation—will be unlikely if we do not simultaneously also address ideology and discourse. The often-corporate diversity and inclusion training or antiracist self-help books are not a panacea for society's ills. Yet, like Roediger, I also see how this attention to racist ideology and discourse can work akin to the consciousness raising practices of 1970s feminism. Thus, attention to ideology and discourse may not be the solution to forging a just, equitable world, but it is a critical, necessary intervention.

As for the second critique, that calls for civil dialogue mask and magnify unequal power positions and silence forms of critique, I agree. *Rules for Reactionaries* and its author have an ambivalent relationship with calls for civil dialogue. I remember well a day when neo-Nazis protested across the street from my campus. As a matter of full disclosure, they were protesting me and my class on everyday white supremacy. As I stood across the street watching, a university administrator walked past me, looked me in the eye, and said, "They have the right to say what they want. I have the right not to listen." While legally speaking, he was correct, this embrace of freedom of speech and a marketplace of ideas for white men like him, me, or the neo-Nazis does not account for how students and colleagues of color may have felt danger and unfreedom as they were forced to walk through a scrum of hate on their way to class or work.

My ambivalence regarding deliberative democracy and its role in forging social justice emerges from the way that the calls for a national conversation that opened this introduction perform the work of "cruel optimism." According to Lauren Berlant, cruel optimism names a relation that "exists when something you desire is actually an obstacle to your flourishing."[39] In this case, calls for national conversations invite those invested in reactionary entrenchment to participate in shaping the contours and direction of what justice can look like and how it may be achieved. These calls erroneously assume that all act in good faith and with similar goals. As such, the romantic desire for a national conversation to heal our wounds often works to maintain the status quo.

Despite this cruel optimism, I find value in the study of rhetoric and justice efforts when deliberative democracy is reframed not as a linear process that will simply result in an imagined equality but rather when it is understood to be a never-ending process and relation between people. This theorization of deliberative democracy is too expansive to take up in detail in this introduction. Thus, after the majority of *Rules for Reactionaries* identifies specific rhetorical maneuvers and explores their cultural logics, I return to this question of deliberative democracy in the conclusion as an opportunity to explore both its danger and its potential.

Guidebooks and Our National Conversation

Aside from public hearings, op-eds, political speeches, and interpersonal dialogue, in the last few years, the national conversation on race has found expression in a collection of what are often marketed as guidebooks aimed at those who are interested but feel unprepared to engage race-talk and race-work. These works seek to introduce the uninitiated into the national conversation. Indeed, Clinton's Advisory Board helmed by John Hope Franklin released a dialogue guide along with the commission report. The *One America Dialogue Guide* offered strategies for citizen-readers to consider how to best engage in meaningful deliberation. These strategies were pragmatic in nature, asking readers to consider their goals, what form the community dialogue might take, who would be included, which questions may prove most fruitful, challenges that may arise, and how the dialogue leader may overcome them. More recently, since 2018, a spate of books have been published aimed at a broad, white audience and seeking to draw readers into the national conversation on race and encourage a commitment to antiracism. Works like Robin DiAngelo's *White Fragility*,

Ibram X. Kendi's *How to Be an Antiracist*, Ijeoma Oluo's *So You Want to Talk About Race*, Layla Saad's *Me and White Supremacy*, and Patricia Roberts-Miller's *Speaking of Race* intervene within a legacy of racial inequality and intransigence.[40] However, these works emerged specifically during the collapse of the postracial façade of the Barack Obama–era by widely publicized extrajudicial, state-sanctioned killings of Black people and the rise of Black Lives Matter as well as the emergence of the 2016 Trump campaign and subsequent presidency characterized by increased detentions and family separations of migrants, white supremacists marched openly in the streets, and the racialization of the pandemic, to mention but a few points of racial and historical context.[41] Although at times these works have been critiqued for reinforcement of feel-good white liberalism, the popularization of these books marks an inflection point in the potential national conversation on race.

These five how-to guidebooks are perhaps the most well-known of a larger body of public-facing antiracist introductions. To be sure, each has notable strengths and weaknesses, and each is shaped by a slightly different purpose. DiAngelo, Kendi, and Roberts-Miller are certainly more firmly grounded in scholarship, and Oluo and Saad are, on average, more accessible texts, although all five are public-facing. These texts offer readers an approachable way of entering the national conversation on race with an antiracist sensibility, providing an understanding of basic concepts that are foundational to race-talk and race-work. But just as the 1990s call for a national conversation on race was met with another side, an underside, to the conversation, one that rejected the need for racial healing and justice, there is also another body of how-to guidebooks.

This body of public-facing antiracist writing may be counterposed to another set of purported guidebooks by right-oriented commentators and media figures such as Ann

Coulter and Ben Shapiro. Coulter's *How to Talk to a Liberal If You Must* is largely a collected volume of previously published columns with an introduction that promises "this book will explain how to argue with liberals by example, not exegesis."[42] From this disclaimer, Coulter offers "ten simple rules" for talking to liberals. These rules include advice like "You must outrage the enemy," "Never apologize, at least not for what liberals what you to apologize for," and "Always be open to liberals in transition" (or who are persuadable), among other tactical wisdoms.[43] Ben Shapiro's twenty-one-page tome *How to Debate Leftists and Destroy Them* takes a more exegetical approach. Shapiro advocates such strategies as framing the debate, pushing one's opponent to answer questions, admitting when you do not know something, and others. Although Coulter's and Shapiro's *How Tos* were published prior to the recent spate of antiracist guidebooks, they suggest active strategizing of how to communicate for their given political purpose.

What distinguishes these two sets of guidebooks is not simply their political orientation but their very approaches to race and dialogue. The antiracist guidebooks range from deep considerations of *how* one should engage in conversations to primers on key concepts, fostering a shared language to enable conversation and understanding. Coulter and Shapiro's *How Tos* make passing gestures at being willing to recruit one's opponents to align with reactionary beliefs, their main thrust evidences demagoguery over deliberation. Roberts-Miller explains that "*Demagoguery is a polarizing discourse that promises stability, certainty, and escape from the responsibilities of rhetoric through framing public policy in terms of the degree to which and means by which (not whether) the out-group should be punished and scapegoated for the current problems of the in-group.*"[44] Simply put, Coulter and Shapiro are not invested in fostering deliberative democracy. Rather, their efforts, consistent with the rhetorical strategies explored throughout this book, are focused on stabilizing reactionary identities and mobilizing them for political gains. Inheritors of the intellectual and political tradition that sought to obstruct and derail Clinton's Advisory Board's national conversation on race, Coulter and Shapiro do not propose a *dialogue* with fellow members of the community but a *debate* with an opponent (out-group) who must be defeated (by the in-group).

Within reactionary rhetoric, racism, sexism, and other societal challenges are not issues to be overcome together but tools for dividing the world cleanly into "us" versus "them" and maintaining the status quo. This is particularly evidenced in the ways Coulter and Shapiro engage race in their *works*. For example, Coulter advocates racial profiling after 9/11 and suggests that it is perfectly acceptable to teach white children to bully Muslims.[45] Moreover, when discussing school desegregation, Coulter evokes racist tropes when she asserts "Illiterate students knifing one another between acts of sodomy in the stairwell is just one of the many eggs that had to be broken to make the left's omelet of transferring power from cities to the federal courts."[46] For Coulter, the only problem with racism emerges when liberals decry conservatives as "racist" or "fascist."[47] Here the political out-group (liberals) stabilizes and reinforces the boundaries of the political in-group (conservatives). Moreover, Coulter maps racial categories onto these groups wherein Muslims, Black and Brown communities, and their white allies form a liberal out-group and conservative white Americans are the besieged in-group. Like Coulter, Shapiro's *How To* seeks to counter claims that the political right is racist, or sexist, or homophobic. Like many before him, Shapiro frames the Klansman as the epitome of racism, and if one opposes the Klan, they cannot be tarred as racist. Moreover, he contends that there is no value engaging with someone who calls him or his readers racist.[48] For Shapiro, assertions of racism demarcate the boundaries of in-group and out-group. Not only does he reject the Klan but he fashions a political identity by rejecting those would challenge him or his readers for investing in racism.

Coulter and Shapiro's reactionary *How To*s also forge a sense of solidarity between author and readers by cultivating a sense of pleasure in reactionism. Roberts-Miller, Cristina Beltrán, and George Lipsitz have all noted how punishment, cruelty, and "recreational hate" create pleasure and a sense of identity within reactionary politics.[49] While many justice-oriented readers may find the tone of these *How To*s distasteful, Coulter provides her readers pleasure in her snark and purposefully inflammatory remarks. Similarly, Shapiro promises readers the ability to debate and *destroy* Leftists. In both cases, Coulter and Shapiro cultivate a sense of group solidarity from the pleasures of "owning the libs."

Placed side by side, these antiracist and reactionary guidebooks illustrate a model of our national conversation in action. One may be tempted to see discussions of race occurring on each side, and there are. But these sides are engaged in divergent projects. One set of texts seeks to foster dialogue and engagement to undo inequality, inviting any interested party into the conversation. The other promises belonging and pleasure at the expense of Others and through the promise of maintaining the status quo.

Rules for Reactionaries identifies and examines reactionary rhetorical strategies in hopes that their hold on popular and political discourse can one day be disrupted. It seeks to expose the language strategies used to obstruct social change by outlining a heretofore unwritten guidebook on rhetorical strategies of political, social, and cultural entrenchment.[50] And in this way, *Rules for Reactionaries* pays homage to two guidebooks that explored political organizing and oppression in the mid- to late twentieth century. Saul Alinsky's *Rules for Radicals* offered community organizers and activists a handbook of strategies, advocating pragmatic tactics for effectively mobilizing aggrieved communities against the powerful.[51] Likely influenced by Alinsky, José Angel Gutiérrez's *The Gringo Manual on How to Handle Mexicans* identified and explained the often-unspoken rules that white people used to disempower Chicana/os and other people of color.[52] Inspired by Alinsky and Gutiérrez, each chapter of *Rules for Reactionaries* begins with an often-unspoken rule expressed as if the book is a guidebook for reactionary entrenchment—for example, a key rule is to *define* "racism" or "sexism" as something extreme and then *disavow* that extreme in order to obscure one's participation in racism and/or sexism. Written as a faux guidebook, the book seeks to make the hidden underside of our national conversations legible. Following the rules, each chapter of this book ruminates on how and why these rules work. Here, the book shifts from identification to analysis so that readers can hone their metacognition. For example, rather than hearing someone claim that they are simply not racist or reading something that laments the multicultural feminist present and internalizing these discourses, readers are propelled by this book to consider how these discursive maneuvers retain entrenched power and inequality. In this way, *Rules for Reactionaries* serves as an analytical guidebook to the unwritten rhetorical guide for reactionary entrenchment.

In order to identify and interrogate this reactionary repertoire, *Rules for Reactionaries* operates with three core methodological precepts. First, like the systems of inequality that they seek to maintain, these rhetorical practices do not exist solely at the fringes of society. Rather, as I will explain in the first chapter, these discursive maneuvers pervade and structure social and political life in the United States. For example, the rhetorical strategies underwriting white supremacy and antifeminist manifestos might also be found within some bestsellers. There is simply no clear dividing line between the extreme and mainstream. A second and related precept: there is no impervious border separating the political from other discourses. Language, and the ideologies it carries, permeates all aspects of society. Thus, to examine reactionary rhetorical strategies requires the ability to move between a diverse range of sources, from politicians' comments to celebrity news, from activist writings to debates within sports culture. Finally, reactionary rhetorical strategies are not simply bound to one ideological position or system of oppression. Just as an appeal to reason or an ad hominem attack are tools that exist in every rhetor's toolkit, so too do these strategies of entrenchment transcend specific ideologies and systems. For example, while white supremacy and antifeminism may not always align in terms of their objectives, they share common rhetorical maneuvers that allow for alliances to form. Indeed, perhaps because the diverse and intersecting freedom struggles of the mid- to late twentieth century shared common strategies that the social movements that seek to obstruct and roll back gains share common strategies as well. Because of these precepts, I treat these rhetorical maneuvers as a connective tissue that draws together diverse reactionary projects and allows them to permeate and shape the contours of US culture.

Chapter 1 analyzes the rhetorical strategy of "define and disavow" whereby individuals are able to escape accountability for their actions through the folk understandings of racism and sexism that categorize people into good and bad subjects. The second chapter, on "weaponized victimhood," explores how reactionaries deploy a sense of "aggrieved entitlement" to erase their own privileged standing and legitimize harassment, mistreatment, and violence toward women, people of color, and other underrepresented communities. Chapter 3 exposes how the imagining of "reactionary utopias" allows political and cultural workers to critique the gains of social justice movements, romanticize a past based on inequality, and offer a call for building a future predicated on the past. Chapter 4 interrogates how reactionary rhetors depict social justice efforts as extremist while claiming to occupy a reasonable, moderate terrain. Chapter 5 examines efforts to shift the debate surrounding large, complex social issues by blaming singular, convenient causes. Through identifying these rules and exploring their undergirding cultural logics, *Rules for Reactionaries* provides a model, an approach, for how scholars and activists may call attention to, understand, and disrupt reactionary rhetorics. As noted earlier, calls for national conversations may serve as cruel optimisms actually hindering social transformation. The conclusion returns to this dilemma, exploring the possibilities and limitations of dialogue and social transformation once the reactionary strategies are accounted for. The conclusion also identifies potential counterstrategies. A brief appendix outlines other rules of entrenchment for future interrogation.

Imagined as a faux handbook for maintaining inequity, *Rules for Reactionaries* is loosely organized around two principles. First, some rules are foundational to the operation of others. Second, the dynamics that underpin and need to be explored to understand some rules must be unearthed and investigated prior to interrogating other rules and their dynamics. For example, recognizing how one defines white supremacy and heterosexism is a crucial step to understanding the seemingly (but not actually) race-gender-power-neutral discourse of family values or nostalgia. Thus, chapters within the book build on each other and speak to one another in often indirect and loosely structured ways, just as specific strategies within the sprawling reactionary discursive repertoire often support one another. With this understanding, we may turn our critical attention to one of the most widely deployed rules and how it works: "Define and Disavow."

RULE #1

Define and Disavow

Follow the pattern. Someone has objected to something you said or did. Perhaps you told an off-color joke about Asian immigrants. Perhaps you said that a young Black man shot by police should have worked harder in school. Perhaps you donned brownface, wore a sombrero, and carried a bottle of tequila as your Halloween costume. Regardless of the situation, someone has claimed that your words, actions, and character are "racist." Here is how you respond: define and disavow. Establish a narrow, rigid identity category of "racist." This identity category is like a conceptual box. It contains only the foulest, most egregious characteristics of racism. Despite and because of its extreme attributes, others can easily agree that this box defines the parameters of racism—this is what racism looks like. Once racism is defined in this narrow, limited way, you simply disavow it. By placing yourself outside of the box, you can assure yourself and others that you are a reasonable, good person. Despite how some may have taken your words and deeds, you are a racial centrist, a potential ally of people of color and, above all, a fair and neutral arbiter of the situation.

In a January 2019 article, *The New York Times* reported Representative Steve King as saying, "White nationalist, white supremacist, Western civilization—how did that language become offensive?"[1] These comments caused an immediate firestorm as Democrats *and* Republicans spoke out in condemnation. However, these comments were far from King's first foray into racism. He long touted anti-Latina/o/x immigration policies.[2] He conflated migrant border-crossers with cartel members.[3] He promoted the Great Replacement conspiracy theory, which posits that immigrants of color are migrating and reproducing in large numbers while white Americans have a declining birthrate, causing the United States and other Western nations to undergo a radical racial transformation and eventual collapse. He befriended far-right European politicians and promoted neo-Nazis on social media.[4] To those who follow and study US politics, there was little surprising in King's defense of Western Civilization and white supremacy. His transgression was likely the fact that he explicitly named white supremacy and white nationalism in his defense rather than simply relying on coded terms like "Western Civilization" and "American culture and values."[5] Indeed, after the *Times* published the article, King disavowed "white nationalism" and "white supremacy" while simultaneously deploying more palatable terms by calling himself a "nationalist" and "defending his support of 'Western civilization's values.'"[6]

After, doubling down in defense of nationalism, King was stripped of his committee assignments. Two weeks later, the House of Representatives voted 421 to 1 to condemn King's words in a resolution "Rejecting White Nationalism and White Supremacy." In an unusual move, King spoke on the

House floor in support of the resolution. He disavowed white supremacy and white nationalism, saying that he would have preferred stronger language in the resolution and that white supremacy never enters his mind: "That ideology never shows up in my head. . . . I don't know how it could possibly come out of my mouth."[7] After the vote, the controversy subsided until the next time King said something in public that aligned himself with white supremacy. This happened nine days later, when King asserted that "there are 60 million babies that are missing in this society" due to declining birthrates and abortions among Americans.[8] This statement echoed the key elements of the Great Replacement theory espoused in white supremacist and nativist circles.

In an era popularly described as one of "diversity, equity, and inclusion," as well as one of "cancel culture," how is it that any one of these incidents did not force King's resignation and immediately end his political career?[9] Indeed, King only left office when the loss of his committee appointments opened a path for a viable primary opponent to challenge and defeat him in 2020. Does King's political longevity and influence actually evidence the pervasiveness of white supremacy in US culture? Perhaps. More critically, however, the example of King illustrates a recurring pattern of events and exposes a key discursive strategy used by those who wish to avoid being held accountable for their promotion and defense of inequality. Like many before him, King drew on popular definitions of racism and white supremacy as morally corrupt, extreme, and as bound to individual actors. Doing so allowed him to disavow the white supremacy he had previously defended and the racism he spent years cultivating. What makes King's example so significant is not its uniqueness. This is a highly common and effective strategy. Opening with King exposes how this definition and disavowal can work even for those who many would readily recognize as practitioners of racism. The example of King, like so many others, illustrates a foundational rhetorical rule of reactionary entrenchment, a strategy of *define and disavow*. Through drawing on and advancing common yet narrow definitions of racism, individuals are able to unshackle themselves with Houdini-like skill from being held accountable for their words and actions.

This chapter explores how and why this strategy of define and disavow works so effectively. Examining this rhetorical strategy is crucial for two reasons. First, this discursive maneuver actively forestalls meaningful dialogue about social injustice. Second, it relies on and exposes the linkages between mainstream and extreme forms of white supremacy and other reactionary efforts. In order to examine the dynamics of "define and disavow," this chapter begins by illustrating how this rule has been deployed in various moments and contexts, making it a recognizable pattern and social ritual with common constituent elements. Then, the chapter interrogates how this rhetorical strategy relies on and manipulates folk theories of inequality that rely on fixed conceptualizations of identity. Moreover, define and disavow rests on an often-unspoken premise that people and complex social life can be categorized into binary ways of thinking (e.g., good-bad, nonracist-racist, mainstream-extreme). In order to contest this foundational logic, the chapter advances a different model of conceptualizing white supremacy and other systems of inequality that does not rely on static categorizations of identity but allows for a more nuanced understanding of how diverse forms of inequality may be linked and how people may participate in them. Finally, it gestures toward how define and disavow can be found not just in the terrain of white supremacy but also in other realms of inequality such as heteropatriarchy.

Variations on a Theme, or, It Was the Ambien Talking and Other Ritual Expressions of Innocence

Before examining why this strategy is so effective, it is crucial to recognize that Rep. Steve King's investment in white supremacy and subsequent disavowal are far from unique. Consider a few examples from twenty-first century US popular and political culture. In 2013, celebrity chef Paula Deen admitted using the n-word and considering hiring a team of all Black waitstaff for a "southern plantation theme for her brother's wedding."[10] As pressure grew, sponsors fled, and her show was cancelled, Deen urged "people to understand that my family and I are not the kind of people that the press is wanting to say we are. . . . Your color of your skin, your religion, your sexual preference does not matter to me."[11] In 2018, star of the then-top-rated primetime sitcom, Roseanne Barr blended white supremacist tropes, tweeting that Obama advisor Valerie Jarrett was the mixed child of the Muslim Brotherhood and "The Planet of the Apes."[12] Barr later claimed that the tweet was failed humor and the result of her taking too much Ambien to help her sleep.[13]

Returning to the world of politics, Rep. Mark Meadows defended President Donald Trump from accusations of racism by Trump's former attorney Michael Cohen. Meadows invited Lynne Patton, Trump supporter and a Black official from the US Department of Housing and Urban Development, to stand behind him as he spoke for her, stating, "You made some very demeaning comments about the president that Ms. Patton doesn't agree with. . . . I asked Lynne to come today in her personal capacity to actually shed some light. . . . She says that as a daughter of a man born in Birmingham, Ala., that there is no way that she would work for an individual who was racist."[14] When Rep. Rashida Tlaib criticized the moment of political theater as itself insensitive and a "potentially racist" act because Meadows used "a Black woman as a prop," Meadows defended himself by stating that he had nieces and nephews who were people of color and Democrat Elijah Cummings spoke up for Meadows stating that he was one of his best friends.[15] These are just a handful of examples of public figures engaging in racism and then quickly disavowing it to avoid accountability, but the list goes well beyond these few eruptions of US popular and political culture.[16]

From navigating various assertions of racism, the underlying structure of this discursive maneuver remains consistent. The *disavowal* is explicit, forceful, and charged with emotion. The *definition*, however, may be more subtle, implicit, gliding below the surface. Consider how our rogues' gallery of examples defined racism. In order for King to vote to disavow and condemn white supremacy, he needed to implicitly define white supremacists as those who had let the ideology enter their heads. One would need to actively and consciously believe in and endorse white supremacy to be a white supremacist. For Paula Deen, being racist required that the color of one's skin matter and matter entirely for how she would view someone. For Rosanne Barr, racism required a conscious malicious intent and derogatory speech not facilitated by prescription medications. For Mark Meadows, being racist means never having even one Black friend, relative, or employee. For the House Republicans and Democrats who condemned Tlaib for calling Meadows to task, racism exists outside the halls of congress and calling attention to it is not done in polite company. In each of these cases, the disavowal of racism hinges on an implied definition that exculpates those invested in inequality. To say or do something racially offensive, something that indicates an embrace of white supremacy, is not to be a racist because the *real* racists are bad people, and no one wants to identify with *them*.

From this brief menagerie of examples, one thing is evident. Disavowing one's participation with systems of inequality through implied, narrow, and rigid definitions of white supremacy is far from a rare or isolated incident. This is a very common discursive practice that falls into a regular, predictable pattern, a social ritual of racism and disavowal.[17] While I focused on a handful of high-profile, public cases, similar manifestations of this rhetorical strategy can be found in everyday life: interactions with friends, charged situations with coworkers, an encounter with a religious leader or social service provider. Drawing on these public examples does not indicate a realm to which these discursive maneuvers are limited. Rather it simply offers common ground upon which we may explore how define and disavow works. To understand how define and disavow is so effective and pernicious requires examining the folk theory that provides a popular definitional framework for racism and other systems of inequality.

What We Talk about When We Talk About Racism

What do we mean when we say "racism"? It's a big word, a heavy word, a capacious word. When I ask a general audience "What comes to mind when you think of the words 'racist' or 'white supremacist'?," they often mention images of the Ku Klux Klan, burning crosses, or swastikas. In essence, they associate white supremacy with the more overt manifestations of the white power movement. In recent years, the iconic image of racism has included tiki-torch-wielding, khaki-clad young men and the president who referred to them as "very fine people."[18] This addition indicates the shift white supremacy has taken over the last few years. In contrast, scholars have demonstrated that white supremacy pervades society in more subtle, everyday forms: disproportionate police violence against communities of color, the racial wealth gap, and the re-segregation of schools, to name just a few examples. This critical understanding of white supremacy as an everyday system undergirds much antiracist work today.

These competing definitions of racism—one overt, the other insidious; one popular, the other academic and antiracist—underwrite define and disavow and its remarkable effectiveness. Despite the regular debates about racist incidents, we rarely have open, honest examinations of what constitutes racism. Rather, in white spaces we often rely on folk theories—or common understandings—of racism and key aspects of these arguments are left unstated. According to Jane Hill, a "folk theory" names the popular (i.e., nonacademic) way in which a community explains a phenomenon. Hill notes that the folk theory of racism has three central attributes. Race is a recognizable biological category. Racism is found in individual acts of prejudice and ill will that reveal the poor character and ignorance of the racist perpetrator. And, despite tremendous social progress over the years, racism itself is natural and some forms of interpersonal bigotry will continue on into the future.[19] Together these tenets obfuscate addressing more subtle and systemic forms of racism. The elements of the folk theory coalesce to render racism as both aberrant and abhorrent yet something that is somehow a natural fact of human social relations. Moreover, the folk theory imagines racism not as existing within policies and institutions but within people. As such, the folk theory renders a racist Other who can be disavowed. While Hill uses the folk theory to elucidate the intransigence of everyday white supremacy, analogous folk theories structure other forms of inequality and support the strategy of define and disavow in similar ways, as I will explore later in this chapter.

Folk theories of inequality are often crucial in defining and disavowing racism and other systems of inequality. These social frames focus on the proverbial "content of one's character" rather than policies, actions, or even the words one may deploy. As such, the folk theory relies on and reinforces a system of categorization: one is either a racist or one is not. Hill notes that this reliance on an identity-based model shapes the ritual of moral panics.[20] Individuals and their allies will attest to their character: *"I'm a good person," "I have a Black friend,"* and so on. Iterations like these seek to obscure what racism is, disavow one's responsibility, and deflect accountability. According to the folk theory, to say that one is a "good person" means that they cannot also occupy the category of "racist." Moreover, such statements hew closer to the ancient Greek concept of *apologia*—a defense of one's character—rather than an apology initiated for the purpose of reconciliation.[21] Ultimately, these efforts to "bolster" one's image in the minds of others contribute to the maintenance of the racializing process because such maneuvers implicitly rely on what a broader public (read: the dominant group) can agree is racist or otherwise oppressive.[22] In other words, the folk theory and this form of disavowal are rooted in identifying and distancing from a lowest common denominator of oppression.[23]

In the folk theory of racism, violent extremists often occupy an outsized role, hindering the ability for people to recognize and confront white supremacy in its more everyday, accretional forms. Indeed, there is such a gravitational pull to examples like the Klan and Nazis that even extremist white power activists have sought to rebrand themselves. For example, while many saw the 2017 "Unite the Right" rally in Charlottesville as a clear example of white supremacy and Donald Trump's equivocation afterward as a siding with racial hate, rally organizers deflected claims of white supremacy by branding themselves as merely "nationalists."[24]

While the folk theory remains popular, for decades, scholars have focused their attention to addressing systemic inequalities. They have long recognized that white supremacy is not the product of a few bad actors. These ideologies and systems have endured in part because those invested in them fail to see their investments because they see themselves as good people, a characterization they see as incompatible with identity rooted in racism. For example, Steve Martinot has explored how narratives of white saviorism blend messianic self-image with the logics of imperialism and supremacy—military invasions and assimilationist social programs are underwritten with a sense of benevolence.[25] Shannon Sullivan has exposed how this imagining of and investment in "good white people" hinders everyday white folk from recognizing and confronting their complicity with white supremacy.[26] This investment in the notion of white goodness and white innocence is not simply an unstated part of the folk theory; it is an anchor that stabilizes the ability to define and disavow.

This disjuncture between the folk theory and the critical theories is a crucial problem for two reasons. First, because the folk theory has hegemonic standing in US culture, its pervasiveness is crucial for defining and disavowing. Even though the folk theory and its tenets are fundamentally flawed, practitioners of antiracism must recognize how the folk theory shapes and constrains discussions of racism if they are going to successfully challenge racial inequality. Second, while communities may be joined in arguing about and against racism, the often unstated element of the argument means that they are having two distinct, parallel conversations. Even as a vast majority of Americans may fully believe that racism is wrong, there is likely a significant cleavage when a specific incident is explored. For example, most would see the 2014 police choking death of Eric Garner as a tragic event. However, in order to charge it as resulting from racism, those adhering to the folk theory would feel the need to gaze into the head and heart of Daniel Panteleo, the New York Police Department officer who choked Garner. Should Panteleo have Black family or friends attest to his good character, these adherents of the folk theory may see the death as tragic but without racism. In contrast, for those embracing the critical theory, the internal thoughts of Panteleo could have little to do with the matter. Panteleo could have been a Black man himself, and the death of Garner could be tied to racism because of the way institutional and unconscious racism pervade US society.[27] From this perspective, patterns of police abuse and the disparate impact on communities of color evidence the endurance of racism, often without conscious racist intent.

To be clear, although I am asserting that there are two competing ways of conceptualizing racism, I am not suggesting that these views have equal merit. The critical theory of racism is both more capacious and nuanced. It provides a foundation for combating racism and fostering meaningful dialogue. However, one must also recognize that the folk theory is the culturally dominant way of viewing white supremacy. One cannot contest white supremacy without recognizing and addressing the wide-reaching impact of the folk theory.

Because the folk theory has hegemonic standing, it is rarely openly articulated. One need not say that racism is an exceedingly rare force in contemporary society, a remnant of a bygone era, occupying the corrupt hearts of a select few. Rather, it is often safe to assume that most white people in the United States will view race in this way. Indeed, because whiteness is an ideological and discursive system, it is not unusual for people of color to subscribe to this limiting way of understanding racism. Consider the examples of Lynne Patton and Elijah Cummings explored earlier. The folk theory is so pervasive that even a committed civil rights activist like Cummings may be recruited to serve reactionary purposes within certain contexts.

The ubiquity of the folk theory fosters a dynamic wherein the definition that precedes the disavowal of racism tied to conscious or extreme identities is often rooted in the logic of an enthymeme.[28] An enthymeme is an argument wherein a premise that structures the argument is left unstated. When Rep. Steve King denied and disavowed his embrace of white supremacy and stated that white supremacy "never shows up in my head," the unstated premise was that to be racist, white supremacy must enter one's heart and head and be a conscious part of one's identity.[29] Enthymemes perform a critical communal function in these iterations. The rhetor relies on the audience to complete the missing element of the argument. And the audience complies. In order for this to work, the rhetor and audience must both belong to a shared discursive and ideological community. Not only does the rhetor draw on a commonly held belief in the unstated premise, but as the audience silently completes the enthymeme, they reinforce the sense of shared "imagined community."[30] As the enthymeme is offered forth and the silent premise gestured toward, the rhetor and audience share an unspoken moment of dialogical interpellation.[31] When King asserts that white supremacy and white nationalism never enter his head, his supporters may consider that they too have never thought of themselves as white supremacists—to do so would be to recognize that they are "bad people," and his supporters, like most people, see themselves simply as good, everyday folk. Both rhetor and audience are ideologically aligned, making their beliefs about inequality commonsense. Recognizing the communal element of the enthymeme extends Hill's argument of the folk theory. Not only is this theory of racism held by the folk, this theory simultaneously constitutes the folk. This dynamic highlights the challenge of confronting racism through dialogue, for not only is the folk definition of racism often held by those who benefit from racial inequality but the definition both remains unstated and forges a sense of collective moral identity for the very people invested in systems of inequality.

In an era marked by the rise of overt racism, it may seem counterintuitive to focus on more subtle iterations of oppression. Here the folk theory may gain more currency—"*Those are the racists over there; they are abhorrent and extreme and must be condemned.*" Why spend time addressing the poor word choice of a politician or celebrity when hate groups are gathering in US cities and assaulting people? With limited attention and resources, shouldn't we focus the extreme manifestations that everyone can agree on? Simply put, the answer is no. First, the imagining of an abject racist Other allows even those who are members of recognized hate groups to rebrand themselves as the alt-right or nationalists. Second, attending disproportionately to extreme forms of oppression or on fixed identities inadvertently gives a pass to the broader systems of inequality because white supremacy and other forms of reactionary entrenchment rely on a variety of manifestations in order to persevere. Emphasizing the extreme obfuscates the everyday nature of systemic inequality. Moreover, attention to extremist examples reinforces the unstated premise essential to define and disavow—the racist Other provides discursive cover to the racist Self, racist policies, and racist acts. In order to contest define and disavow, we must reject the logic of simple categorization.

Beyond Binaries: Mapping the Ideological Terrain of White Supremacy

If the strategy of *defining* merely activates the often unstated but commonly held understanding of and category of "racist," then *disavowal* forges a distance. Disavowal cleaves space between rhetor and racist, asserting that "*I am (or they are) not that type of person.*" Thus disavowal is a double move, categorizing one's identity through the rejection of the racist Other. Steve King must be a good person because racists are those who consciously believe in and own their white supremacy, and he does not even allow those ideas to even enter his head. The act of disavowal relies on and reinforces binary thinking where "racist," or the "extreme," occupies one side of the dyad and "nonracist," or the "mainstream," occupies the other. This structure requires an oppositional, dependent identity wherein one sees themselves in contrast to the perceived identities of others and not as an outgrowth of one's own actions, experiences, or beliefs. This binary is depicted in figure 1.1.

Because in actuality there is no clear dividing line between racists and everyday people, the binary thinking upon which disavowal relies obscures significant manifestations of systemic inequality. If a racist is an active white power activist, where does one locate those who counter assertions that "Black Lives Matter" with "All Lives Matter" or "Blue Lives Matter"? Such assertions obfuscate the urgency of Black protest and replace cries against racism with colorblind platitudes. They are manifestations of what Hannah Noel describes as "deflective whiteness."[32] Where does one locate someone who promotes school choice initiatives, policies that often reinforce the segregation of schools? Clearly neither of these positions fit simply into either side of the nonracist-racist binary because they both uphold elements of white supremacy *and yet* do not fall into the category of

BINARY MODEL	
Everyday People	Racists
Mainstream	Extreme/Fringe
Good	Bad
Self	Other

Figure 1.1: The binary model forges a clean distinction between the purportedly good, everyday, nonracist Self and the bad racist Other. As long as one disavows the latter, they may define themselves in a way that escapes accountability.

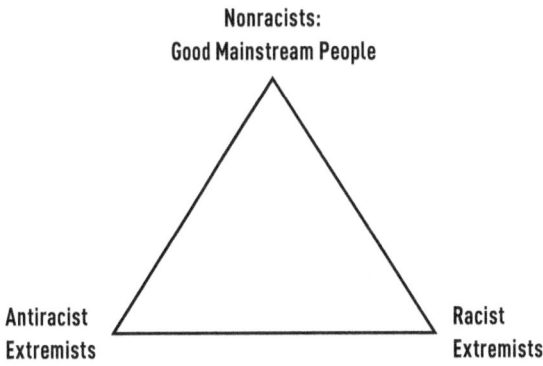

Figure 1.2: This triad model illustrates how those claiming nonracist status can position themselves against racists and antiracists, allowing them to condemn racism while opting out of committed action.

white power activist. Making assertions that distract attention from the impact of state violence on Black lives or advocating for policies that will expand the opportunity gap for students of color are but two ways in which white supremacy may manifest in colorblind ways and thus evade categorization on the racist side of the binary.

Although the binary model forges a simplified distance between the racist Other and everybody else, there is another variation of this model that seems to offer more nuance while maintaining the basic structure of the folk theory. When those claiming nonracism distinguish themselves from antiracists and racists, the binary model shifts to a triad. Figure 1.2 consists of three interlocking binaries. As with the initial model, nonracists and antiracists position themselves against the racist Other. However, what distinguishes this model is the way nonracists achieve bystander status by also rejecting antiracism. There are activists and extremists on both sides, they may say. By highlighting differences between themselves and racist and antiracist Others, those claiming to be nonracist are able to reject racism while simultaneously doing nothing to combat it. When this triad model is flattened out, it gives the appearance of a spectrum of identities and nuanced relationships of inequality. However, rendering this interlocking set of binaries as a triad depicts how those embracing nonracism position themselves above the fray. Critically, we must remember that there is nothing stable or fixed about these identities. As I demonstrate in a later chapter, reactionism gains tremendous force by cloaking itself as neutrality, whether that is done with sincerity or in bad faith.

Critically, the logic of fixed identities and binary and triad thinking that undergirds the rhetoric of disavowal can also be found within social justice activism, underscoring how reactionary impulses traverse political ideologies. Since the 2000s, the discourse of allyship with aggrieved communities has achieved a heightened currency. Individuals and organizations proudly identify as allies of people of color, women, LBGTQ folks, and other communities engaged in social justice struggles. However, this allyship also has severe limitations.[33] The discourse of being an ally (or "co-conspirator" or "woke") relies on a fixed notion of identity. Here allyship rhetoric finds common ground with the folk theory discussed earlier. One can be a racist, sexist, bigot, or one can be an ally. The well-intentioned popularization of allyship discourse reinforces the rigid identity categories of the binary and triad models. This too-simple categorization allows the ally to see social problems as outside the Self and located within the oppressive Other. As such, claiming to be an ally allows one to reject those cast as extreme—*"I'm not a racist; I marched for Black Lives Matter."* In these manifestations, allyship is less about social transformation and more about reactionary entrenchment. The speaker asserts their investments in moral goodness at the exclusion of some non-ally (and thus presumably bad) Other.

Like King's assertion that white supremacist thoughts never enter his head or Deen's claim that she does not care about skin color, uncritical embraces of "ally" as an identity provide a Teflon coating through which these people may escape implication in systemic oppression. However, these identities do not just work by rejecting the extreme. Those who claim this status may also compete as to who is a true ally, rejecting mainstream and other justice-minded proponents of antiracism and feminism through the competition of virtue signaling. This inversion of the oppression Olympics works not to dismantle inequality but to entrench its hierarchies while in the guise of struggle.

Whether discussing those who simply see themselves as nonracist (e.g., Rep. Steve King and Paula Deen) or those who see themselves as allies for social justice, these identities and their capacity for justice fail because they seek to too simply categorize humans into stable, rigid identity categories. As Patricia Williams suggests, "That life is complicated is a fact of great analytic importance."[34] Drawing on Williams, Avery Gordon theorizes the concept of complex personhood: "Complex personhood means that all people (albeit in specific forms whose specificity is sometimes everything) remember and forget, are beset by contradiction, and recognize and misrecognize themselves and others. Complex personhood means that people suffer graciously and selfishly too, get stuck in the symptoms of their troubles, and also transform themselves. Complex personhood means that even those called 'Other' are never never that."[35] If we recognize the complexity of human life as Williams and Gordon insist, then we must also recognize that the purported racist Others "are never never that." Or to put it a different way, those who consider themselves good white people share much in common with the racists they seek to reject.[36]

Ultimately, the impulse to categorize racists and racism as somehow aberrant and abhorrent—as in the folk theory—or ourselves as good white allies—as in many social justice circles—replicates the logical structure of white supremacy. Drawing on the work of David Theo Goldberg and Abby Ferber, Kenneth Ladenburg argues that "the categorization of racist groups and racist discourse into hierarchical strata that signify a 'degree' of racism (e.g., *alt-right*, *white supremacist*, *far-right*) is often based, especially outside of academia, on ambiguous or shallow criteria that requires the presence of overtly prejudicial language or symbolism to be present to classify a person or group as outside the *mainstream* or *racist*."[37] As such, these models of categorization elide more subtle and supple forms of white supremacy. While Ladenburg recognizes that categorization holds significant social and psychological value, he notes the tragic irony of using a rigid system of categorization to identify and bracket off people, groups, and ideologies when white supremacy itself emerges from the impulse to categorize humanity.[38] This, of course, is not to say that white supremacy should not be rejected. Rather it should not be rejected as somehow Other. Underwriting Ladenburg, Goldberg, Ferber, and numerous others is the need to recognize the everyday nature of systemic injustice and how we participate in it. Rigid categorization of white supremacy as somehow Other allows the good, nonracist, antiracist, mainstream Self to escape introspection, a move that allows white supremacy, both everyday and status quo, to maintain its entrenched power.

As noted earlier, I find it more useful to conceptualize systemic injustice taking the shape of discursive, ideological, and sociopolitical terrain. Rather than fixing ourselves and others within a binary or triad framework, the metaphor of terrain allows us to recognize that we occupy various positions throughout our lives.[39] The terrain itself is not fixed but always shifting beneath our feet and transforming through our actions, even when, like erosion, we do not see the immediate impact. And our identities, moving across coordinates on the terrain, continually unfold and develop in relation to the system that we inhabit.[40]

Here a note on terminology is critical. While this rendering of white supremacy and other systems of oppression may be more accurate, much of the popular discourse relies on the binary or triad models that rigidly construct a mainstream and extreme. How then does one describe and examine these interactions without simultaneously reinscribing the logic of the folk theory and the enthymeme that allow for easy disavowal and the forestalling of meaningful dialogue? For my work, I sometimes still reference extreme and mainstream manifestations of white supremacy. However, I do this with a significant caveat. I treat these as relational categories. When former Fox News host Tucker Carlson asserted that immigrants make the United States a dirtier nation, he voiced the same argument often found by more overt white power and nativist groups.[41] However, to a large segment of the US voting public, Fox News is a mainstream media outlet. In this instance, Carlson's claims were both mainstream and extreme, and a less rigid, territorial imagining of ideology allows the nuance and relationality to be explored. Moreover, the purported mainstream and extreme are not simply relational to one another but also in regard to the one reading the map of the ideological terrain. For example, if I view Carlson's assertion about immigrants as extremist, this interpretation illustrates that I may hold pro-immigrant views. Others may take my interpretation of Carlson's words as extreme as an indication that I am an extremist, out of touch with the mainstream perspective that Carlson voiced. Thus, my analysis is rooted in this territorial model even as I actively reference terms like mainstream and extreme that often invoke a binary, triad, or spectrum.

Why do I advocate for a territorial model when the binary and triad are so pervasive that it is difficult to discuss inequality without referencing flawed terms like mainstream and extreme? At its core, the territorial model allows individuals to recognize that people do not occupy stable ideological categories but rather may actually traverse a vast terrain. This movement across the terrain of inequality suggests the possibility that people, the system they build, and the ideology they inhabit may evolve over time. In contrast, the binary and triad models and their indexing of extreme and mainstream fix humans to general, limiting categories of good and bad people. When we imagine our identities and commitments and the identities and commitments of others to be fixed and unchanging, we lack a reason to practice introspection or deeply engage others. And we cannot work to change the terrain that we inhabit if we do not first map it and understand our location.

Social Rituals of Define and Disavow

Thus far, I have explored how the strategy of define and disavow relies on the folk theory of inequality and a rejection of a somehow bad Other. There is, however, another component that may be deployed should outright disavowal prove ineffective at quelling a moral panic: a rhetor may apologize. An individual has done something to stir controversy, they are called to account for their actions, they define and disavow, but the controversy continues, and they offer a heartfelt—but more often, a tepid—apology, and the opportunity for meaningful dialogue closes. While apologies seem a crucial part of accountability—someone commits a wrong, the wrong is identified, they apologize, and they are forgiven—focusing on the requisite apology propels the situation forward through the predictable discursive pattern. As Jane Hill noted about moral panics, when individuals are called out for racism, the discussion almost immediately shifts to the character of the individual: "*I don't have a racist bone in my body*"; or a third party offers testimony: "*I know*

John and he is a good person." Calling for an apology may very well seem like the logical step. However, the demand for apology often locates the transgression within the individual: John has committed a social sin, he must atone, and all will be forgotten.[42] Such individual atonement forestalls broader, unfolding explorations of inequality. Should the individual take responsibility for his actions, an apology ushers in the cessation of dialogue. In other words, an apology is a form of disavowal.

As John Hatch has demonstrated, these disavowals and apologies hew more closely to the ancient Greek concept of *apologia*, a defense of one's character or ethos. Rather than attempting an apology of reconciliation wherein the aggrieved party's honor is restored, a commitment to empathy is established, and forgiveness is hoped for but not a foregone conclusion, racial apologia offers a defensive posture that forecloses conversation.[43] Thus, it is unsurprising that numerous communications scholars have exposed how racial apologia does not lead to healing but often reinforces racial systems and maintains the status quo.[44]

Because apologies can be highly structured, they can circumvent the messiness and human complexity so often needed. For example, when the Paula Deen controversy erupted, Deen made three video apologies. The first two were directly in response to the controversy, and the third was to apologize to Matt Lauer for cancelling an appearance on *Today* to address the controversy. According to a member of Deen's public relations team, Deen recorded the first video on her own without a production team, but the video did not capture what she wanted to say.[45] While the first video was later edited, Paula Deen took responsibility for her words and actions: "I want to apologize to everybody, uh, for the wrong that I've done. Uh, I want to learn and grow from this. Inappropriate, hurtful language is totally, totally unacceptable. I've made plenty of mistakes along the way, but I beg you, my children, my team, my fans, my partners, I beg for your forgiveness. Please forgive me for the mistakes that I've made."[46] Deen's team later released a second, unedited video where she focuses the attention to her strong character and asserts that the words and actions she has been accused of do not reflect who she is.

> Hello, y'all, I'm Paula Deen. . . . The pain has been tremendous that I have caused to myself and to others. And so, I'm taking this opportunity now that I've pulled myself together and am able to speak to offer an apology to those that I have hurt. I want people to understand that my family and I are not the kind of people that the press is wanting to say we are. I have spent the best of 24 years to help myself and others. Your color of your skin, your religion, your sexual preference does not matter to me. But its what's in the heart, what's in the heart. And my family and I try to live by that. And I am here to say that I am so sorry. I was wrong. Yes, I worked hard, and I've made mistakes, but that is no excuse. I offer my sincere apology to those that I have hurt, and I hope that you forgive me because this comes from the deepest part of my heart.[47]

Neither response quelled the outcry. However, the second video adheres more closely to the logic of define and disavow. She states that "my family and I are not the kind of people that the press is wanting to say we are"; this second apology embodies more a defense of Deen's character (and financially lucrative media image) than an attempt to restore honor to and reconcile with those she has harmed. In marked contrast, the first video seems more honest and opened up the possibility of meaningful engagement. Deen acknowledged the wrongness of her words and deeds and she did not equivocate or deflect. Unfortunately, the social pressure for apology and the economic drive for the situation to go away converged in the second video where she emphasized the goodness of her heart and character.

Recognizing that apologies can function as a form of disavowal raises a challenging question: If demanding an apology is a means for seeking accountability, how can someone be held accountable when apologies are forms of disavowal? Perhaps, just as we must reject the folk theory that injustice is aberrant and the fault of an abhorrent Other, we also must avoid emphasizing the need for and demanding apologies.

To be clear, I am neither advocating that people should not be held accountable nor am I suggesting that people do not apologize for hurtful deeds. Rather, I am cautioning against an undue emphasis on apologies. Ultimately, apologies may actually work against social transformation. Just because the conversation has ceased does not mean that healing or transformation has taken place. By simply ending the dialogue, apologies may leave the hurt and harmful acts lingering like a "seething presence" to haunt social situations.[48] If apologies are a critical point in moral panics and usher in the cessation of meaningful dialogue, we must shift the conversation away from apologies in order to hold open a space for meaningful dialogue. Such a move would break the predictable pattern. When someone causes a moral panic, we must focus our attention on their words, actions, and the underlying logics. If they are "good people" that is beside the point. If they apologize, that's lovely, but we must turn attention back to the words, actions, and logics, decentering the individual and focusing on the system that makes inequality possible. For example, when Steve King said that white supremacy "never shows up in my head," his vote to support the resolution ended the conversation, until he said the next racist thing. Rather, than offering the resolution as a condemnation and apology, what if reporters asked why was King invested in white supremacy? Why are his feelings not unique? What does a pride in white nationalism offer him and others? These questions might not sound like they could hold Steve King accountable. They may not garner an apology. But they could help those seemingly "good" whites see how they are implicated in a system of racism by exposing the shared cultural logics that make the terrain of inequality possible.

Beyond Racism: Define and Disavow in Other Regions of the Terrain of Inequality

Define and disavow has become an entrenched element of US popular and political discourse, but it also permeates interpersonal conversations where one party seeks to address inequality and another seeks to disavow their investment in it. In these cases, rhetors rely on binary thinking and the widely shared folk theory, activating unstated beliefs about injustice and oppression to disavow their and others' culpability. Perhaps the most frustrating aspect of define and disavow is that it appears to offer an overt conversation about inequality while in truth this maneuver actively shuts down meaningful dialogue.

Throughout this chapter, I have grounded my discussion of define and disavow in examples of how people evade charges of racism. Yet I have also gestured toward a broader terrain of inequality that is constituted by not just white supremacy but other systems of injustice too. If we are to keep with our model of a terrain of inequality, each of these discursive, ideological, and sociopolitical systems work like tectonic plates pressing against, sliding across, moving away from one another to shape the more visible terrain of inequality that we see before us, the terrain we inhabit. In truth, define and disavow is a rhetorical strategy more easily identified with discussions of racism in

US society. However, as central to the thrust of this book, these systems share discursive strategies, routes, that help them maintain power. A more complete analysis of define and disavow, then, would account for the similar and different ways this strategy manifests around other forms of inequality. While it is not feasible to trace all the permutations of define and disavow in this chapter, let us briefly consider its use in discussions of sexism.

Here, prominent New Atheist Sam Harris serves as a useful example. In 2014, Harris was interviewed at an event at George Washington University by *Washington Post* reporter Michelle Boorstein. Their exchange was contentious as the atheist public intellectual and the religion reporter disagreed about the prevalence of Christian fundamentalism in US society. Boorstein then questioned Harris as to why the New Atheism movement seems to be predominantly male and if it has a sexism problem. Harris joked that the atheist gender imbalance was likely due to his lack of sex appeal and earnestly contended that his confrontational and brash style of argumentation was "to some degree intrinsically male and more attractive to guys than to women. . . . The atheist variable just has this—it doesn't obviously have this nurturing, coherence-building extra estrogen vibe that you would want by default if you wanted to attract as many women as men."[49] When Boorstein published these remarks and attention to sexism in the New Atheism movement was highlighted, Harris responded with a post on his website. In the post titled, "I'm Not the Sexist Pig You're Looking For," Harris doubled down and expanded on the reasoning he offered Boorstein. But he also told of an exchange with an audience member at the book signing after the event. After Harris and the female attendee went back and forth about what Harris said and what he meant on stage, according to Harris, the exchange ended like this:

> SHE [AUDIENCE MEMBER]: You should just know that what you said was incredibly sexist and very damaging, and you should apologize.
>
> ME [HARRIS]: You really are determined to be offended, aren't you? It's like you have installed a tripwire in your mind, and you're just waiting for people to cross it.
>
> SHE [AUDIENCE MEMBER]: No. You're just totally unaware of how sexist you are.
>
> ME [HARRIS]: Listen, I was raised by a single mother. I have two daughters. Most of my editors have been women, and my first, last, and best editor is always my wife. If you really want to know the truth about me, I tend to respect women more than men. I'm not saying that's a good thing, but it's actually an honest statement about my psychological biases. I'm not the sexist pig you're looking for.[50]

In the blog, Harris then acknowledged the weakness of such a response, and that weakness is telling:

> I knew that this honest (and admittedly desperate) confession could be cynically viewed as a version of the "Some of my best friends are black!" defense. (It isn't. I'm not saying that my fondness for certain women proves that I'm not sexist. I'm saying that I actually respect women more than men by default. Again, I'm not saying that this is necessarily good; I'm saying that it is a fact.) However, I don't think I'll ever forget the mixture of contempt and pity my words elicited from this young woman. Her expression of disdain for me couldn't have been any more intense had I said, "Listen, honey. I go to strip clubs every week. I love women—especially when they're covered in oil."[51]

The example of Harris demonstrates the common way define and disavow can be deployed within the realms of sexism and racism. When he is accused of sexism and promoting it via his platform, Harris disavows sexism, asserting that his *relationship with* and *respect for* women precludes him from being a sexist. While I do not doubt Harris's sincere belief in his feminist bona fides, the unstated premise of his argument is that to be sexist one cannot have loving relationships with or respect for individual women—he does not treat sexism as a pernicious system that has shaped every facet of modern society, affecting our lives in ways that often escape conscious attention. Moreover, Harris deploys the binary model as a crucial escape from charges of sexism. He identifies true sexists as pigs, fashions an image of the sexist Other as a man leering at women writhing in oil, and, later in the essay, juxtaposes his support of Malala Yousafazi against real sexists like Islamic extremists and Muslims more broadly. Harris is rhetorically savvy, and he recognizes the potential critique of relying on women in his life as an escape from charges of sexism. And his comparison to the assertion "Some of my best friends are black!" illustrates the shared structure between his arguments and those discussed earlier in this chapter.

What is clear about Harris's effort to refute sexism is that he conceptualizes it as an identity, one explicitly tied to overt subordination of women. Viewing sexism this way reinforces and is reinforced by a binary or a triad model of sexism that mirrors the thinking that pervades discussions of racism. However, Boorstein and Harris's unnamed interlocutor seems to recognize the capacious nature of sexism. The terrain of gender inequality is broad enough to include sexual objectification of women, female genital mutilation, offhand comments about sex appeal, and vociferous critique being a masculine trait. Harris may not believe that women should be denied an education, but that does not mean that he does not inhabit the terrain of sexism. We all do. Rather Harris's definition and disavowal of sexism simply illustrates that he does not realize he inhabits this terrain.

Although there is significant overlap in how define and disavow can be deployed to escape claims of racism and sexism, there may be a significant difference. While both rely on a folk theory model, sexism lacks the easily agreed upon image of the sexist Other. In contrast, when defining and disavowing racism, one need only draw on and distance oneself from iconic images like the Klan or neo-Nazis. When Harris asserted that he is "not the sexist pig you're looking for," he humorously and tellingly included an image of an actual pig walking on the beach. Later, to construct the sexist Other he could then disavow, he had to render the image of an exotic dancer slathered in oil—here, the object of the verbal gaze is as much the woman as it is the ersatz leering man. Then Harris positions Islamic fundamentalists as the true sexist Others. These repeated gestures illustrate that sexism may lack easily agreed upon, iconic representations that discussions of racism often silently invoke, for Harris must look to animals, strippers and their clientele, and religious extremists outside of the United States to forge identifiable, disavowable sexist Others.

I am not trying to say that Harris is the same type of sexist as those he positions himself against. Nor am I asserting that Harris's brand of sexism is the equivalent to Steve King's brand of racism. This is not about where one falls on the grand scale of oppression. I am arguing, rather, that ideological investments in inequality share common discursive strategies, means for maintaining social power, rules of reactionary entrenchment. Moreover, these diverse systems interact like tectonic plates, giving shape to the terrain of inequality. Define and disavow relies on and exposes common logics across the terrain. Whether found within white supremacy, antifeminism, heterosexism, or other systems, define and disavow hinges on folk theory beliefs that oppression is aberrant and the territory of those of bad character and malicious intent. The definition gestures toward that racist, sexist Other. Then the rhetor disavows this Other as a means of protecting oneself from accountability.[52]

Interrupting and undermining this rhetorical strategy requires a fundamental reimagining of how inequality persists and thrives in contemporary society. White supremacy, heteropatriarchy, and other forms of inequality are not located within a few bad actors. They constitute the vast terrain we all inhabit. Even efforts to hold people accountable by demanding an apology may work to foreclose meaningful dialogue and reinforce the status quo. There is no longed-for silver bullet, charged with a mythic power to disable an enemy interlocutor. The folk theory, with its emphasis on fixed identities, and rituals of disavowal and apology promote reactionary entrenchment. But if define and disavow relies on distancing oneself from the racist or sexist Other by asserting that one's character is indeed pure and good, the next strategy extends this logic. *Weaponizing victimhood* allows rhetors to assert that they are the truly aggrieved party, a logic that inverts power relations in order to galvanize and mobilize political identities.

RULE #2

Weaponize Victimhood[*]

A group of people is working for the acknowledgment of, and redress for, historical wrongdoing and fighting for equality today. They may be calling attention to forms of privilege. Perhaps they want a secularization of schools or the government to honor multiple faith traditions. Maybe they have intimated that a community to which you belong has benefitted in the past or continues to benefit from social inequalities. They clearly want to change the status quo—they want to disrupt society as you know it and your position within it. How do you respond? Simple. Assert that these efforts are attacks on innocent people. Contend that those claiming to fight for justice are really the ones dividing society by race, gender, sexuality, religion, class, and so on. Frame this conflict as a war: they are the aggressor; you are the victim. Once you claim the status of victim, weaponize it. After all, if you and your community are being targeted and your social standing is under threat, isn't it logical to fight back? Asserting your position as victim will provide a valuable sense of identity for your community, and, if used properly, weaponizing victimhood can mobilize your community to retain the social order.

---

[*] An earlier version of this chapter was first published as "Weaponizing Victimhood: Discourses of Oppression and the Maintenance of Supremacy on the Right," in *News on the Right: Studying Conservative News Cultures*, ed. Anthony M. Nadler and A. J. Bauer, 64–83, Oxford: Oxford University Press, 2019.

Patrick Buchanan and Lou Dobbs warned of an ongoing Reconquista where the Mexican government, Mexican immigrants, and radical Chicanos are politically and culturally taking over the United States.[1] Rush Limbaugh bemoaned the way "feminazis" pushed their agenda of politically correct speech and "confusion of traditional gender roles."[2] White supremacists decry diversity and multiculturalism as "white genocide." David Horowitz, Elisabeth Hasselbeck, and Turning Point USA's "Professor Watchlist" website warn of liberal professors indoctrinating the minds of American youth.[3] Bill O'Reilly and Glenn Beck report on the latest skirmishes of the "War on Christmas" where Christian values are under attack from a secularist mainstream.[4]

Placed side by side, these examples evidence four common characteristics: they deploy hyperbole, they assert a moment of crisis, they claim victimhood, and they appear on the right but may find common ground across political identities with those who feel a loss of status. This discursive maneuver of weaponized victimhood transcends media formats and finds expression within diverse political identities, from white supremacists and nativists to evangelical Christians and men's rights activists. Across these various groups, weaponized victimhood is deployed to maintain power and privilege in the guise of powerlessness and justice. As such, weaponized victimhood has become a dominant structure in reactionary media and political thought, a rhetorical strategy that both shapes and reveals the key logics of the contemporary reactionary entrenchment.

Consider the perennial War on Christmas. Coined by the nativist Peter Brimelow in 1999 and the topic of John

Gibson's 2005 book, the "War on Christmas" narrative was spread by Bill O'Reilly over twelve years on his highly rated Fox News program *The O'Reilly Factor*.[5] Soon the discourse permeated reactionary politics—the War on Christmas has been a focus on *Fox and Friends*, *The Blaze*, and other right-oriented media. The battles stretch across the United States from the cashier at the local store wishing someone "Happy Holidays" to public schools honoring multiple cultural traditions in their holiday pageants. Sometimes the War involves the removal of religious iconography and language from public or governmental spaces; other times the War takes place in the marketplace, such as the 2015 brouhaha when Starbucks released a plain red cup for its ~~Christmas~~ holiday season.[6] And strangely, the War on Christmas seems to begin a bit earlier each year.

More than a catchy slogan developed to sell a political fantasy, the War on Christmas exposes how metaphors shape thought.[7] Framed as a war, contemporary debates about public celebrations and recognitions of holidays take on a specific structure. Like other wars, there are "battles," "targets," and "aggressors," a struggle between "us" and "them," "good" and "evil," and potentially a "clash of civilizations." As a frame, the metaphorical lens of war transforms each new manifestation. Logically, not only will there be "battles" and "fronts," but when a school removes references to religion in their rendition of "A Charlie Brown Christmas," Bill O'Reilly or others will call it "terrorism," and do so with a straight face, for he and others are merely following the train of logic.[8] Critically, the War on Christmas frames Christians as victims. After all, the War does "target" their holiday, and by extension their identity and faith. As such, assertions of a War on Christmas are simultaneously expressions of victimhood. The claim that "they" are attacking "us" positions Christians as besieged victims—and, more importantly, as victims, they have the moral authority to fight back.

The War on Christmas is not an outlier but a critical manifestation of reactionary logic that can be found elsewhere. Indeed, as I revised this chapter in 2023, the United States had been roiled by a slate of state and local anti-trans and anti-LBGTQ bills and efforts to restrict the teaching of US history and social dynamics under the guise of anti–critical race theory laws and policies. These issues along with efforts to end pandemic-related mask mandates were framed as protecting children from the public institutions like schools that purportedly pose a threat to youth by affirming their or loved ones' gender identities and sexualities, teaching them about the complexities of US history, and mitigating their risk of viral infection. This weaponization of victimhood resulted in numerous incidents where school board members, administrators, and educators were harassed, threatened, and intimidated because that is what a logic of victimization underwrites and requires of its adherents.

Weaponized victimhood has emerged as a dominant discursive and ideological structure across the media formats and constituent elements that make up and extend beyond the political right. Moreover, because these otherwise potentially disparate groups are asked to see themselves as victims under siege, their shared logic makes mobilization and coalition based on perceived grievances possible. Moving beyond the War on Christmas, this chapter explores how victimhood is expressed within two other constituent communities and ideologies: men's rights activists and white supremacists. Together, these examples show not just how disparate actors may deploy victimhood but also how this rhetorical maneuver undergirds specific political agendas across reactionary politics. From there, this chapter examines how victimhood is weaponized for strategic effect within three interconnected realms: the discursive and ideological, the psychoaffective, and the sociopolitical. Paying attention to these manifestations of victimhood exposes how common logics and strategies connect otherwise discrete political actors and ideologies. However, before examining weaponized victimhood, one must understand how it emerges at this moment in time and how language shapes thought.

Theorizing Victimhood

Weaponized victimhood did not emerge out of whole cloth in the late twentieth century. Systems of oppression have long rendered others as potential and actual threats to those in power. The massacre of Indigenous people was underwritten by the potential threat they posed for settlers—caused by the settlement on and expropriation of Indigenous lands. Proslavery advocates declared abolition—and not the brutal system of chattel slavery—as the cause of slave uprisings from which white southerners needed protection. Today's victimhood discourse and its logic stretch across social power relations, from gender and religion to race and nationality. Moreover, this heightened prevalence of victimhood has coalesced on the US political right, growing in force from the 1960s onward.[9]

Critically, weaponized victimhood is qualitatively different from social movements that have fought for equality. Weaponized victimhood is not about working toward a more equitable world. Rather, it often adopts the rhetorical practices of aggrieved communities in order to maintain and regain standing in the social hierarchy.[10] Moreover, those weaponizing victimhood are not socially marginalized, or at least not in the way that they imagine themselves to be. Rather, they *feel* the *potential* loss of standing above others as a form of loss and grievance.

Weaponized victimhood has come to prominence as a strategic rhetorical reaction to the social tumult of the mid-twentieth-century United States. Various liberation struggles from the African American and Chicano civil rights movements to women's liberation and LBGTQ equality efforts claimed grievance against systems of power. In response, those in positions of relative power appropriated a discourse of victimization to secure their position within a system of inequality.[11] For example, Mexican Americans demanded desegregated schools and curricular representation, and politicians invested in whiteness claimed that ethnic studies programs teach hatred for white people.[12] Women's rights groups asserted the need for domestic violence shelters, and men's rights activists claimed that those shelters discriminate against men.[13] These examples share a similar logic and structure. They claim victimization and fairness in order to secure inequality. One could see this as a cold, calculated, and effective rhetorical maneuver to obscure systems of power through adopting and adapting a rhetorical cache of twentieth-century liberation struggles.

Another complementary and reinforcing explanation also exists: one that does not rely on political actors' full consciousness of their rhetorical strategy. Weaponized victimhood does not simply respond to the rhetoric of twentieth-century liberation struggles but also to the ideological, social, and political transformation those struggles brought about. The multifocal shifts of the mid- to late twentieth century discussed earlier precipitated a multifaceted crisis for those in positions of relative power as well as the ideologies and discourses that sustain them. This is not to suggest that white supremacy, patriarchy, and Christianity have lost their privileged standing in the United States. Rather, they have undergone significant transformation, a transformation that upends those invested in those systems. Thus, weaponized victimhood neither emerges ex-nihilo nor in response to one axis of social change but in response to a constellation of social change.

Despite being shaped by social tumult and the gains of liberation struggles, reactionary investments in victimhood cannot be attributed to a simple backlash. According to the backlash thesis posited by Susan Faludi and Thomas Edsall in the 1990s and still embraced today by thinkers like Angela Nagle, conservativism ascended in the late 1970s after its constituent elements felt they were pushed too far by the gains of the left in the mid-twentieth century.[14] This pendulum model has been challenged by scholars like Joseph Lowndes and Julian Zelizer who have exposed a longer history of conservative thought and that right ascendancy does not necessarily equate to a vanquishing of the left.[15] Rather, these old intellectual and political traditions grow and develop together. Weaponized victimhood is not the result of a backlash in the sense that those on the right have been simply pushed too far. However, weaponized victimhood embraces discourses of "backlash" as rhetorical position because it claims to have been pushed in order to legitimize its efforts in pushing back. The rhetorics of backlash and victimhood promote the idea that efforts of reactionary entrenchment are merely defensive, thus using social identities like whiteness, masculinity, heterosexuality, and Christianity to draw those who may otherwise identify with the center or left into alignment with reactionary politics.

While appearing new, weaponized victimhood emerges from the genealogical tradition of Richard Hofstadter's paranoid style and Michael Rogin's countersubversive strategies. Like Hofstadter's paranoid style, those who weaponize victimhood today are convinced that their "political passions are unselfish and patriotic" which intensifies their "feeling of righteousness and his moral indignation."[16] As with Rogin's formulation of countersubversive demonology, weaponized victimhood is part of mainstream political culture that actively dehumanizes and stigmatizes its political foes with a faux defensive stance.[17] However, marking a shift from these earlier manifestations, weaponized victimhood does not require a fear of an eventual takeover or a shadowy conspiracy. Rather, because of the near hegemonic gains of the cultural left, weaponized victimhood calls attention to attacks on "traditional values" happening in plain sight.

In this way, weaponized victimhood forms an outward expression of what Michael Kimmel has called "aggrieved entitlement." Kimmel theorizes aggrieved entitlement as the emotional reaction to the loss of privilege and entitlement: "Aggrieved entitlement can mobilize one politically, but it is often a mobilization toward the past, not the future, to restore that which one feels has been lost. It invariably distorts one's vision and leads to a misdirected anger—often at those just below you on the ladder, because clearly they deserve what they are getting far less than you do."[18] Through Kimmel's formulation, aggrieved entitlement names the outrage Bill O'Reilly feels and generates in his audience when a school changes its Christmas concert to a holiday concert. Aggrieved entitlement names the resentment felt when a woman or person of color is cast in a role traditionally designated for a man or white person.[19] That is, the feeling that one has lost ground triggers and generates claims to victimhood. But the dynamic works in the other direction as well—articulations of victimhood give expression to feelings of power lost. If aggrieved entitlement is the emotional state, weaponized victimhood is the rhetorical maneuver. For scholars, weaponized victimhood marks the expression of aggrieved entitlement; for those who deploy it, weaponized victimhood functions as a way of consciously or unconsciously maintaining social hierarchies.

A critical caveat: rhetorical actors may not be fully aware of their rhetorical choices. Because language and ideology are intertwined through interpellation, the language of victimhood exposes conscious and unconscious elements of political thought. At one level, weaponized victimhood is one form of what Roberts-Miller has termed "cunning projection." Drawing on social psychology, Roberts-Miller argues that cunning projection "is generally an unconscious process, and that it gets much of its power from the way that it resolves unconscious, even suppressed, anxieties"; moreover, "This cunning strategy of rhetorical projection rationalizes the bad behavior of the rhetor, in that it makes the aggressive behavior seem, at worst, defensive."[20] As she explains, proslavery rhetors "projected" their fears and anxieties onto northern abolitionists. Roberts-Miller's theorization recognizes projections—like asserting that those in marginalized positions are victimizing the privileged—emerge out of anxieties and a desire to use language to maintain the status quo or return to a more idyllic time. Aggrieved entitlement and its manifestation of weaponized victimhood echo what Richard Hofstadter and Seymour Martin Lipset described as status anxiety.[21] According to Hofstadter and Lipset, social mobility within the US and uncertainty of stable social standing fosters a status anxiety within those who then seek to define their Americanness against immigrants or the elite. This aggrieved entitlement and sense of weaponized victimhood follows a more specific trajectory. Rather than originating from a timeless social instability that characterizes the United States, today's anxieties stem from the perceived, and at times actual, loss of power and social standing emanating from the multifocal ruptures of the mid- to late twentieth-century freedom movements. Moreover, while multiculturalism, feminism, and secularism are blamed for lowering public and psychological wages, neoliberalism has brought about the decline of social wages.[22] With this in mind, weaponized victimhood is not simply deployed to win over an oppositional group. Rather, it seeks to establish and reinforce group identity.[23] In the projection of victimization, there is no room for a middle ground; one must either identify with the oppressor or the oppressed. Ultimately these rhetorical moves arise out of psychological, social, and political anxieties that hold the purpose of delineating an "us" from a "them."

With this theoretical background established, weaponized victimhood takes shape through four identifiable stages. First, there is a real or perceived challenge to the status quo or a community's hegemonic social standing. Second, this perception triggers a sense of aggrieved entitlement. Third, people mobilize in public performances of victimhood. Fourth, this victimhood is weaponized to justify politics, policies, and social practices of entrenchment to retain or regain positions within a social hierarchy.

Expressing Victimhood in Two Case Studies: A Manifesto and a Moment

Over the last few decades, deploying victimhood by those in positions of privilege has become culturally dominant. Without coming to terms with this, we are ill-prepared to understand how reactionary entrenchment works. The following pages examine two case studies in which reactionary arguments rely on victimhood: Richard F. Doyle's 1976 *The Rape of the Male* and the 2015 privilege controversy at Appalachian State University.

Some may think this an odd pairing: a decades-old self-published men's rights manifesto and the racial backlash stemming from discussions of white privilege. These cases emerge in different forms and as part of distinct political projects. This seeming disconnect, however, is central to the argument of the chapter. A common rhetorical maneuver, weaponized victimhood fosters connections between otherwise disparate political efforts. Others may come to this analysis with a different concern: men's rights activists and white supremacists? Aren't they the same people? Pathetic, angry white men sitting at their computers trolling away into the wee hours? While there have certainly been overlaps between these groups, particularly within recent manifestations of the alt-right, there is no requirement that because one is invested in patriarchy, one must simultaneously support white supremacy, nor that if one is a proponent of white supremacy does one need to subscribe to heteropatriarchy.[24]

Until the early 2000s, white nationalist and men's rights movements had not coalesced. Men's rights activists disdained both political parties, and white nationalists found men's rights activists' concept of masculinity to be lacking. However, these movements converged in 2006 during the media frenzy of the Duke Lacrosse rape case, when an African American woman accused team members of raping her.[25] While white nationalists saw this as a case of antiwhite media hysteria, men's rights activists saw the media attention operating under a logic of misandry. Notably, both elements found evidence of their supposed victimization in the case, the mainstream media's rush to judgement, and the eventual dismissal of the charges. Indeed, both Richard Spencer and Stephen Miller, two figures heavily associated with the alt-right, gained media experience and their political ascendancy through the case.[26] Although there is nothing predetermined about the alignment of white supremacy and antifeminism, the Duke case proved a critical convergence, and today the men's rights community has become a fertile recruiting ground for white supremacy.[27]

The men's rights movement has long claimed and weaponized victimhood as a critical component of its ideology and discursive repertoire. In the United States, the men's rights movement emerged in the 1960s and 1970s in response to changing gender and economic developments such as women's prevalence in the workforce, the decline of the family wage, the proliferation of no-fault divorce, and rise of second-wave feminism. The men's rights movement today intersects with and diverges from a constellation of other male supremacist discourse communities, from fathers' rights and divorcee rights to pick up artists and involuntary celibates (INCELS). Since its origins, the men's rights project has held two structuring beliefs. First, society is in decline and only a recuperation of a "traditional" masculinity (read: heteropatriarchy) can restore order. Second, contrary to popular and scholarly opinion, men are the oppressed sex.[28] Rather, men's rights activists contend that feminism has overreached and targeted men for oppression. From the 1970s to the 1990s, the men's rights movement developed key organizations like Coalition of American Divorce Reform Elements (CADRE), the Men's Right's Association, and the National Center for Men as well as a constellation of intellectual leaders such as Richard Doyle and Warren Farrell. The advent of the internet has allowed like-minded men to find one another with greater ease. Today the men's rights movement is known for its online presence with its male supremacist fellow travelers, sometimes referred to as the "manosphere."

Examining weaponized victimhood within an ideological and discursive community that has existed for over fifty years and now spreads across media and platforms is a challenge. For this chapter, Doyle's *The Rape of the Male* serves as a representative example of how men's rights discourse deploys victimhood. *The Rape of the Male* is hardly unique. Indeed, one could easily locate Doyle's ideas and rhetorical moves within later texts of the movement such as and Warren Farrell's *The Myth of Male Power*, Imran Khan's "The Misandry Bubble," and other men's rights polemics. What makes *The Rape of the Male* such a useful text is its publication in the early years of the men's rights movement and the way its arguments do not stand out as significantly distinct from later men's rights works.

The Rape of the Male advances the notion that women and the legal system victimize men and privilege women. Responding primarily to changes in divorce laws, women's growing economic independence, and second-wave feminism, Doyle contends that men are victimized by sex prejudice and that he is merely fighting for equality. Doyle dedicates the book "to all the victims of sex prejudice, including my shattered children."[29] Doyle argues that he is making a critical intervention because "sex discrimination against men" is "little recognized."[30] His positioning of male victimhood allows him to assert that his screed against women is merely an effort "intended to unashamedly and unequivocally present the other side of the coin."[31] In this way, victimhood allows Doyle to position himself as an invested but fair arbiter of gender equality in the United States.

Doyle grounds his understanding of male victimhood by recounting his personal experience with marriage and divorce. According to Doyle, he had married a woman named Marge who he had known in high school and began dating two years after graduation. He describes Marge as a fun, sexually experienced girl, who was used to being flattered. In contrast, Doyle casts himself as a "square," a virgin, and only wanting to "build a comfortable home and make some good, healthy children."[32] The marriage quickly soured as Marge's "Halloween mask" falls and she reveals her true person.[33] There are incidents of domestic violence that Doyle asserts Marge either instigated or deserved: she tells him that his "cock wasn't big enough for her" and she cheats on him numerous times. Once they divorce, she is awarded custody of the children and turns them against him as he is required to pay child support.[34]

Reading Doyle's narrative, one cannot hope to ascertain a definitive truth behind why and how the marriage fell apart. More interesting and useful is how this narrative rhetorically positions Doyle as an innocent victim.[35] Doyle uses his victim status to support conclusions about what must change in regard to gender and society. Doyle is keenly aware that the legal system and those who knew him and Marge "branded [Doyle] as the villain in the whole affair, and Marge the innocent victim of my [his] 'cruel and inhuman treatment.'"[36]

Facing a loss of friends and social isolation, Doyle finds community when attending a meeting of "divorce *victims*" and later discovers sex discrimination in divorce and other realms of society when he connects with other early men's rights activists.[37]

From his testimonial, Doyle shifts to an argument of how society victimizes men. Perhaps unsurprisingly, Doyle begins his exploration of societal victimization by focusing on the problems with marriage and divorce. Regarding marriage, Doyle laments the immaturity of women and men who rush into marriage, but he also notes that marriage is a means for women to harm men.[38] He contends that brides see marriage as a form of economic security and collateral.[39] Moreover, Doyle frames women as bitter and willing to take advantage of weak men.[40] Further casting women as the victimizers, Doyle argues that sometimes other women instigate the trouble, convincing a wife to find unhappiness where there should not be any. Through his rumination on marriage, Doyle disproportionately places the cause of unhappiness on women, their laziness, bitterness, and meddlesome nature. If marriage is often bad in Doyle's vision, divorce is worse. In cases with a contested divorce, Doyle asserts that the courts and community automatically privilege the woman, treating her as a "damsel in distress" and "the male defendant—the villain."[41] With the introduction of no-fault divorce laws in the 1960s and 1970s, Doyle contends that the victimization of men does not get better. In this new era, divorce is easier to achieve, and, according to Doyle, because women receive favorable treatment in terms of custody of the children, alimony, and child support, divorce can place men in a position of "human bondage."[42]

Notably in his exploration of marriage and divorce, Doyle does not address the social inequalities that targeted women and paved the way for alimony and preferential treatment in custody battles. Rather, claiming to embrace equality while ignoring inequities, Doyle is able to consistently position men as victims. One must wonder: If modern marriage and divorce open men to victimhood by (ex-)wives and the legal system, what exactly do Doyle and his fellow men's rights antifeminists want? From Doyle's writing, he clearly wants a return to an older, traditional, patriarchal masculinity wherein men are in charge of the family and women have little autonomy.

After positioning men as victims, Doyle contends that men must fight back. Doyle advocates that men should avoid marriage, but if they get married, the men should take lead.[43] Doyle also favors divorce reform, but this goes beyond issues of child custody and the end of alimony. Doyle asserts that rape and abuse laws also need to be addressed, for, he suggests, some women have a "rape wish" and many times women deserve to be struck by their husbands.[44] Through this logic, if these laws are changed, men will be able to take their rightful position in the family and no longer be victimized by women. Until his vision of legal reform takes place, Doyle offers other ways men can fight back. They should liquidate and hide their assets when a divorce arises. When men do not receive custody and cannot see their children, they should become ex-fathers, emotionally shutting themselves off and treating their children as if they do not exist.[45] Beyond issues directly relating to marriage and divorce, Doyle argues for a host of social and legal changes. For example, the United States must end the integration of women into men-only establishments.[46] Women should have limited access to the work force or securing loans independently.[47] And men should have equal access to abortion rights.[48] If these changes are not made through peaceful means, Doyle warns that some men will fight back through violence. Indeed, he notes some already have as he glosses an example of men who have turned their anger at victimization into violence against wives, lawyers, and judges who they feel have wronged them.[49]

Despite some of the appalling statements that Doyle makes, Warren Farrell credits Doyle as a significant influence in Farrell's mainstreaming of men's rights in the 1990s.[50] Today many of the arguments made by Doyle in 1976 can be found articulated by men's rights antifeminists in the manosphere, a collection of websites, discussion boards, and online communities focused on men's rights and how men must navigate a society dominated by feminism. In other words, Doyle's male victimhood persists at the center of men's rights discourse nearly five decades later.

While a manifesto offers a rich case for unpacking victimhood discourse, another way of uncovering the workings of victimhood is to turn to specific historical flashpoints, moments of moral panic wherein media converge their attention to one incident to claim and articulate victimhood. The 2015 privilege controversy at Appalachian State University serves as a useful example. In spring 2015, an Appalachian State residence advisor put up a bulletin board to raise privilege awareness. The board mixed humorous memes found on the internet with explanations: white, male, able-bodied, heterosexual, and Christian forms of privilege.[51] In early March, Laurel Littler, a student who did not live in the dorm, complained about the bulletin board's content online. On March 16, *Campus Reform*—an online platform that, along with *The College Fix*, pays students to expose supposed left-leaning politics on campus—published an article claiming that the bulletin board was designed to "shame" students.[52] Similar articles soon appeared on *The Daily Caller*, *College Insurrection*, Fox News' *The Insider*, and *The Blaze*. When interviewed on Fox News, Littler repeated her claim that she felt targeted by the bulletin board: "When I looked at the board I instantly felt shameful for my heritage and my upbringing because of my life choices. And it just concerned me that it was in a dorm."[53] Moreover, Littler agreed that the bulletin board had "intimidated" her. Littler also claimed that since she had posted on social media and spoken to the press, she had been victimized again by cyberbullying.[54]

In response to the media attention, Appalachian State posted other privilege awareness bulletin boards across campus and held fora and panel discussions.[55] Seizing on the media attention, a white supremacist organization the National Youth Front (NYF) initiated "Operation Bully Board."[56] Overnight NYF members posted fliers across Appalachian State's campus that defended and/or refuted the concepts of white, Christian, and male privilege. Although the NYF campaign brought more attention, Appalachian State did not back down. In August 2016, the university posted a privilege awareness bulletin board at the center of university life, the Memorial Union, and the media hysteria erupted again.[57] The Appalachian State privilege controversy illustrates how victimhood discourse traverses media formats and these assertions of victimhood travel across and bridge elements of the political right.

Critically, Appalachian State was not an isolated incident. Colleges, their faculty, and staff have been targeted as victimizers for years. The same semester as the Appalachian State controversy, Saida Grundy and I were both targeted by *Campus Reform*, Fox News, other right media outlets, and the National Youth Front.[58] Since then, Cheryl Matias, George Yancy, Tommy Curry, and many others have come under the same media focus.[59] While not all of these incidents have involved the pressure of neo-Nazis on campus, they have all involved right-oriented media attention, harassment, and death threats. Moreover, university administrations have engaged diverse response strategies—some have defended their employees, and others have condemned them under pressure.

The Appalachian State controversy and others like it reveal not just a shared discourse community invested in victimhood but a variety of ways that victimhood can be articulated. One may trace diverse manifestations from the aggrieved students to the conservative media to the white supremacist group. The two Appalachian State students who complained framed their grievances along two lines. As Littler asserted to *Campus Reform*, she felt the bulletin board targeted her based on her immutable identity: "I can't help that I'm Caucasian. Will they be happy if I change the color of my skin so I don't have my 'white privilege' anymore? I want to be comfortable in my own skin. You can't preach equality if you aren't willing to let a people group feel accepted as they are."[60] Through this logic, Littler and other white students are targeted and shamed for something they have no control over. Littler deployed a logic commonly found in popular understandings of racism as the mistreatment of someone based on racial ancestry. In this way, Littler positions being called out on one's privilege as similar to being the target of racial animus, and thus, she is a victim. Along with Littler, another student, Mike Herbert, engaged a different yet complementary argument, contending that such conversations about privilege may be legitimate on campus but not in dorms and not when instigated by resident advisors. Herbert told *Campus Reform*: "It was like a slap in the face. . . . Although a lot of us have similar views as he [the resident advisor] does, we feel like it's a giant middle finger to us."[61] For Herbert, the dorm was a safe space and advisors should remain neutral. This assertion positions Littler and other potentially privileged students as victims in that the bulletin board targeted them in a place that should have remained off-limits to sociopolitical debate. Moreover, the resident advisor, according to Herbert, was counterproductive because of his tone: "It's his job to make sure we don't burn down the place and go to school. It's not his job to flaunt his own personal and political views, even if we agree with him."[62] Together, Littler and Herbert position white students as victims of shame and harassment in what should have been an otherwise safe, neutral (read: privilege reinforcing) space.[63]

While *Campus Reform*, Fox News, and other outlets adopted the same victim framing as Littler and Herbert wherein the students were shamed by an advisor abusing his position in the safe space of their own dorms, the right-oriented media also positioned the bulletin board within a broader conflict. For reactionary media, the bulletin board was not a one-time maligning of white people, Christians, and men. Rather, as pointed out by *Campus Reform* and Elizabeth Hasselbeck of Fox News, the bulletin board was an outgrowth of the "Check Your Privilege" campaign started by professors at the University of San Francisco.[64] By tying the bulletin board to the "Check Your Privilege" campaign, the victimization at Appalachian State is part of the ongoing culture war in higher education—just the most recent battle in which whites, males, and Christians have been targeted for shame and harassment. Indeed, in an interview, *Campus Reform*'s Kaitlyn Schallhorn connected the bulletin boards at Appalachian State to the attitudes of those who would criticize Indiana's anti-LBGTQ "religious freedom" law.[65]

If reactionary media framed Appalachian State as part of a broad liberal plot to harass and shame, the National Youth Front took the victimization to its logical conclusion. For years white nationalist groups have argued that immigration and diversity programming constitute a "white genocide." Common slogans such as "anti-racist is code for anti-white" and "diversity equals white genocide" run rampant within these discourse communities. When *Campus Reform*, Fox News, and others asserted victimhood via the Appalachian State bulletin board, the NYF recognized this as a battle and stepped up to defend whiteness, Christianity, and patriarchy. Rather than a sense of personal shame or discomfort, or a fight against liberal educators, the NYF saw the bulletin board as a skirmish in the broader fight for the survival of the white race. John Angelo Gage, the then-leader of the NYF, argued that his efforts were in line with the spirit of the 1964 Civil Rights Act.[66] While Gage, the NYF, and others of his ilk fall clearly within the categories of neo-Nazis and white nationalists, it is critical to note that he engaged a "defensive" rhetoric that is enabled and legitimated by positioning whites and others bearing relative privilege as victims in an ongoing war.[67] In this way, Gage and his white supremacist brethren share much in common with more mainstream right-oriented media, and even, albeit perhaps unknowingly, with students like Laurel Littler.[68]

While Doyle's *The Rape of the Male* demonstrates how victimization sprawls within and permeates an ideology, this moment of the Appalachian State bulletin board controversy shows how victimhood may be claimed in differing ways by those who may not see themselves as ideologically in line as part of a collective effort. Despite the distinct ways each participant asserted victimhood, they legitimized each other. Right-oriented media outcry hinged on the authority and complaints of two offended students. Likewise, the students and media give a cloak of mainstream legitimacy to white supremacist groups like the NYF, suggesting that their concerns and worldviews are not fringe but commonplace amongst aggrieved whites.[69] Although the NYF and other white supremacists gain legitimacy by latching onto more mainstream assertions of victimhood, right-oriented media and the students strengthen their legitimacy by not embracing or engaging explicit articulations of white supremacy. This allows students and conservative media to occupy a position of mainstream "reasonability" in contrast to fringe-oriented white supremacists. Fox News and other reactionary media outlets ignored the actions of the National Youth Front. To cover "Operation Bully Board" would require reactionary media to either disavow white grievance or to acknowledge their role in spurring on the white supremacist fringe. Ultimately, understanding the way victimhood discourse underwrites and mobilizes communities who may not see themselves as in common or ideologically aligned explains why this weaponization is so effective.

Victimhood Weaponized: Three Realms of Reactionary Entrenchment

To many, these assertions of victimhood may appear ludicrous. Indeed, many of these beliefs are demonstrably false or rely on obvious logical fallacies. Despite the sociopolitical tumult of the mid- to late twentieth century, white people, men, and Christians continue to disproportionately occupy positions of symbolic and material advantage in the United States. However, we must treat this discursive practice seriously because it pays significant dividends. These dividends take shape across three distinct yet interrelated realms: the discursive and ideological, the psychoaffective, and the sociopolitical.

In a discursive and ideological realm, assertions of victimhood flatten out or invert social hierarchies and make them illegible. This strategic obfuscation operates through the following logic: the oppressed are not really oppressed, but if they are, the privileged are oppressed in equal or greater ways; therefore, any emphasis on social transformation should be aimed at decreasing the marginalization of the privileged. While this may appear logically incoherent in the abstract, consider how this logical structure underwrites the claims to victimhood in specific cases. The 2015 Starbucks Christmas cup kerfuffle rendered Christians as victims and occluded the fact that other religious and nonreligious identities rarely receive an elevated social standing in the United States. Here victimization did not signal marginalization, denigration, or oppression, but a loss of assumed status and power. When Fox News frames white students as victims of privilege awareness campaigns, they obscure the real disadvantages experienced by communities of color, flattening out and then inverting racial power dynamics so that they position whites as oppressed as much as, if not more than, students of color. Similarly, Doyle's manifesto positions women as fake victims in comparison to a true victimization of men. Moreover, *The Rape of the Male* reveals the discursive and ideological endgame for these claims of victimization: a return to patriarchal authority, reducing women to a form of dependency, subservience, and property where they can be beaten or raped by husbands without consequence, where the man's control of finances underwrites his control of the home and family, and where women can no longer have autonomy over their reproductive health. One can imagine a similar argument extending out of the War on Christmas or white privilege controversies wherein systems of inequality are seen as neutral to those that benefit from them. That is, these reactionary cultural workers all seek a return to the status quo ante wherein they benefited from an unquestioned privilege. Scholars have warned against aggrieved communities competing in an "oppression Olympics," for doing so only reinforces systems of power.[70] Here we see that those in positions of relative power and privilege also compete in the oppression Olympics and doing so allows them to nullify and blind themselves to the experiences of others.

Exploring this use of victimization within a discursive and ideological realm exposes how language shapes and limits the contours of human thought. Social systems of power and inequality are rendered natural, rational, and unrecognizable to their beneficiaries.[71] Critically, weaponized victimhood closes off potential alliances. While men can make many legitimate grievances—such as their historical expectations to serve in the military and other high-risk professions—the root causes of such issues are more accurately attributed to hegemonic notions of masculinity and economic exploitation and not the hegemonic rise of a mythically oppressive radical feminism. Indeed, 1970s women's liberation and men's liberation agreed on the belief that patriarchy victimized both women and men, albeit in different ways.[72] A key difference is that men are not only victims but also the beneficiaries of patriarchy. As such, men's rights discourse denies oppression at the hands of patriarchy and claims victimization at the hands of feminism and feminists. Not only does this position feminists, if not all women, as always already potential enemies, but it exposes that men's rights activists would rather choose the limited benefits of patriarchy over liberation from economic exploitation and hegemonic masculinity. Within the discursive and ideological realm, both unearned privilege and potential alliances in the struggle for a better world are rendered illegible. Social justice is imagined as social power wherein like pie all must compete for the biggest slice and the other's gain is your loss. While this discursive and ideological realm is foundational, the weaponization of victimhood does not end here.

Within a psychoaffective realm, weaponized victimhood gives language to felt experience and forms individual and collective identity. These assertions of victimhood are verbal expressions of "aggrieved entitlement," the feeling of loss and grievance when systems that ensure one's privilege have started to erode.[73] For those in positions of privilege, the fruits of privilege feel like they were earned through merit.[74] When social inequality is addressed, even incompletely, those in positions of privilege may *feel* oppressed. Kimmel's framework aggrieved entitlement makes particular sense when placed in conversation with the "wages of whiteness." According to W. E. B. DuBois, working-class whites during reconstruction received not just economic benefits but public and psychological wages for distinguishing themselves from Black people.[75] In essence social privileges paid psychological wages. Working-class whites could see themselves as superior to their laboring brothers and sisters, a psychological wage that made up for their own economic exploitation and secured a cross-class alliance with elite whites.[76] Placing these ideas in conversation, one finds analogous systems of power. Men in patriarchy experience psychological wages as do whites living in white supremacy. When those systems undergo crisis, those in relative power express aggrieved entitlement, victimized at the perceived loss of unearned privilege. In contrast to the psychological wages of the past, aggrieved entitlement becomes a wage for those who feel they have lost social status. This manifestation of weaponized victimhood strips away personal accountability and occludes systems of power, instead placing responsibility for one's struggles onto imaginary others and a mythical world of upside-down social relations. For example, an individual may receive a psychological wage from stating that "a woman or minority took my job" not because it is true but because it relieves the speaker from interrogating their actual social standing and potential shortcomings.[77]

This framework exposes the psychoaffective dynamic behind antifeminist, white supremacist, and other fallacious assertions of victimhood. Doyle and others may claim that women are unfairly privileged in marriage and divorce, given the benefit of the doubt in sexual assault and domestic violence cases, and fail to become committed partners with chivalrous gentlemen. *Campus Reform* and Fox News may assert that white students undergo daily psychological assaults on campus, Allan Bakke and Abigail Fisher may assert that they did not get into their desired school because of people of color, and white supremacists groups may see diversity programing as an ongoing "white genocide." Clearly these claims are questionable at best. However, they do not have to be objectively or empirically true. What matters is that they *feel* true. That is, weaponized victimhood allows for the expression of grievance even when there really isn't one. And weaponized victimhood pays the psychological wage of exploring why one's own struggles are the fault of others.

Through the psychoaffective realm, claims of victimhood are more than expressions that let off the steam of grievance. These expressions forge and maintain individual and collective identity. Antifeminists like Doyle imagine and assert what it is like to be a man during the rise of feminist hegemony. White supremacists claim a white racial identity in the looming face of diversity and multiculturalism. Evangelical Christians declare their righteousness through their persecution in an increasingly secular and diversely religious society. In an era when it may be seen as déclassé to openly assert white, male, Christian, or straight pride, although this does happen, casting oneself as a victim through these identities makes them more acceptable to the mainstream. These assertions of victimhood, however, provide a sense of identity for more than the rhetors themselves. These expressions interpellate audiences and imagine them into community. Francesca Polletta and Jessica Callahan argue that telling and sharing stories "can build collective identity," "provid[ing] pleasure and strengthen[ing] group membership."[78] Even if a feminist, multicultural, or secularist dystopia exists only in their minds, reactionaries can imagine it into existence and express a "besieged solidarity" together. As George Lipsitz has suggested, the identity and psychological wage accrued through this sense of "besieged solidarity" may be just as valuable as any social or political victory.[79] For example, when reactionaries decry diversity efforts in hiring or higher education, they promote a narrative and identity often seductive to those invested in whiteness who seek to make sense of their own dissatisfaction and failings.

In its most dangerous form, this faux victimhood can be weaponized to organize and mobilize attacks on marginalized people and the social apparatuses that support them. Within the sociopolitical realm, victimhood is deployed to directly impact the lives of others either through formal, legal approaches or though less formal, extralegal means. Lawsuits and legislation embody the most formal approaches to using victimhood for sociopolitical gain. For example, men's rights groups have engaged in numerous lawsuits to eliminate what they see as the privileging of women and the victimization of men. In 2002, a group of men's rights activists including lead plaintiff Scott Booth and Richard Doyle sued the state of Minnesota to eliminate women's domestic violence shelters.[80] The plaintiffs contended that men were equally likely to be victims of domestic violence and that the state ignored this and discriminated against male victims. The objective was not to secure protection for men but to eliminate services used by women.[81] Although this lawsuit failed, others have been successful. For example, over the last four decades, there have been many lawsuits regarding "ladies' nights" at bars and nightclubs. These cases argue gender-based price discrimination, and many of the lawsuits have been successful.[82] These lawsuits find an eerie parallel in anti–affirmative action cases wherein plaintiffs like Allan Bakke and Abigail Fisher have contended they were victims of racial discrimination. Whether turning on the axis of race or gender, these examples illustrate how positions of relative privilege are recast as victimhood, pushing for the maintenance of racial and gendered hierarchies. Sometimes these assertions of victimhood find legislative sponsorship. In 2010, conservative lawmakers and editorialists claimed that the field of Mexican American studies taught high school students to hate white people to justify Arizona's anti–ethnic studies law. Whether successful or not, this litigious and legislative weaponization feeds back on and reinforces a sense of individual and collective identity based on perceived victimization.

This victimhood may also be weaponized through harassment campaigns and other extralegal means. Here, the Gamergate controversy serves as a well-known example. In 2014, video game developer Zoë Quinn was accused by her former boyfriend of having an inappropriate relationship with a journalist. This post signaled to antifeminist gamers that the attention to Quinn's *Depression Quest* game was due to her gender. Thus began a harassment campaign that targeted Quinn, fellow game developer Brianna Wu, critic Anita Sarkeesian, and other women. As noted earlier, numerous ethnic studies scholars have been attacked in similar ways.[83] This harassment involves more than online threats and hate mail. As in the case of Gamergate and many of the professors under attack, this mobilized harassment often takes the form of doxing, death threats, false 911 calls, threatening visits to one's home, and, in the case of targeted women, threats of rape. The objective of these efforts is more than harassment for the joy of making the target's life miserable, a psychoaffective wage. Rather, the harassment also seeks a sociopolitical gain, making it so that the target and other like-minded individuals will retreat from the public sphere.

The most extreme forms of weaponized victimhood occur when individuals turn to violent rampages to correct their perceived mistreatment. In 2014, Elliot Rodger murdered six people and wounded fourteen others before killing himself. He targeted women because he believed the gender to have wholeheartedly rejected him, and he targeted men in order to enact vengeance for their sexual activity that he could not achieve. The manifesto he left behind details a sense of victimhood common to men's rights discourse wherein he claims to have suffered at the hands of women because they did not see value in him.[84] Likewise, Dylann Roof murdered nine Black worshippers at Emanuel African Methodist Episcopal Church in Charleston, South Carolina, and contended that he had to do so because of the rates of violent crimes committed by Black people against white folks. Patrick Wood Crusius shot forty-six people, killing twenty-three, in an El Paso, Texas, Walmart because he felt that the United states was under siege from a "Hispanic invasion."[85] It may seem unfair to group murderers like Rodger, Roof, and Crusius with men's rights activists, white nationalists, and reactionary media and politicians. While violent rampages may be the exception rather than the rule, a sense of aggrieved entitlement underwrites all these manifestations of antifeminism and white supremacy. Rodger, Roof, and Crusius may be outliers but they exists in the same discursive and ideological communities as Doyle, Farrell, the National Youth Front, Fox News, those who initiate lawsuits to end affirmative action and halt women's domestic violence shelters, those who harass women and people of color online, and those who propose laws outlawing an accurate, multiracial history of the United States.[86] Structuring all of these actions is a sense of victimhood, weaponized.[87]

Mapping weaponized victimhood across three realms illustrates the discrete workings as well as how each realm feeds off and reinforces others. Moreover, this mapping suggests how disparate historical incidents and seemingly fringe tactics are underwritten by mainstreamed reactionary cultural logics. As Anthony Nadler and Doron Taussig have argued, grievance operates at the center of right-oriented political culture, and the storytelling of grievance found in weaponized victimhood functions as the "movement's engine" from which "popular loyalty and energy come."[88]

Understanding how seemingly discrete reactionary elements—antifeminism, white supremacy, and conservative evangelical Christianity—weaponize victimhood for the maintenance of social hierarchy and relative forms of privilege exposes a common pattern of beliefs, attitudes, and behaviors underwritten and structured by a victimization frame. Critically, however, this dominant cultural logic does not solely reside and thrive on the moderate and extreme right. A sense of victimhood and this framing may find fertile soil in political moderates and on the left. Anyone with the potential for perceiving a loss of privilege is vulnerable to the feelings of aggrieved entitlement. For example, white respondents from numerous studies and polls have articulated how they felt whiteness was a hindrance in academic and career success.[89] In other words, they perceived themselves as potential victims of antiwhite racism. Similarly investing in victimhood, Kierra Loki Anderson has shown how men within ecoanarchist circles in the Pacific Northwest responded to charges of violence and sexism by claiming that they were the target of a "feminazi witch hunt" and being "persecuted by 'dramafreaks'" and radical feminists.[90] It would be foolish to simply categorize these survey respondents and leftist environmental activists as belonging to the extreme right. Rather they more accurately express the values of whiteness and patriarchy that transcend limited and limiting definitions of extreme and mainstream. In these moments, the speakers draw on, recirculate, and give legitimacy to reactionary narratives and the efforts of entrenchment that they underwrite.

Weaponized victimhood seizes these feelings and anxieties of a hierarchal social order in tumult, transforming them into ideology, identity, and mobilization. Anyone who benefits from white supremacy, patriarchy, or Christian hegemony in the United States is susceptible to the seductive power of the victim frame, whether they consciously identify with the right or not. As the next chapter illustrates, because weaponized victimhood is bound to a sense of loss, it often manifests through a temporal dimension wherein the past was Utopian and the present is dystopian, and in the future, reactionaries take their "country back" or "Make America Great Again."

RULE #3

Build Reactionary Utopias

You find yourself in position of alienation and aggrievement. Things are not the way you believe they should be. Perhaps you find yourself in competition with others who in years past would have been excluded from your school, career, or neighborhood. Maybe you struggle to find purpose and happiness in your workaday life and feel that you deserve more respect and deference. Possibly you listen to the radio or watch the news and see a world reflected back that differs from the way you think it should be, the way you remember it being before. Something is not right, you think; the world is spiraling out of control, the center did not hold, and we are on the precipice of dystopia. Recall a past when these problems did not exist. A past when gender norms were firm and fixed, when men were strong and chivalrous and women did not see a need for feminism. A past when the history of the United States was filled with the heroic deeds of those who looked like you. A past when you or your children were not made to feel guilty about the actions of ancestors. A past when you did not have to push #2 for English or when you would hear a Midwestern accent when you called customer service. Seize upon this past, hold it up as a mirror to critique the present. Use this romanticized past to call forth a new utopian future, a return to the tradition and the values of yesteryear. Contend that we are at a crossroads; tomorrow will be too late. Assert that we must reject this brave new world and build the future on the stable foundation of the past.

In August 2019, *The New York Times Magazine* released a project commemorating the 400th anniversary of the first arrival of enslaved Africans in the future US colonies. "The 1619 Project" consisted of essays, poetry, and stories that reimagined the US past and present with slavery and the experiences of Black people at the center. "The 1619 Project" was accompanied by reading and discussion materials that would support the project's use in educational and other settings.[1] While many of the ideas found in the project were commonplace in the fields of African American studies, American studies, and ethnic studies, this was a significant departure for *The New York Times Magazine*, and the imprimatur of *The New York Times* offered a wider distribution and sociopolitical credibility to the centering of Black life in the United States. Notably, the project did not operate on a model of inclusion wherein underrepresented people are added to an already established narrative of the United States that centers the sociopolitical elite, the way US history has largely diversified in schools since the 1980s. Rather, "The 1619 Project" "disturbed the peace" by offering a dramatic restructuring of the US narrative.[2]

Centering Black life in this public-facing project created an immediate sensation where "The 1619 Project" was hailed as groundbreaking and revolutionary. While the project was generally lauded, three trajectories of critique quickly emerged. First, five disciplinary historians criticized the project for Nikole Hannah-Jones's interpretation of slavery being central to the founders' decision to seek independence from England.[3] A second critique emerged among ethnic studies scholars, but often outside of African American studies, wherein they questioned the notion that there should be a single center of US history. This critique recognized the importance of "The 1619 Project" but also recognized the simultaneous centrality of Indigenous and other experiences in the formation of the United States. A third, longer-lasting critique emerged from politicians and cultural workers who saw the centering of slavery and racism (and Blackness) as an attack on US history and values. This response to "The 1619 Project" was but a flashpoint in the larger culture wars and dovetailed with vocal opposition to antiracism and Black Lives Matter. For the purposes of this book, this third line of critique is particularly interesting, for it illustrates a form of reactionary entrenchment.[4] While "The 1619 Project" offered a corrective to dominant interpretations of US history, reactionary cultural workers developed a *counter*-counternarrative, one that bears a temporal logic wherein the past is drawn on to critique the present and build a future.

A year later, in September 2020, President Donald Trump announced the creation of his administration's 1776 Commission. The group's purpose was to contest the "twisted web of lies" surrounding the United States and systemic racism taught in schools.[5] For Trump and his adherents, the 1776 Commission would mark a return to patriotic education. Four months later, the Trump administration released "The 1776 Report." However, the attention it received was short-lived, for it was released the same month as the failed insurrection at the US Capitol and Trump's second impeachment trial and two days before Trump left office. On January 20, 2021, the Biden administration removed "The 1776 Report" from the official White House website. During its short, two-day official online presence, scholars and other public figures lambasted the commission and report for failing to include professional historians, misreading primary documents and secondary sources, and politically mischaracterizing Martin Luther King Jr.[6] Rather than looking to how the report fails, I am intrigued by the cultural, ideological, and rhetorical work the report performs. "The 1776 Report" is not unique in its effort to romanticize the past, critique the present, and gesture toward and imagine a future. Indeed, this temporal logic is a common rhetorical strategy of entrenchment found within the reactionary politics. The tension and discordance between "The 1619 Project" and "The 1776 Report" are but yet another expression of the ongoing culture wars. Emerging in response to the social movements of the 1960s and 1970s, the "culture wars" names the debates surrounding what constitutes American culture, what the narrative arc of US history is, and who is included in the category "American."[7] Read through this frame, the paired 1619 and 1776 narratives are not simply histories as accountings of past events: they are accounts of the past charged with value, political meaning, and utopian ideations that make claims about the nature of "America."[8]

Some may write off "The 1776 Report" as bad history or more American myth-making and treat it as of little consequence. To do so would be a mistake. Despite its short official online tenure, "The 1776 Report" illustrates both a refutation of "The 1619 Project" and a resuscitation of American exceptionalism in order to entrench domestic inequalities in the twenty-first century. While neoconservatives marshalled American exceptionalism to promote wars and "export" democracy in Afghanistan, Iraq, and elsewhere, "The 1776 Report" turns its focus inward, imagining the United States as the pinnacle of democratic equality and thus immune to claims of injustice.[9] And it does so through emplotting and deploying a usable past to critique the present. "The 1776 Report" turns to the Declaration of Independence as the nation's founding document.[10] The report contends that "the core assertion of the Declaration, and the basis of the founders' political thought, is that 'all men are created equal.'"[11] This emphasis allows the Report to establish a two-part frame for understanding the trajectory of US history: The United States was founded on the Enlightenment's tenets of individual rights and these rights are not granted by government but bestowed by God.[12] From this premise, "The 1776 Report" seeks to explain the United States' struggle with slavery and inequality as a means of refuting "The 1619 Project." The report contends that the American founders, many of whom were enslavers, by and large did not want slavery to continue, and while they could not abolish it immediately, they ingeniously planted the seeds for abolition within the country's founding texts.[13] As such, the report fashions a progress narrative wherein the true American nation is one that values individual rights from which equality may flourish. Notably, this narrative relies on selective inclusion of historical facts and key quotations as well as the elision of others. For example, while the report centers Thomas Jefferson's language in the Declaration of Independence that "all men are created equal," it fails to mention, let alone grapple with, Jefferson's remarks about Black folks in *Notes on the State of Virginia*, wherein he both recognized the need to end slavery and advocated for an inherent white supremacy.[14]

The report contends that, in contrast to this hallowed American tradition of individual rights, current efforts for social justice are actually rooted in group rights, and group rights are antithetical to American values and tradition.[15] The report introduces the concept of group rights with John C. Calhoun and his advocacy for continuing and expanding of slavery.[16] From there, the report asserts a lineage of group rights within progressivism, fascism, and communism.[17] Ultimately the report locates Martin Luther King Jr. and the Civil Rights movement as manifestations of the struggle for individual rights—of course quoting King's often decontextualized line where he dreams of a world where his children "live in a nation where they will not be judged by the color of their skin but by the content of their character."[18] "The 1776 Report" positions the United States at a critical juncture. Today the American values of individual rights and religious freedom are under attack by communist-inspired academics and group rights-oriented social justice activists.[19] Despite this dystopian present, there is potential in the nation's future: "As we approach the 250th anniversary of our independence, we must resolve to teach future generations of Americans an accurate history of our country so that we all learn and cherish our founding principles once again. We must renew the pride and gratitude we have for this incredible nation that we are blessed to call home."[20] Here, the report offers a future in the past, calling for a return to traditional values and education.

"The 1776 Report" is not unique in its temporal logic. During the 2016 campaign, Trump captured the essence of building the future in the image of a romanticized past in the slogan "Make American Great Again." Opponents and commentators asked when exactly Trumpism hoped to return. Was it prior to the deindustrialism and neoliberalism that arose in the 1980s? A time when the immigration system had national origin quotas or restricted legal immigration and naturalization to white people? The era before the Civil Rights movement? But the details did not matter to Trump's supporters. They understood the logic that the nation's best days were behind them, but also those days could somehow be brought back in the future. This is a temporal logic of entrenchment, one that resists the ongoing social transformation of the present and finds the promise of a better tomorrow in the carefully crafted reminiscences of yesterday. The past is a stable, valued tradition; the present is a moment of tumult and loss; and one must fight to make the future in the image of the past.

To explore how this rhetorical strategy works, this chapter first turns to the temporal imaginings of four sample texts from the reactionary projects of white supremacy and antifeminism. These texts illustrate common features of what I term reactionary utopias from disparate yet connected ideological projects. From there, I examine how the temporal logic evidenced in these texts is bound to the concept of utopia as both a critical and rhetorical function. That is, utopias serve to forge a critique of the present world and mobilize people toward establishing their perceived world. I then demonstrate how reactionary utopias work to maintain inequality, spread ideology, and forge sociopolitical identities.

Gone Today, Here Tomorrow: Four Instances of Searching for the Future in the Past

As a rhetorical strategy, using an idealized past to critique the present and imagine the future did not emerge with the rise of Trumpism. This rhetorical maneuver can be found in other reactionary movements forged on aggrieved entitlement and a desire to return to a status quo ante. A complete cataloging of these discursive moments would be impossible, but it may be useful to briefly explore textual examples where this temporal logic operates. Here I offer a quick gloss of four texts that deploy this rhetorical strategy. Within each text, an idealized past is juxtaposed to a dystopian present to form a critique. From there, reactionary authors gesture toward two possible futures: a social collapse if we continue on our current path or the utopian balance found in returning to bedrock elements of the past.

Robert Bly's 1990 bestseller *Iron John: A Book About Men* looks to a past storytelling tradition as the basis for a mythopoetic recuperation of a masculine ideal. Some may question my inclusion of Bly's work in a discussion of reactionary utopias. Bly does not explicitly blame women for a present-day emasculation of men, and he cautions against framing men as victims.[21] However, as Jill Johnston has noted, Bly's

Iron John relies on an exclusion of women and locates the feminization of men not just on the absence of fathers but on the hyperpresence of mothers.[22] Moreover, Bly's assertions about the lack of fatherly rolemodels and initiation into manhood as a prime cause of social ills like street gangs and domestic violence echoes the discourse of other reactionary thinkers. Even if one does not place Bly squarely within men's rights antifeminism, he clearly influenced that discursive community.[23]

Drawing on Jungian psychology, Bly sought to address a twentieth-century crisis in masculinity. Bly contends that in 1990, the "images of adult manhood given by the popular culture are worn out" and adult men know that "images of the right man, the tough man, the true man . . . do not work in life."[24] Although Bly lauds the women's movement in recuperating and honoring the strength of women, he believes that the feminist movement push for men to discover their feminine side inadvertently created "soft men" who are not happy and often lack energy.[25] Bly rejects both rigid notions of a tough man (i.e., hypermasculinity) and the invention of "soft" (i.e., feminized) men and argues for a healthy masculinity built around the image of a sacred warrior, one that recognizes his strength but keeps it moderated.[26] Bly locates this crisis in masculinity as arising from the Industrial Revolution when fathers left the home to work elsewhere and sons no longer saw their fathers labor.[27] Bly posits that what is missing in society is an initiation ritual and process whereby boys are brought into the community position of manhood.[28] Ultimately, Bly locates numerous contemporary problems—"street gangs, wife beating, drug violence, brutality to children, and aimless murder"—as emerging from a lack of focused male energy and initiation.[29] By turning to the story of Iron John, one of the Grimm brothers' fairytales, Bly seeks a way of recovering a traditional masculinity. According to Bly, this story may be thousands of years old, offering insight into traditional masculinity. Throughout *Iron John*, Bly offers a reading of the fairytale that explores different characteristics of a healthy masculinity and the process of initiation that the young hero of the tale goes through as a model for young men today. The temporal logic of *Iron John* is clear. Society is at a crossroads: it must either choose the dystopian future of soft men and uncontrolled warrior energy, or it can rescue its past to build a utopian future of masculine energy and initiation.

In 1995, Peter Brimelow published his national bestseller *Alien Nation: Common Sense about America's Immigration Disaster*, a nativist polemic that repeatedly locates the American national (i.e., ethnoracial) character as emerging from its colonial origins wherein the citizenry was overwhelmingly of Western European heritage. A naturalized US citizen who worked as an economic journalist and had been an editor at *National Review* and *Fortune*, Brimelow has been a fixture within racial nativism in the United States for three decades. In 1999 he formed V-Dare, an online nativist and white nationalist website that features work by a host of anti-immigrant and white supremacist writers.[30] Deploying a strategy central to white supremacy and nativist political projects, *Alien Nation* crafts a usable past wherein the origins and foundation of the US is unquestionably Western European (i.e., white) emerging from what he describes as the "colonial-stock population."[31] *Alien Nation* develops a narrative of US history wherein some immigration has been acceptable in the past. As waves of immigrants arrived, those waves were met with pauses and restrictions on immigration that allowed for newer immigrants (e.g., the Irish and Southern Europeans) to assimilate fully into the otherwise Anglo-American cultural stock of the United States.[32] However, Brimelow locates a turning point in the 1960s. Since the removal of national origin quotas in the 1965 immigration act, the majority of migrants coming to the

United States are from "third-world" countries, thus challenging the Anglo-American core of the nation.[33]

While Brimelow laments the cultural differences between today's migrants and his true America rooted in a Western European core, there is also a clear racial dynamic. For example, he compares the US immigration system to Dante's *Inferno* and then states, "When you enter the INS waiting rooms you find yourself in an underworld that is not just teeming but is also almost *entirely colored*."[34] Here, Brimelow does not fall back on colorblind nativist concerns of wage depression or draining social services. Rather, he clearly asserts the racial difference of these newer immigrants as essential to the problem they pose. Moreover, lest one think that Brimelow's dystopic present is caused solely by immigrants, the book's title also refers to US-born people of color who feel alienated from society (white society) and are fighting to change the nation. For Brimelow, the threat to the United States—the *whiteness* of the United States, that is—is both the immigrant population and Americans of color.[35] They are wreaking havoc on the long-held centrality of whiteness. Brimelow's present is one of whiteness as lost status, and he gestures toward two potential futures: in one, the United States continues on its path and collapses under the weight of diversity: in the other, immigration restriction flourishes and white population booms so that the Anglo-American core of the US nation can be saved.[36] For Brimelow, a future based on the present is dystopian whereas a future based on the past is utopian.[37]

The temporal logics that I have outlined in these 1990s bestsellers also permeate more recent, fringe works. For example, written under the pseudonym Imran Khan, "The Misandry Bubble" typifies how these temporal logics structure men's rights antifeminism. The article was published online via the technospeculative site *The Futurist* in 2010. Sites within the Manosphere link to "The Misandry Bubble" as a foundational reading for the men's rights movement.[38] Khan begins with the lament that things have changed with the rise and reign of feminism. In years past, men could be unabashedly masculine and patriarchy as a system of gender balance was embraced. Khan locates this utopic time in previous popular culture depictions of masculinity like Rocky and The Fonz from *Happy Days*. Yes, Arthur Fonzerelli signifies a utopian masculinity of the past. For Khan, today is a near dystopian world of misandry. Women emasculate men and cheat on them, but men also suffer through the "glass floor" of more dangerous professions and heightened suicide and prison numbers. While things are bad for men today, according to Khan, the gender imbalance is only going to get worse in the future. The rampant misandry today will lead to an economic and civilizational collapse: "The Western World has quietly become a civilization that has tainted the interaction between men and women, where the state forcibly transfers resources from men to women. . . . This is unfair to both genders, and is a recipe for a rapid civilizational decline and displacement."[39] Khan suggests that one strategy for men in overcoming this misandry is for men to move to more traditional societies in order for them to find nonfeminist wives and for them to have the law on their side. Khan contends that Islamic courts have become a way for men to counteract the Western misandrist laws and notes that "almost every American man who relocates to Asia or Latin America gives a glowing testimonial about the quality of his new life. A man who leaves to a more male-friendly country and marries a local woman is effectively cutting off a total of three parasites in the US—the state that received his taxes, the potential wife who would take his livelihood, and the industries he is required to spend money on (wedding, diamond, real estate, divorce attorney)."[40] Like with Brimelow's *Alien Nation*, Khan foresees an unmitigated nightmare in the future based on the dynamics of misandry he locates in the present. Only by taking action—changing laws and culture, fighting feminism—can men stave off this nightmarish future and save civilization by returning to the past.

Notably, the role of "traditional societies" marks a divergence from the white supremacist thinking of Brimelow. While Khan locates those cultures as a reprieve and a site of replenishing gender hierarchy, Brimelow would characterize those nations as "third-world," "colored," or nonwhite. Although Khan and men's rights antifeminism may deploy a shared temporal logic with those invested in white supremacy, the specific contents of their utopian imaginings and plans for how to achieve them may diverge. That being said, this does not mean that race and racialization is absent from Khan's writing. Rather, like white supremacist discourse, he notes the breakdown of Black family structures and identifies a crisis in US urban centers like Detroit. However, what is different for Khan is that he contends that the root of these issues is not racial or cultural deficits but misandry, and if this misandry continues, the problems he locates within Black families and urban communities will also reach crisis levels within other communities. Thus, while Khan may locate a different cause of the crisis, his use of Blackness and urbanity allows him to foster ideological and discursive common ground with white supremacists.

As a final example, Jack Donovan's 2018 *The Way of Men* illustrates how the use of the past to imagine and build a future can be used across reactionary politics and create sites of coalition. Donovan is known for his men's rights antifeminist writings, his affiliation with white supremacist groups like the Wolves of Vinland, and his status as an influential figure in the alt-right.[41] Donovan has contended that women domesticate men, advocated a pansecessionist ideal where smaller ethnonationalist enclaves would govern themselves, and rejected "gay" as an identity despite acknowledging his attraction to men because the term names what he sees as an identity and culture that feminizes men.[42] Similar to the divergent projects of Bly and Khan, Donovan's *The Way of Men* argues that masculinity is in crisis and under attack in the present. For Donovan, men are asked to reject violence, embrace their emotions, and see no difference between themselves and women.[43]

Donovan locates the utopian past much earlier than the industrial revolution or the rise of second-wave feminism in the late twentieth century. Donovan's utopian moment predates civilization and is rooted in men's evolutionary nature when men originally banded together to hunt and protect the perimeter of their nascent communities.[44] For Donovan, this traditional masculinity is founded on strength, courage, mastery, and honor.[45] In some ways, his approach echoes Bly's mythopoetic approach, yet like fellow antifeminist Mike Cernovich, Donovan claims men must be in tune with their inner primate—we must be true to how we evolved and our attendant instincts, otherwise we will go against nature and be miserable.[46] Donovan casts men's brutish evolutionary nature as in conflict with modern civilization. For centuries, men were able to adapt the core survival elements of masculinity to fit the needs of civilization: men could be knights, warriors, and other heroes. For Donovan, the present moment has not just rejected the brutish, primal masculinity but the adaptation of other traditional forms of masculinity as well. For men to find happiness and purpose, they must return to the source and reclaim masculinity through what he calls "the way of the gang."[47] This is the only thing that will save mankind from the hypercivilizing forces of feminism and "globalism" of now and a more dystopian future.[48]

Looking to recuperate the essential evolutionary elements of masculinity and build a utopian future, Donovan urges that men start their own gangs: "The gang is the kernel of masculine identity.... it is also the kernel of ethnic, tribal, and national identity. The culture of the gang in, as author bell hooks wrote in a rather different context, 'the essence of patriarchal masculinity.'"[49] As with "The Misandry Bubble," Donovan sees civilizational collapse in the near future, and building gangs ensures both the embrace of masculinity and survival through "gangs of men ... restart[ing] the world."[50] Notably, Donovan asserts that gangs must be built on commonalities—religion, ethnoracial identity, shared ideology—and proximity. In other words, Donovan's future salvation rests on a return to barbarianism and brotherhood, but the formation of an "us" of the gang relies on some organic level of identarian sameness.[51] Donovan's embrace of a pre-civilized, pre-social-contract past allows him to imagine a future built on masculinity and ethnonationalism.

Despite their differing political content, each of these reactionary examples shares a common temporal structure. Looking back to an idealized and stable past, the authors critique the ongoing social transformations of the present. In order to stave off the crisis of the present, they seek a future built in the image of the past.

Utopian Dimensions of Time, or Temporality and Sociopolitical Critique

Understanding the deployment of usable pasts to critique the present and build reactionary futures requires recognizing time as an *expression* of the political imagination. As a tool of entrenchment, narrative and rhetorical time is not neutral, objective, or apart from sociopolitical machinations. The procession of time is not simply one damn thing after another. Rather, time in this case is carefully emplotted—aspects of the past are remembered and forgotten, sifted and shaped by the political imagination.[52] Likewise, one's perspective on the present and future is forged in part through one's sociopolitical position. In a way, time—through its rhetorical usage and narration—is charged with value and meaning in order to leverage sociopolitical critique. This is the utopian dimension of time. Time becomes the landscape where communities can imagine utopias and dystopias as a means to articulate their sociopolitical desires and foster an identity that can be mobilized. To understand how time structures forms of critique, one must turn more directly to the concept of utopia.

In its original usage, utopia was not located in time but rather in space. In 1516, Sir Thomas More used the term "Utopia," meaning "no place," to describe a land without private property, where everyone receives the goods that they need, and each person contributes to the collective labor of society.[53] As a place that does not exist, More's *Utopia* rendered a perfect society elsewhere and offered a contrast with the world of More and his readers. Notably, writing at a moment of global exploration, trade, and expansion allowed More to imagine Utopia as existing in what would be known as the Americas, a place largely unknown (to his readership) to construct his fantasy. However, according to Ernst Bloch, in the eighteenth and nineteenth centuries, writers began imagining utopia not as a place but within a temporal dimension. With More's Utopia, one can say *I am not in that perfect place*; however, "when it is transposed into the future, not only am I not there, but utopia itself is also not with itself."[54] In this view, the perfect society is located elsewhere in time. For utopian writers of the eighteenth and nineteenth centuries and afterward, the elsewhere was the future. Shifting utopian thought from a geographic to a temporal dimension allowed writers and readers to imagine the future possibility of a perfect or at least better world, as if to say utopia is not here, utopia is not now, but utopia can exist one day.

But what exactly is utopia? What does a better world look like? Much of the creative and scholarly work on utopia in the last fifty years has explored utopia as an imagined space and time wherein social inequalities related to race, class, and gender can be overcome. However, these "freedom dreams" are not utopian for all.[55] For those invested in systemic inequality, these utopian visions may well be dystopian. Consider how Chicano recuperations of Aztlán as a symbol of cultural pride and rightful belonging has been read by some as a nightmarish plan by Chicana/os, Mexican immigrants, and the Mexican government to reconquer the US Southwest.[56] Or, recall how Nikole Hannah-Jones's assertion in "The 1619 Project" that Black experience is central to the creation and understanding of America was seen as divisive and as an attack on white people and America.[57] These and numerous other examples illustrate how justice-oriented, multiracial, and feminist utopias form the basis for what Edward Chan has termed "multicultural dystopias."[58] From William Luther Pierce's *The Turner Diaries* and *Hunter* to Dave Arendt's *Reclaiming Aztlan* and Ben Shapiro's *True Allegiance*, there is an entire genre of multicultural dystopian novels that allow for the rendering of violent, reactionary political fantasies.[59] Of course, the existence of multicultural (and feminist) dystopias exposes the possibility of reactionary utopias, the imagined future worlds rooted in an idealized past that seek to either maintain social hierarchies or return society to the inequalities of the status quo ante.[60] Reactionary utopias embody "the possibility of hope" for entrenchment and revanchism.

Most scholars have unsurprisingly assumed that the utopian imagination through which literary and nonliterary works are read should be a then and there (i.e., time and place) of equality, justice, and happiness. But how does one read the utopian imaginings of reactionaries? Although texts like *Alien Nation* or "The Misandry Bubble" may not offer utopian worlds for many, these works capture and articulate the fears and the desires of white supremacy and men's rights antifeminism. They may not be *your* idea of utopia or *mine*, but they certainly carry what some would see as utopian impulses. As Theodor W. Adorno has suggested, "There is nothing like a single, fixable utopian content."[61] In order to make these utopian impulses legible, we must shed our preconceived notions of what a perfect world may look like and foreground the critical, rhetorical function of utopia that signals both the important and the evaluative work that utopias perform.[62]

Utopia is inseparable from its critical function. In conversation with Adorno, Ernst Bloch contended that "the essential function of utopia is a critique of what is present."[63] Moreover, evaluation and fault-finding of the present bears a "utopian impulse": "What is true is that each and every criticism of imperfection, incompleteness, intolerance, and impatience already without a doubt presupposes the conception of, and longing for, a possible perfection."[64] That is, when a text like "The 1776 Report" leverages a critique of the present and the move away from individual rights (or, more accurately, the effort to address centuries of systemic inequality), embedded within this critique is the premise of a utopian future wherein patriotic education has been renewed.

While Bloch underscores utopia's critical function, Marlana Portolano contends that a concept of utopia has been embedded in rhetoric since the beginning. For Portolano, this utopian impulse has existed since antiquity, well before Thomas More's initial coining of "Utopia." In her description of a "rhetorical function of utopia," Portolano states,

> Without naming it "utopia," rhetorical theorists have consistently referred to an imagined, often idealized aspect of place as part of ethos, the artistic rhetorical proof that is drawn from an audience's collective character. In a corresponding vein, rhetorical practices are inherent in what utopian theorists Herbert Marcuse and Ernst Bloch

have called the "utopian impulse." ... For the purposes of my argument, "utopia" is not an impossible political dream or a philosophical ideal but, rather, any kind of symbolic expression of hope for a better world, whether in a concrete future or in fictional or spiritual realms, and no matter if that expression is considered in a positive or negative light.[65]

Emphasizing the critical, rhetorical function of utopia provides a lens for investigating those utopian impulses found in literary and nonliterary texts and exploring the cultural work they perform. These reactionary utopias are not simply paranoid anxieties or extremist fantasies. They are expressions of hope, critiques of the present world, and efforts to forge identity and mobilize community to build a future. Through Bloch and Portolano, we see two interrelated functions of utopias: they foster a critique of the present, and they imagine and potentially mobilize a shared communal identity through the rhetoric of a "hope for a better world."[66]

Recognizing the critical, rhetorical function of utopia offers a new dimension to and transcends scholarship on the political uses of history in the late twentieth and early twenty-first centuries. Since the 1980s, the United States and other Western nations have been embroiled in what are often described as the culture wars, an ongoing war of position over which narratives, symbols, and values fashion a national character.[67] In Australia, this debate is often described as the "history wars" because the struggle over contemporary politics is rooted in and finds expression in competing historical narratives.[68] The phrase "history wars" may more adequately name a critical dimension of the US culture wars; that is, the contestation over what is "American" is bound to competing usable pasts.

Here, I resist the positivist frame that considers usable pasts as anathema to disciplinary history.[69] Rather, usable pasts may be largely fictions or they may be grounded in historical research, but they emerge from and demonstrate the exigencies and questions of the present. In divergent ways, both "The 1776 Report" and "The 1619 Project" function as usable pasts. "The 1776 Report" draws on American exceptionalism to select specific elements of US history to forge a narrative useful for reactionary politics today. While more disciplinarily rigorous than "The 1776 Report," "The 1619 Project" also advances a usable past by asking what the story of the United States would be if we reconsider the national story as indelibly linked to the story of slavery.[70] These usable pasts are dialectically backward looking. As Genaro Padilla noted about nostalgia, these ruminations on the past are simultaneously critiques of the present.[71]

The critical, rhetorical function of utopia opens these usable pasts in a new temporal direction. While utopia may look backward for inspiration, it exists always in the unfolding future. Looking at these texts, sometimes the future orientation is merely implied or gestured toward and sometimes it is more fully fleshed out. Nikole Hannah-Jones's introduction to "The 1619 Project" renders a vision for America where Black folks and their experiences are an essential part of the nation's fabric and may lay claim to the United States and its symbols without blindness but in recognition of injustice past and present. While drawing on the past, Hannah-Jones points toward a future where Black people lay equal claim to belonging. As a reactionary project, "The 1776 Report" seeks to recenter whiteness within the national imagination as it calls for a rebirth of patriotic education that will instill a love of country and sense of exceptionalism. In other words, these usable pasts are solely about neither history nor the present. They both evidence utopian imaginings of the future, but it is the reactionary utopia that seeks to build a future that echoes the past, forging a sense of political identity beholden to the status quo ante.

Reactionary Utopias and the Fashioning of Political Identity

To explore how utopian imaginings forge political identity, to understand their political and cultural work, one must recognize these as *reactionary* utopias and explore their relationship to ideology. Karl Mannheim argued that ideology and utopia both share a common core element but are largely discrete phenomena. For Mannheim, both are explanatory perceptions of the world that are incongruous with the state of reality.[72] In other words, these are the precepts and narratives that shape people's perception of and relationship to the world around them. However, according to Mannheim, utopias and ideologies perform fundamentally different sociopolitical work: whereas utopias are wish-dreams for a better world that disrupt the current order and mobilize people for change (i.e., they have a critical function), ideologies stabilize the sociopolitical order, naturalizing the status quo and hindering social change. Because of their divergent functions, Mannheim's framework appears to suggest that ideology and utopia are mutually exclusive entities. However, this is not the case. Reactionary utopias expose how ideology and utopia may indeed be intertwined.[73]

The reactionary utopias under study here illustrate an intersection of ideology and utopia. Reactionaries do not simply want to retain their current status; they wish to reclaim the sociopolitical standing that they imagined they have lost, the status quo ante. Within reactionary utopias today, ideology and utopia appear as mutually reinforcing elements that transcend and act upon reality. Notably, Mannheim recognized the potential connection between ideology and utopia, for he contended that "utopias of ascendant classes are often . . . permeated with ideological elements."[74] While not all groups may deploy utopias, all groups are shaped by and bear ideology. Moreover, as reactionary forces position themselves as sociopolitically aggrieved and ascendant, their utopias become narrative and rhetorical vehicles for their ideologies, propelling their worldview and allowing it to spread. For example, consider how *Alien Nation* and *Iron John* achieved bestseller status within the United States and thus spread ideological precepts of white supremacy and antifeminism.

The interrelationship between ideology and utopia can forge political identity through what Portolano described as utopia's rhetorical function. For Portolano, the "symbolic expression of hope for a better world" "is drawn by the rhetor from the audience's collective character."[75] As part of cultivating and deploying ethos (i.e., credibility, character, the values that unite a community), imagining utopias fosters the relationship and shared worldview between rhetor and audience. That is, in the case of reactionary utopias, when those like Brimelow and others render the present moment a dystopian multicultural hellscape and gesture toward a means of recuperating a core white identity in the United States, they are eliciting and fomenting a sense of shared white supremacist values. When Bly, Khan, Donovan, and others lament the loss of traditional masculinity—whether that be embodied in barbarianism, chivalry, or the Fonz— they advance that society's future depends on the defeminization of men and recuperation of a masculine ideal. Or, in the language of Louis Althusser in his foundational work on ideology, these authors and their writings interpellate the audience as subjects of reactionary politics.[76]

Recognizing that utopias are bound together with and function as vessels for ideologies—creating a locus of ethos where rhetor and audience meet—forges a critical lens for examining reactionary utopias. Consider the reactionary utopias glossed earlier. "The 1776 Report" draws on shared values of American exceptionalism rooted in a glorious and ordained past and asserts concerns regarding racial division and vilification of America, its heroes, and its history. These shared values and concerns are drawn from the "audience's collective character" and establish an ethical intention behind the report's call for a "great project of national renewal [that] depends upon true education—not merely training in particular skills but the formation of citizens."[77] While critics of the report should question the historical value of the document and push back against the connection it makes between nineteenth-century proslavery advocates and social justice activists today, they should also recognize that the report establishes an ethical intention with its audience so that the authors and audience forge a discursive community that imagines itself as good.[78] Readers of "The 1776 Report" are thus able to imagine themselves in community marked by shared values and concerns. Although the report does not depict a concrete utopia, it gestures toward one, for this restoration of patriotic education will provide Americans with the "timeless stories and noble heroes that inspire them to be good, brave, diligent, daring, generous, honest, and compassionate."[79] "The 1776 Report" looks to the future to teach this "accurate history," but it never fully renders what this future will look like.[80] Indeed, this idealized future of national renewal does not need to be articulated, for this utopia exists within the minds of the audience and the rhetor. This utopia establishes their common ground and fosters an ideological and political unity between them.

The reactionary utopia imagined by Brimelow's *Alien Nation* also elicits the shared values and concerns of the audiences' collective character. *Alien Nation* draws on and stokes fears of the changing social order brought about by the Civil Rights movement gains and changes to immigration policy. This white supremacist utopia thus begins by reading a loss of white sociopolitical standing. Brimelow establishes a common value of a white national identity in his audiences' character. Brimelow repeatedly references the colonial-stock (i.e., Anglo-American and Western European) cultural and political heritage of the United States. While Brimelow does not go so far as to say that the US has historically been a white nation, he does point to previous restrictive immigration measures as essential to propelling cultural assimilation and contends that the end of the national origin quota system with the 1965 Immigration Act has fundamentally shifted the current character of the United States and imperils its future. The common ideological ground for Brimelow and his audience requires a belief in the core white colonial stock of the United States and a desire to buttress and strengthen this ethnoracial core in the future through renewed immigration restriction.

While they may bear marked differences, the men's movement writings of Bly and the explicit antifeminism of Khan and Donovan draw on and express the values and concerns they share with their readers. These works view contemporary masculinity as in crisis. For Bly, industrialization and the way it took men away from the home and family, hiding their masculine labor and virtues from their sons, was responsible for many contemporary social issues from gang activity and domestic violence to drugs and "aimless murder."[81] Bly finds an imagined unity with his readership by both noting how contemporary masculinity damages men and locating a healthy masculinity in the past, a powerful site of recuperation. Khan does not locate the masculinity crisis in industrialization per se but within the gains of feminism of the late-twentieth century. Donovan argues that the crisis of masculinity is part of modernity and exacerbated by the gains of twentieth-century feminists. Bly, Khan, and Donovan, each render an idealized form of masculinity located in a past.

Despite the divergences in their approach to feminism, Bly, Khan, and Donovan embody the rhetorical function of utopia in their ethical intention. That is, they premise their arguments on the goodness of their projects and the good intentions they hold in common with their audience. This is perhaps unsurprising for Bly, who appears to want a healthy, liberated masculinity for men. But given the virulent antifeminism of Khan and Donovan, it is critical to note how their "good intentions" are established through their positioning of men as victims of feminism. As Khan deploys this shared ethical character to call for a return to patriarchy, Donovan engages a critical, rhetorical utopia along axes of both gender and race. Through the formation of ethnonationalist masculinist gangs, Donovan imagines with his readers a reactionary utopian response to both feminism and multiculturalism. As such, Donovan exposes how rendering shared values with one community (e.g., antifeminists) can allow one to introduce and foster other constituent elements (e.g., white supremacy) of a reactionary coalition.

It may be helpful to consider the critical, rhetorical function of utopia as less of a blueprint for a harmonious world and more of a rhetorical trope, a common discursive maneuver that points to the possibility of the future and strengthens the identification between audience and rhetor on the grounds of shared ethos. Here, I am reminded of Houston Baker's assertion that "the effective trope . . . is merely a lever long enough for the purpose."[82] If we consider the temporal logics of these reactionary examples, each romanticizes a past and identifies a crisis in the present. The future is split into two tracks: a dystopian continuation of the present and a utopian recuperation and reconfiguration of the past. The rhetorical utopias articulated by Bly, Khan, and Donovan imagine a common character that unites the rhetor and audience into a discursive community. The authors depict the divergent tracks and through the trope-as-lever ask the audience to choose their future.

Each example evidences that reactionary utopian futures are built on romances of the past.[83] The reactionary utopias that I explore in this chapter are characterized as such because of their investment in systemic inequality. While they each look to the past to build a future, it is not their rootedness in the past that structures their reactionary projects. The past may also be a fertile ground for imagining liberationist utopian futures.[84] What "The 1776 Report" and its cohort of examples expose is how reactionary utopias are not simply rooted in the past to conserve some narrative content or values that have been lost. Rather, they turn to the past to stave off changing power relations in the present. That is, reactionary utopias find no inherent value in the past of the nation's founding, mid-twentieth-century gender roles, or biologized, pre-social-contract racial and gender dynamics. Reactionary utopias merely turn to those pasts because they are the necessary levers to alter the future trajectory of the present, a present in which reactionaries see themselves as under siege. As such, reactionary utopias are political and ideological tools with flexible content.

Shared Structures and Reactionary Alignments

Beyond articulating and potentially mobilizing a communal identity with one's readers, the temporal structure to reactionary utopias allows for alignments between distinct sociopolitical projects. The authors explored in this chapter may not see themselves as contributing to the same political project of others in this grouping, yet they are aligned at a deeper level through a discursive and ideological structure. For example, although Michael Kimmel and others in masculinity studies position the mythopoetic work of Bly as distinct and apart from the political dimensions of men's rights antifeminism, both Bly and Khan assert a crisis in masculinity in the present and deploy usable pasts to build a future.[85] Moreover, across axes of race and gender, Brimelow and Donovan would be horrified by Khan's location of a future revivification of patriarchy through Asian and Latin American (i.e., nonwhite) nations. This disjuncture exposes the unnatural, uneasy alliance between white supremacy and men's rights antifeminism. Although they may both be forms of reactionary politics, their coalitional possibilities are far from a foregone conclusion. However, while this treatment of race and migration clearly diverge, their understanding of time—the utopian past, the dystopian present, and the uncertain future—structures both discourses and ideologies allowing readers and adherents to potentially traverse and bridge these communities. That is, the specific content of these narratives may differ in crucial ways, but their overall structure and points of connection make reactionary politics legible across differences and fosters the possibility of coalition. Moreover, other reactionary utopias and potential alignments exist. Romanticizations of a preindustrial past—one associated with nature and the natural—are common in anticapitalist, antivaccine, and some environmental discursive communities. These utopian pasts can facilitate unexpected alignments such as when environmentalism and white supremacy coalesce to fashion ecofascism.

Critically, the texts explored in this chapter need not each specifically depict and explore all three temporal components of the past, present, and future, but these works fit together and reinforce each other because they draw from and reinforce aspects of the temporal-ideological structure. That is, the emphasizing of discrete aspects of time actually evidences how these texts may work together in complementary fashion without directly addressing each other. They rely on an unspoken metastructure of past, present, and future charged with utopian and dystopian value. Each text is both an entity into itself and part of a larger discursive and ideological machinery. Each iteration of this reactionary rule need not fully engage all three temporal locations. Like pieces of a mosaic or components of an assemblage, these iterations rely on others to further their work. Moreover, the specific contents of these temporal imaginings need not be the same. Even as Khan and Donovan imagine drastically different futures, the fact that they both find men presently emasculated by feminists allows them to both occupy space in the discursive and political community of men's rights antifeminism. Like with the moments of seeming disjuncture discussed earlier, members of the discourse community have their ideologies and identities shaped by these works, and these distinct yet interconnected discourse communities perform the critical work of creating the connective tissue that holds these sociopolitical projects together.

Because of their rhetorical power, these reactionary utopias can perform critical cultural and political work. First, they forge a basis for imagining community. However, unlike "homogenous empty time" of the present or curated narratives of the past, reactionary utopias also open up hope for a future.[86] The future may be a return to patriotic education called for in "The 1776 Report" or increased immigration restriction and assimilation into the colonial-stock America offered by *Alien Nation*. Second, like the weaponization of victimhood, these utopias fashion an identity of loss and aggrievement, but they also orient toward the future, calling for an active challenge to the present conditions. Consider how loss of standing is at the core of *Alien Nation* and "The Misandry Bubble." Third, as carriers of ideology, reactionary utopias do not simply solidify a common ground between audience and rhetor. Rather, these utopian futures and their critiques of the present interpellate their audience, drawing ideological subjects into community. These works circulate, some on bestseller lists and others in underground discursive communities, shaping the culture and language of reactionary politics. Finally, because they share a common overarching structure but have flexible content, reactionary utopias may smooth over potential fractures between reactionary coalitions. For example, Bly may not see *Iron John* as contributing to men's rights antifeminism, and Khan's "Misandry Bubble" may imagine a future of patriarchy in "third-world" countries that diverges from the futures imagined by *The Ways of Men*, but the shared critique of the changing sociopolitical conditions of the present along with the romanticization of the past and the gesture toward a future allow for reactionary alignments and potential coalitions.

RULE #4

Label Your Opponents Extreme (so that You Can Appear Reasonable)

All around you people are pushing the world to change. Perhaps they are calling for greater gender and racial equality. Maybe they are advocating for a more level economic playing field. They may be pushing for greater representation in school curriculum and acceptance by society. These calls for change threaten to disrupt the world as you know it and your place within that world. What do you do? Go on the offensive! Label these agents of social change as extremists. You may dredge up terms that resonate as deeply, historically anti-American (e.g., "Nazis" and "Communists") to a broader public and tie your opponents to these terms. Or you may deploy terms that are beyond the pale, like "baby killer" and "groomer." After you label social transformation as extreme, you can assert your stance as one of reason, moderation, and common sense. Reactionary entrenchment is, then, the only reasonable position. Your audience will be compelled to respond to calls for social change with desire to keep things as they are or return to a simpler time. Let the backlash ensue!

In 1977, former singer turned antigay activist Anita Bryant founded the anti-LBGTQ organization Save Our Children and argued that because same-sex relationships could not biologically reproduce, the LBGTQ community needed to recruit children, stoking fears and conflating queerness with pedophilia. During the early 1990s, radio host Rush Limbaugh popularized the term "feminazis" to describe feminists, forging an imagined world wherein those seeking gender equality were man-hating fascists.[1] In 2020, conservative activist Christopher Rufo initiated a campaign against critical race theory (CRT), purposefully using the term to signal not just an academic area of study but also efforts within ethnic studies, antiracist education, and diversity, equity, and inclusion (DEI) initiatives. The effort framed this imaginary CRT as inherently antiwhite and anti-American.[2] In 2022, Florida Governor Ron DeSantis drew on Bryant's playbook and signed into law a provision prohibiting "school district personnel from discouraging or prohibiting parental notification & involvement in critical decisions affecting student's mental, emotional, or physical well-being; prohibit[ing] classroom discussion about sexual orientation or gender identity in certain grade levels."[3] When the Walt Disney Company, a major Florida employer, came out against the law and in support of the LBGTQ community, Rufo and other reactionaries accused the company of supporting the "grooming" and "sexualization" of children.[4] Taken in isolation, these appear to be discrete moments, separated by time, place, issue, and agents. However, placed beside and against one another, the pattern emerges.

These examples share a common rhetorical structure. How does it work? In each case, reactionary rhetors ascribe a label that renders their targets as "extremists." Feminists are "Nazis." LBGTQ folk "recruit" children for the purpose of sexualization. Antiracist activists and scholars are "un-American" and aligned with "communism." For each of these labels to stick, there must be a kernel of truth within them, even if that kernel is infinitesimally small. There are feminists who identify as radical although they are probably not trying to eliminate men as much as patriarchy. LBGTQ folk do offer community to younger generations because young LBGTQ people are often not accepted within heteronormative and homophobic homes, schools, and other institutions. Antiracist scholars and activists do indeed want the United States to do better and often take class analysis into consideration. By distorting these kernels of truth and labeling their targets as extremists, reactionary rhetors are able to assert a position of reasonability and moderation to their audiences. Through this positioning, reactionary entrenchment renders efforts to fight against inequality and injustice as dangerous and radical and efforts to maintain the status quo as rational, moderate, safe, and commonsense.

To understand this rule as a purposeful strategy aimed at demonizing others by waging a cultural war, one need only turn to recent comments by Christopher Rufo. In the case of the recent anti-CRT campaign, Rufo has been remarkably candid about his strategy. On social media and in interviews, Rufo has made explicit the often-hidden reasoning behind this discursive strategy. First, as he told Benjamin Wallace-Wells of *The New Yorker*, reactionaries needed a "new language" to frame the debate: "'Critical race theory' is the perfect villain. . . . Its connotations are all negative to most middle-class Americans, including racial minorities, who see the world as 'creative' rather than 'critical,' 'individual' rather than 'racial,' 'practical' rather than 'theoretical.' Strung together, the phrase 'critical race theory' connotes hostile, academic, divisive, race-obsessed, poisonous, elitist, anti-American."[5] After repackaging a host of disparate scholarly and activist projects—from the actual scholarship of critical race theory and ethnic studies to the institutional efforts of diversity, equity, and inclusion programming and antiracist activism—into the label of CRT, Rufo tweeted: "We have successfully frozen their brand—'critical race theory'—into the public conversation and are steadily driving up negative perceptions. We will eventually turn it toxic, as we put all of the various cultural insanities under that brand category. . . . The goal is to have the public read something crazy in the newspaper and immediately think 'critical race theory.' We have decodified the term and will recodify it to annex the entire range of cultural constructions that are unpopular with Americans."[6] Rufo's imagined CRT is an elastic label, a "semantic Hefty Bag" pliable enough to encapsulate anything racial that appears out of the ordinary or unpopular to mainstream audiences.[7] Critically, Rufo acknowledges that his efforts are concerned not with providing intellectual honesty but tarring racial justice efforts to wage a cultural and political war. But labeling his opponents as extreme was only the first step.

Rufo also fashioned his own reasonability and trustworthiness through key strategic moves. He claims to be an "investigative journalist" who was uncovering these otherwise little-known racial justice efforts. However, his exposé that launched this campaign was merely a 650-word blog post that decried as totalitarian and a "racial-justice shakedown" a program aimed at helping white city workers work against systemic inequality.[8] A later article that received significant traction was simply four sentences that framed a training document as "explicitly endorsing principles of segregationism, group-based guilt, and race essentialism—ugly concepts that should have been left behind a century ago."[9] He claimed to have discovered the linkages between contemporary antiracist efforts, CRT, and the Marxism of the Frankfurt school by engaging in the scholarly practice of following the footnotes.[10] However, as David Theo Goldberg points out, the Frankfurt school's discussion of racism was limited to antisemitism and the early writings of CRT did not reference thinkers from the Frankfurt school.[11] Moreover, Laura Meckler and Josh Dawset note that many of the allegations that Rufo makes in his articles are not substantiated by the evidence that he offers.[12] Rufo likely relies on his readership not being critical readers or not examining the evidence that he provides at all.

Rufo's assertion of faux reasonability also foreshadowed a pivot in his political strategy. In January 2022, Rufo tweeted that the next step was to push for "curriculum transparency": "The Left will expect that, after passing so-called 'CRT bans' last year, we will overplay our hand. By moving to curriculum transparency, we will deflate that argument and bait the Left into opposing 'transparency,' which will raise the question: what are they trying to hide?"[13] After having maligned racial justice efforts, Rufo's embrace of curriculum transparency would put his opponents on their heels. Who after all would argue against parents' rights to know what their children are learning? Of course, curriculum transparency was just a guise to instill greater surveillance of and fear of harassment within school officials.

Here, one must note that the end goal of Rufo and his compatriots is not simply to demonize their opponents and appear reasonable in doing so. Rufo has advocated "lay[ing] siege to the institutions" of society.[14] He has expressed that "to get universal school choice you really need to operate from a premise of universal public school distrust."[15] In other words, this discursive maneuver, like all reactionary rhetorical strategies, is about maintaining and wielding social and political power.

While Rufo offers a clear articulation of the reasoning behind this discursive strategy, this chapter turns to James

Lindsay's *Race Marxism* to examine how this rhetorical strategy is put into practice. Running with Rufo's anti-CRT campaign, Lindsay's work draws on anticommunism and racial fears to advance an investment in the status quo ante and nullify critiques of inequality. After exploring Lindsay's deployment of "labeling others extreme," this chapter interrogates the cultural logics of how this rule works to shape the possibilities of political thought. Placing the concept of the Overton Window in conversation with the ideas of Antonio Gramsci, Stuart Hall, and Jacques Rancière exposes how this rule is crucial to forging and wielding social and political power. But first, the chapter turns to Lindsay's *Race Marxism*.

Race Marxism: Repackaging Anticommunist Fears for a Twenty-First-Century Racial Anxiety

Trained as a mathematician, James Lindsay came to prominence when he and collaborators Peter Boghossian and Hellen Pluckrose engaged in a Sokal-esque hoax targeting academic journals in the fields of gender, sexuality, and ethnic studies. Lindsay and company submitted manuscripts with falsified data and purposefully inflammatory conceits in order to discredit what they termed "grievance studies."[16] As with Rufo, media organizations often failed to question the legitimacy of Lindsay and his collaborators' claims, and when journalists and scholars pushed back on Lindsay and his cohort, their critiques did nothing to tarnish these reactionary hoaxsters as legitimate experts on race, gender, and sexuality studies in conservative media. After the hoax, Lindsay and Pluckrose coauthored *Cynical Theories*, a culture war primer that argues postmodernism has infiltrated the humanities and social sciences and corrupted the scholarship emerging from ethnic, gender, and sexuality studies.[17] Despite demonstrating, or because of this demonstration of, a rudimentary and facile understanding of the subject material, *Cynical Theories* quickly became a bestseller and an influential text within reactionary social media. The initial hoax and the publication of *Cynical Theories* cemented Lindsay's status as culture war expert within the conservative mediasphere. When the Rufo-influenced backlash against DEI and antiracism took shape as an anti-CRT campaign, Lindsay was poised to perform the role of expert for conservative news and on social media. Lindsay's *Race Marxism* demonstrates how one can label their opponents as extreme so that one can appear reasonable. As a cultural worker operating as a conduit between extreme and mainstream reactionary politics, Lindsay deploys this rhetorical maneuver to make social justice, and particularly racial justice, efforts unpalatable and promote a logic where entrenchment within the current order of things appears to be the only reasonable, American approach.

Like Rufo, Lindsay joins under the banner of critical race theory a host of related projects: the academic and legal scholarship of CRT, ethnic studies, antiracist activism, DEI trainings and initiatives, and recent flashpoints where race and racism were central to conflict. In doing so, Lindsay renders CRT a unified effort to undermine the lives and worlds of his readers. The central conceit of *Race Marxism* is that CRT is a Marxian project wherein class divisions have been replaced with racial ones.[18] Lindsay locates this shift in the work of Herbert Marcuse, who saw hope for social transformation in the organizing potential of working-class people of color and, as Lindsay is fond of reminding readers, was Angela Davis's dissertation director.[19] For Lindsay, not only are Marxism and critical race theory characterized by the fomenting of conflict, whether based on class or race, but both projects are marked by irrational and conspiratorial thinking.[20] Ultimately, Lindsay depicts CRT as a civilizational threat, contending that CRT is but "the tip of a one-hundred-year-long spear that is being thrust into the side of Western Civilization."[21] For Lindsay, Western Civilization is characterized by liberal democracy, capitalism, colorblindness, and an adherence to the status quo. Through the spear metaphor, CRT is but the latest subversive invention aimed at destroying this way of life. Because he views CRT as merely the tip of the spear, Lindsay argues that one must move backward through intellectual history, excavating the origins of this dangerous movement.[22] While CRT is the tip of the spear, and the critical theory of the Frankfurt School and advent of postmodernism form the shaft, "W. E. B. DuBois is the hands on the shaft of the spear" and Marx, Hegel, and Rousseau are the "two-hundred or more years of muscle behind it."[23] Together, these thinkers function as a project that seeks to undermine and destroy the stability and status quo of Western Civilization today. Unfortunately, Lindsay does not extend his metaphor further to explore if Immanuel Kant, Plato, and Aristotle are the hips and legs respectively, from which the true power of the spear thrust comes.[24]

As a scholar steeped in CRT, ethnic studies, and the discourses of antiracist activism, I find it tempting to rebut every intellectual misstep in *Race Marxism*. This rebuttal may begin with simple questions: What is Marxist thought if not a central thread within Western Civilization? Isn't the nefarious dialectic that Lindsay identifies as a threat to society as we know it simply the core structure of intellectual history?[25] How can CRT be reductive to racism as the sole reason for inequality if CRT also promotes intersectional analyses?[26] These questions elucidate serious errors in Lindsay's thinking for any reader with a thorough understanding of the fields Lindsay is critiquing. And there are numerous other questions one may ask to unravel the semblance of logical coherence that *Race Marxism* purports. However, two caveats must be made. First, Lindsay does occasionally offer legitimate critiques of what he calls

CRT; critiques that if he were more well-read and honest, Lindsay could point out have already been made by the CRT scholars he seeks to tar.[27] However, Lindsay's strategy relies on depicting CRT as a fairly unified and monolithic movement, not a heterogenous set of projects constellating around common concerns. Second, it is not necessary to identify all Lindsay's errors and fallacies, for he is not speaking to scholars situated within these fields. Lindsay is reaching an audience with a more limited knowledge of CRT and intellectual history than his own. That is, *Race Marxism* is not seeking to make an intervention in an intellectual project. The book is Lindsay's effort to educate, or miseducate, his readers into his political project. Thus, in the following pages, I find it more useful to demonstrate how his logic functions to position reactionary entrenchment as rational and normal through labeling those who advocate for social justice as radicals and extremists.

The central argumentative trope of Lindsay's *Race Marxism* is that Marxism has been repackaged and transformed into contemporary racial justice movements through CRT. Here, two questions immediately emerge: What is Marxism to Lindsay? And how does he see elements of CRT align with Marxism? First, it should be noted that Lindsay does not see Marxism as an academic approach seeking to understand how labor, capital, and the production of value shape social dynamics. Rather, he reads any articulation of Marxism through a lens deeply influenced by Cold War rhetorical legacies.[28] For Lindsay, Marxism sees the world cleanly divided along class divisions where material conditions determine one's identity, concerns, and political interests. Lindsay contends that Marxists seek to foment division in society: "The goal of all Marxian Theory is to alienate and exploit some lower class from society until they hate it, mostly by projecting that the society itself is that which is alienating and exploiting them."[29] For Lindsay, Marxists are not actually concerned with economic exploitation and inequality but with fostering conflict and using the working-class to gain power for themselves. Lindsay rightly notes that for Marxists, this conflict is the prime force propelling history. Central to his argument, Lindsay warns against "negative thinking" whereby Marxists identify an aspect of the world that needs to change in order for a better, more egalitarian, utopian world to come about. For Frankfurt school intellectuals like Max Horkheimer and Marcuse, critique and negative thinking were foundational to forging a better future out of the conditions of the present.

For Lindsay, highlighting society's contradictions and inequalities is but conspiratorial, paranoid thinking aimed at changing the status quo. CRT replaces Marxism's emphasis on class division and economic exploitation with an emphasis on racial conflict and injustice. In this way, Lindsay maps his perceptions of CRT onto his understanding of and anxiety about Marxism. According to Lindsay, CRT positions race as the solitary and prime conflict underwriting history. CRT's focus on race and hope for a better world (i.e., negative thinking) make it a paranoid and conspiratorial intellectual project.[30] Lindsay sees this effort not as one to understand historical and contemporary inequality but as an effort by scholars and activists to exploit the pain of people of color in order to seize power.[31] Moreover, because he sees CRT as a paranoid effort that stokes racial conflict in order to seize social and political power, Lindsay casts CRT as a racist endeavor.[32] Echoing Marxism's theorization of a dictatorship of the proletariat, Lindsay foretells a coming "dictatorship of antiracists" that is taking aim at whiteness and those not actively committed to antiracism.[33]

Lindsay positions his imagined CRT as extreme and dangerous to the survival of Western Civilization in a few key ways. First, Lindsay clearly builds on Cold War–era anxiety that cleaved the world into an us-them dichotomy between

Western, liberal capitalist countries coded as democracies and their Other: communist regimes. Here, his efforts to map CRT onto Marxist thought are less an intellectually driven project and more an effort to revivify and stoke old anxieties about national and civilizational survival for a new era of racial justice struggles. Crucial to this is Lindsay's invocation of negative thinking, which he ties to Marxism vis-à-vis the Frankfurt School and Horkheimer. Quoting from an interview with Horkheimer, Lindsay recognizes that Marxists may not be able to determine "what a good, a free society would look like from within the society which we now live in. We lack the means. But in our work we can bring up the negative aspects of this society, which we want to change."[34] For Lindsay, the danger of Marxism and CRT is that they wish to change the existing order. Despite Lindsay sounding the alarm, this negative thinking of critical theory can be a moderate and essential force within history. When one sees a problem, they advocate for change. Pointing out and addressing inequality—whether in the form of segregation in the 1950s or police violence today—is not a threat to Western Civilization but a way in which Western Civilization has changed and will continue to change over time. Unless, of course, one's true understanding of Western Civilization is white domination under the guise of fairness forever and always. While many would see the negative thinking of identifying injustice as a common force driving historical change over the course of human history, Lindsay views this desire for changing the world as a threat to the status quo of Western Civilization.

Lindsay contends that CRT's extremism stems from its emphasis on systemic racism. Lindsay and his readership are invested in the folk theory of racism where racism is enacted by purposefully discriminating people and is both abhorrent and aberrant.[35] From the perspective of the folk theory, Lindsay contends that the existence of systemic racism evidences a "particularly paranoid and cynical style" and that "this belief turns liberal ethics themselves into a racist conspiracy theory upheld by whites against racial minorities while positioning race-first identification, identity politics, and, not least, Critical Race Theory as the only possible remedy."[36] To be clear, CRT and its adjacent projects have critiqued Enlightenment ideology as it grew alongside and was consolidated by the development of white supremacy and capitalism. Lindsay, however, does not engage these critiques on their merits. Rather, he recoils, aghast that scholars might point out how communities have been divided by racializing practices and not as autonomous individuals. This becomes particularly evident in his reading of Kimberlé Crenshaw's writing on intersectionality. In "Mapping the Margins" Crenshaw exposed how the US legal system was unable to address discrimination faced by those caught between two (or more) intersecting systems of oppression (e.g., sexism and racism). While Lindsay acknowledges that Crenshaw opens "a challenging but important domain within discrimination law," he rejects the concept of intersectionality, arguing for a remedy based on Enlightenment, liberal thought, one "veering more toward individualism, objectivity, and meritocracy."[37] This moment in Lindsay's thinking is revealing. Racism, sexism, and other forms of systemic inequalities do not target people based on individualism, objectivity, or merit, and thus an emphasis on these liberal attributes alone cannot remedy group-based inequalities.

When Lindsay asserts that CRT is ushering in "Racial Bolshevik Revolution," "Antiracist Cultural Revolution," and "Dictatorship of the Antiracists," he is not simply suturing Marxism and racial justice efforts to draw on Cold War anxieties.[38] He is simultaneously stoking fear over a changing racial order. Of course, this isn't entirely new. As Charisse Burden-Stelly has noted, twentieth-century US anticommunism often intersected with anti-Blackness and anti–racial justice efforts.[39] One need only consider the ways in which redbaiting was used against Martin Luther King Jr. or how rumors of communist-trained guerillas were attached to Reies Lopez Tijerina and the Alianza's struggle for land rights in New Mexico.[40] It is difficult to read "dictatorship of antiracists" in Lindsay and not hear echoes of reactionary utopias discussed in the previous chapter. Existing within the same sprawling discursive and ideological community, "dictatorship of antiracists" invokes the multiculturalist bureaucrats that had ascended to power in *The Turner Diaries* and other reactionary thrillers.[41] Even if they had not personally read William Luther Pierce's white power novel, Lindsay's reactionary readership is familiar with the anxiety that comes from a loss in racial power. By linking previous communist social upheavals to CRT and the quest for racial justice, Lindsay positions CRT as an epochal threat to Western, liberal (read: white and capitalist) civilization.

Lindsay extends his effort to label CRT as extreme and position himself as moderate through repeatedly comparing and then slightly distancing racial justice scholars and advocates to Nazis. Whereas Lindsay imagines CRT as Marxism redirected along a racial axis, his linking of CRT to Nazism is more complicated. He often asserts what he sees as key overlaps between the movements but also steps back to clarify that CRT is merely *like* but not *actually* Nazism. For example, Lindsay connects CRT and Nazism early on when he says that "critical race theory scapegoats whiteness for the problems of society. Moreover, it does so in an almost perfect parallel to the ways Marxists have scapegoated capitalists and National Socialists scapegoated Jewish people, and for nearly identical reasons."[42] Lindsay also contends that traces of Nazism can be found in CRT's use of phrases like "Black folk," "white folk," and "doing the work." Lindsay asserts that the use of "folk" is not merely another word for "people" or "community" but rather illustrates the perfidious influence of German thinkers like Gustov von Schmoller, Johann Gottfried Herder, G. W. F. Hegel, and German *Volkish* nationalists, who influenced W. E. B. DuBois, who in turn shaped CRT. The logic goes something like this: German thinkers = Nazis → DuBois → CRT.[43] At other points, Lindsay's ascription of Nazism is implied rather than explicitly stated. He asserts that CRT fosters "racial tribalism" and is quite similar to "illiberal right-wingers."[44] In these moments, Lindsay relies on his readers to fill the gaps and affix the Nazi label. Whether directly stated or not, ascribing fascist influences and inclinations to CRT positions racial justice advocates as extreme and radical. Moreover, because Lindsay's argument relies on an us-them dynamic, this juxtaposition implicitly renders Lindsay and his readership as moderate and rational through their shared rejection of CRT and Nazism.

Critically, however, Lindsay also steps back from this labeling at key points. Although he does believe that CRT is *like* Nazism, he argues that critical whiteness studies is *more like* Nazism than CRT is.[45] Moreover, critical to establishing credibility, Lindsay recognizes that CRT opposes Nazism even as he asserts that they share key elements. As such, he asserts that CRT is ultimately a form of communism and not Nazism.[46] Why does Lindsay temper these comparisons when he has made the spurious linkages between CRT and Nazism throughout the book? Is he striving for intellectual nuance and walking the line between analyses of CRT and Nazism? No. It is more accurate to state that Lindsay is walking on both sides of the line. He links CRT to Nazism not because there are strong, legitimate connections between them, but as a strategy for demonizing CRT. By sprinkling in a few caveats about these movements not being the same but being similar, Lindsay claims a moderate, rational position in two ways. First, he rejects the positions of both Nazism and CRT. Therefore, he distances himself from those extremes. In this way, Lindsay triangulates himself against two opposing extremes following the triad model discussed in chapter 1. Second, he distances himself from calling racial justice advocates Nazis, although he has laid the groundwork for his readers to make those assertions. Through this rhetorical two-step, Lindsay both proves and seeks to evade Godwin's Law, the online adage wherein the longer a debate ensues the probability increases that one will make a comparison to Hitler and Nazis.

Along with rendering CRT as an extreme position by mapping it onto Marxism and linking it with Nazism, Lindsay frames what he sees as rational, moderate positions through subtle inferences and through an advocation of "Americanism." While rendering CRT as extremist, "paranoid," "cynical," and conspiratorial, Lindsay repeatedly positions himself and his intended audience as "normal people."[47] For example, Lindsay labels CRT's systemic understanding of racism as extreme against "the way *any normal person* uses or understands" racism.[48] In this moment Lindsay contrasts systemic understandings of racism with the folk theory of racism discussed earlier. This, however, is not simply an analytical distinction. Lindsay deploys "normal" to elicit notions of the good, the proper, and the everyday—the location within the triad model that sits above the fray of conflict between extremes. The "normal" works to signal a sense of shared ethos that makes this common, folk understanding of racism one that is trustworthy. Moreover, the "normal" becomes a site of identification and communion. Distancing himself and his audience from antiracists and racists as well as Nazis and communists, Lindsay's deployment of "normal" gestures toward a sense of ideological community that must be defended. Notably, this rhetorical assertion of normalcy aligns with the language practices and ideology of white supremacy. As numerous scholars have noted, whiteness often goes unmarked and is considered the norm against which people of color are judged.[49] Rather than ignoring whiteness, Lindsay is signaling whiteness in a potentially coded, seemingly race-neutral way.

Lindsay's rhetorical use of normalcy is ultimately rooted in maintaining an entrenched social order. Whereas he criticizes Marxism and antiracism for their desires to change the world, Lindsay argues that "normal moral commitments lead us to figure out how to flourish in the world by according with it as it is, whether as a brute fact of Nature or because of how it was ordered by God."[50] Consider this statement. Lindsay ostensibly contends that to be normal one must accept and navigate the world as it is. Efforts to transform society, to create greater equality along the lines of race, class, sex, gender, ability, and so on are abnormal. Thus, they are extreme and must be rejected. Lindsay's articulation and embrace of the normal should be read as an acceptance and endorsement of the status quo (ante) structured by systemic injustice. For Lindsay, calling attention to inequality and injustice as a means for ushering in historical change and a better world is extreme because it rejects the normalcy of the status quo (ante).

Echoing his use of "normal," Lindsay concludes *Race Marxism* by calling for an establishment of (or return to) a "common sensibility."[51] Arguing that intersectionality hinders people from seeing their commonality, Lindsay contends that identity politics must be replaced by . . . identity politics.[52] Under the label of "Americanism," Lindsay offers a colorblind vision that will maintain the status quo: "The magic of this way of thinking is that it puts us all on common ground. We're all individuals, and we are all people. We all share that in common. We all want our societies to flourish, as we hope we will within them."[53] For Lindsay, Americanism is the norm; it is but one particular embodiment of Western Civilization and it must be defended.[54]

In this call to action, Lindsay offers an identity politics in defense of the status quo. Lindsay claims that embracing "Americanism" will heal the divisions within our society.[55] Here Lindsay mistakes causes and effects. Racial, gender, sexual, and other identities are not what divide people. They are the consequential expressions that result from systemic inequalities. To eschew disparate racial, gender, sexual, and other identities in favor of "Americanism" turns on a full-throated embrace of the status quo (ante). While he does not address it, one must recognize that Lindsay's invocation of "normal" and platitudes about US culture can be read as asserting whiteness and romanticized notions of the past and country akin to those found in "The 1776 Report." That is, Lindsay is not rejecting identity politics. Rather he is rejecting the politics of identities that seek liberation in favor of an identity politics of entrenchment.

Of Medieval Fortifications and Rhetorical Countermeasures

With this explanation and example of how labeling one's opponents "extreme" works in tandem with and undergirds claims to moderation, it is critical to understand how this rule operates to foreclose logical responses. Because it contains a kernel of truth, one cannot simply reject the premise as false, no matter how ludicrous. For example, should one make the argument that CRT is not communism with race at its core and that contemporary antiracists are not ushering in a racial Bolshevik revolution—fairly reasonable responses—Lindsay would merely retreat to his kernel of truth. One can imagine him saying that antiracists are not *exactly* communists per se, but they have been influenced by the same Marxist thinkers. This has been evidenced when reactionaries fight the teaching of CRT in K–12 schools only to step back and acknowledge that while the legal scholarship of critical race theory is not in K–12 education, it has indirectly influenced a body of diversity education found in the schools. As Rufo suggested, the goal is to freeze "their brand—'critical race theory'—into the public conversation and . . . steadily driv[e] up negative perceptions."[56]

Labeling a diverse array of projects as CRT allows Lindsay, Rufo, and their confederates to deploy a motte and bailey defensive strategy. A motte and bailey was a medieval European castle design wherein an elevated and walled structure known as a motte was used for defense when the more vulnerable courtyard or bailey was under siege. Nicholas Shackel, a scholar that Lindsay draws on, uses this medieval defensive strategy to depict a rhetorical strategy.[57] In these cases, the bailey is the extreme but indefensible position, and the motte is the moderate and defensible rhetorical position. Two quick examples:

> BAILEY: CRT is race communism.
> MOTTE: Both CRT and Marxian thought attempt to understand and address forms of inequality in society.
> BAILEY: CRT in schools teaches white children to be ashamed of themselves.
> MOTTE: Addressing systemic racism in school curriculum will cause stress responses by those who may benefit from or are invested in inequality.

According to Shackel, "An entire doctrine or theory may be a Motte and Bailey Doctrine just by virtue of having a central core of defensible but not terribly interesting or original doctrines surrounded by a region of exciting but only lightly defensible doctrines."[58] Lindsay's *Race Marxism* consistently foregrounds the bailey, but at key moments he retreats to the motte to appear reasonable as a built-in defensive counter-strategy. Because labeling one's opponents extreme relies on a kernel of truth, rhetors like Lindsay need only retreat to the walled structure of their modest claim—that antiracists were influenced by previous political theorists and cultural critics, or that some feminists have adopted radical politics, or that LBGTQ folks rear children outside of heteronormative families. As such, asserting the fallacious nature of the outrageous claim merely allows the reactionary rhetor the opening to further the argument through a more reasonable claim.

This movement between motte and bailey, between modest claim and deliberately provocative assertion, also forecloses the ability to engage Lindsay as an honest interlocutor. Just as one cannot reject Lindsay as being wrong because of his motte position, so too does his bailey illustrate that he is not arguing in good faith. When Lindsay asserts that CRT is seeking a dictatorship of antiracists, that CRT demands ideological uniformity and political fealty of people of color, and that it scapegoats whiteness (i.e., whites) the way that Nazis did to Jewish people, these are not good faith arguments. They are a mixture of exaggeration, defamation, and lies. As such, one cannot simply respond as if there were legitimate, evidence-based assertions. It would be dangerous to accept these claims at face value and cede the terms of the debate. One does not want to be in a position wherein they accept a dictatorship of antiracists, believe that all people of color should march in lockstep, or suggest that an antiwhite fascism sounds lovely. That is the rhetorical beauty and terror of the motte and bailey. With the opening extreme claim, you are asked to accept or reject an assertion made in bad faith. Regardless of your choice, the result will shift the terrain of sociopolitical discourse.

Claiming the Middle Ground, Controlling the Discursive Terrain

At first glance, labeling one's opponents extreme may appear similar to define and disavow, the rule that opened the book. Both rules rely on rejecting an extreme Other in order to claim the position of reasonability, moderation, and goodness. For example, Rep. Steve King and Sam Harris defined racism and sexism, respectively, as an explicit, purposeful commitment to inequality. However, define and disavow is primarily a defensive effort used to deflect and defuse charges of racism and sexism. In contrast, labeling one's opponents extreme shifts the focus away from one's ideological and discursive kin. Rather than disavowing racism, sexism, and other reactionary commitments as extreme, this rule targets one's ideological and discursive *opponents* as extreme, ostensibly shifting the focus to the other end of the political spectrum. Take the case of Lindsay's *Race Marxism*. Lindsay does not take significant time rejecting white supremacists.[59] Rather, focusing his attention on progressive thinkers and social justice activists, Lindsay positions these opponents as the *real* extremists. Indeed, Lindsay, even actively bends the political spectrum to contend that racial justice activists have significant alignment with the racists and Nazis that they oppose.[60]

Even though these rules identify and target an extreme on different ends of the political spectrum, they both share an effort to claim a seemingly neutral, reasonable middle ground, a crucial location in leveraging control of the discursive terrain. Moreover, Lindsay's work to link critical race theory and antiracism to racism and Nazism underscores an implicit disavowal of extremist white supremacy. That is, if one were to accuse Lindsay of racism, he need only point to his repeated rejections of racism and Nazism that underwrite his critiques of antiracism and CRT. Because both of these rules rely on folk theories of inequality, Lindsay and other reactionaries need only decry *all types of racism and sexism*, forging a false equivalency, asserting that there are bad people on both sides, and that goodness exists in the middle ground where "normal people" and those who see themselves as Americans exists. This is particularly evident in Lindsay's critique of CRT that there is no middle ground between racism and antiracism.[61] Within antiracism circles, this argument is deployed to identify that those who are not actively working against racism are implicitly benefitting from and holding up the system.[62] Lindsay and his confederates reject this bifurcation, preferring a middle ground where one does not need to fight for or against racism but may still benefit from it. Here, one cannot overlook that asserting this middle-ground position is not simply about appearing reasonable; it is also the position of entrenchment, propelling not social transformation but maintenance of the status quo. That is, laying claim to a middle ground between racism and antiracism allows Lindsay and his readers to avoid questioning and challenging systemic inequality. The extremists on both sides can be rejected as one can turn a blind eye to the everyday hurts and injustices of inequality.

Labeling one's opponents extreme, however, does not simply stake a claim to the middle-ground position. Doing so can also shift the Overton Window. In the traditional iteration of the Overton Window (as depicted in figure 4.1), one highlights extremist views so that (slightly) less extreme positions appear mainstream by contrast.[63] For example, underscoring the existence of neo-Nazis and Holocaust denialism and positioning these as anathemas creates space for mainstream iterations of white supremacy like those who merely wish to defend traditional values (i.e., white identity) or back the police (when it comes to disproportionate violence toward communities of color). This is the logic that underpins the rhetorical maneuver of define and disavow.

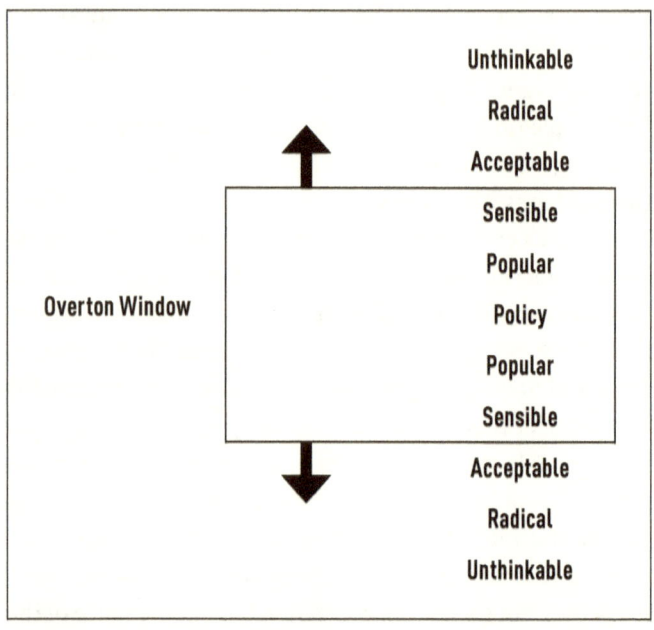

Figure 4.1: As the Overton Window shifts, or "opens," ideas and practices that may seem unthinkable, radical, or acceptable are moved into the mainstream realms of the sensible, popular, and policy. Note how the structure of the Overton Window mirrors the model of the political spectrum and triad where there are extremes on both sides.

In contrast, labeling one's *opponents* extreme shifts the rhetorical force to the other side. By labeling modest social justice efforts as extreme, this strategy pushes that which is rational and acceptable into the realm of the radical and the unacceptable. For example, if learning an accurate, robust, multiracial history of the United States is cast as antiwhite indoctrination, then returning to a celebratory, Eurocentric curriculum—like the one that existed without question prior to the Civil Rights movements of the 1960s and 1970s and multicultural turn of the 1980s and 1990s—is no longer an extremist position. Rather, white-centered history is simply normed as "accurate" "American" history. Or another example; this time along the axis of gender. While there is a vast array of feminisms, few experts would position Hillary Clinton as a radical. Radical feminism is often characterized by a recognition that society is structured by patriarchy, and for society to be reordered, patriarchy must be abolished. Clinton, in contrast, more accurately typifies a liberal feminism that works within the existing political order to reform society. However, when Rush Limbaugh labeled Clinton a feminazi, he shifted the Overton Window making moderate feminisms seem radical, ostensibly neutralizing the term and driving mainstream political identification with a fight for gender equality underground.[64]

In regard to the Overton Window, two aspects of this rule should be readily apparent. First, while labeling opponents as extreme relies on the logic of the Overton Window, the rhetorical pressure is placed on the opposition. Thus, labeling one's opponents extreme is dependent on the same logic that underwrites define and disavow, but it doesn't disavow an extreme of its own ideological perspective. By labeling the opposition as extreme, this strategy is able to implicitly create affirmative—if still unvoiced—identifications with extremist reactionary elements. That is, while Lindsay describes CRT activists as communist and fascist-adjacent, he gives cover to and gives voice to the concerns of white nationalists. This is evidenced when he asserts that CRT is a purposefully antiwhite endeavor, which echoes the white nationalist mantra that diversity equals white genocide.

Second, unlike define and disavow, labeling one's opponents extreme is not only defensive tactic, reacting to assertions of racism, sexism, and so on. This strategy is deployed offensively, proactively framing or reframing public debate. Critically, this claiming of reasonable and acceptable discursive and ideological terrain is not merely about a label but about the political and social power that comes with that label. Here, the reactionary theorization of the Overton Window echoes scholarship in the Marxist tradition. The discursive and ideological terrain that Joseph Overton bracketed off in his window aligns with and names what Antonio Gramsci explored as "common sense."[65] Drawing on Gramsci, Stuart Hall and Alan O'Shea have illustrated how claims to what is viewed as common sense are inextricable from a struggle for hegemony.[66] Gramsci used hegemony to describe the ways the elite maintained the social order and rule through consent. In other words, hegemony is when social power relations—from the roles of capitalists, managers, and labor to gendered expectations or the ethnoracial order—are made to appear as common sense. For Gramsci and Overton, seizing control of the common sense or the reasonable is foundational to establishing the consent necessary for hegemonic rule. Through hegemony, social stratification that benefits some and disadvantages others is rendered not as the result of specific policies, practices, and choices but rather as the naturalized order of things, although there is nothing natural or inherent about the social order.

By labeling their opponents extremists and laying claim to the reasonable, reactionaries are able to recast the fight. Through this framing, racial justice advocates are no longer fighting against police violence, disparate treatment and representation in schools, or access to adequate housing and food. They can be seen as attacking Western Civilization, society writ large, or the common sense that holds the social order together. Framed in this way, reactionaries are able to imagine entrenchment within the status quo (ante) of social inequalities as a backlash, a natural reaction to overreaching extremists. For Lindsay, his claims to normalcy are forever bound to imagining CRT proponents as extremists, and this framing requires that "normal people" who see themselves as "American" defend society from social justice advocates who are implicitly or explicitly rendered anti-American.

Likewise, the book bans and "don't say gay" policies that accompanied the 2020s moral panic are not viewed as entrenching systems of inequality. Rather, their proponents would likely describe them as defensive measures to protect their way of life, the common sense that orders their hegemonic understanding of the world. Ensconcing this position within the terrain of the reasonable makes it nearly impossible for reactionaries to understand social justice advocates. Blind to their own "extremist" positions, reactionaries in this dynamic will only see their fellow humans as opponents and threats to their way of life.

A critical result, this rhetorical maneuver drives identification with social justice efforts underground, making people uncomfortable with expressing their politics. Here Overton's theorization of the terrain of political discourse is reminiscent of Jacques Rancière's concept of the distribution of the sensible. For Rancière, "The distribution of the sensible [is] the system of self-evident facts of sense perception that simultaneously discloses the existence of something in common and the delimitations that define the respective parts and positions within it. A distribution of the sensible therefore establishes at one and the same time something common that is shared and exclusive parts."[67] Rancière contends that "politics revolves around what is seen and what can be said about it, around who has the ability to see and the talent to speak, around the properties of spaces and the possibilities of time."[68] Like Overton's window, Rancière's distribution of the sensible recognizes that the terrain of political discourse can be put under pressure and shifted. As such, labeling one's opponents as extreme and asserting that one's own position is reasonable and commonsense pushes justice-oriented language, ideology, and attendant identities to the margins of the public sphere.

Here, two examples may be useful. I codirect a program for first-year students and during orientation, my collaborator and I both introduce our teaching and research interests to the students and their parents. I had often talked about my work in Latinx studies, critical whiteness studies, and critical race theory. However, in 2021 and 2022, I second-guessed talking about my work in those terms. I was not worried about doxing or harassment, although I had been through that before. Nor was I worried about losing my job; tenure offers significant protections. Rather, I was concerned that by accurately describing my work I may activate the framing that students and their families had already received from the ongoing moral panic led by Rufo, Lindsay, and others. Would I discredit myself in their eyes on the first day? Would I establish an obstacle for our future success in the program? While I ultimately introduced my work with these terms and took the time to explain these scholarly areas, it came with risk and doubt. I suspect that I am not alone, and those who do not have my social and professional privileges may be even more reticent to publicly embrace these projects once they have been transmogrified by political efforts.

Indeed, one finds an analogous dynamic between my hesitancy and the way women have been pushed to deny feminism. I remember teaching in 2008 when a student, let's call her Mary, introduced herself to her peers saying, "I'm a feminist, but I'm not a lesbian or anything. I don't hate men." I was initially taken aback. Were we really worried that feminism was a big, bad thing? Did it really signal to Mary's peers that she might hate men or be attracted to women? Dear readers, these were and are still legitimate concerns in some spaces. Mary had been conditioned to deny her politics to the degree that even as she proclaimed herself a feminist, she chose to distance herself from LBGTQ folk and recognize the anxieties of feminists as man-hating feminazis. Notably, this student's attachment and distress surrounding "feminist" is not unique. As Toril Moi and others have illustrated, antifeminism exemplified by Rush Limbaugh's popularization of "feminazi" shifted the terrain of the sensible, moved the Overton Window, and made it common sense for many women to distance themselves from the label "feminist."⁶⁹

While these anecdotes demonstrate how being labeled extreme can alter the discursive and ideological terrain, driving some identities underground, they also signal an uneasy common feeling between justice-oriented individuals and the reactionaries who embrace the status quo (ante). It has been commonplace throughout the culture wars for reactionary rhetors to argue that conservative voices have been silenced on college campuses often through self-censorship, purportedly limiting conservative views within the public sphere. Yet, here, through labeling their opponents extreme, we see how reactionary rhetors actually engage in silencing those committed to social transformation, attempting to drive them out of the public sphere, and constraining the range of reasonable public discourse. When reactionaries loudly and vociferously proclaim their own silencing, we would do well to not treat these as earnest, heartfelt declarations but as cunning projections made to bolster a sense of group identity.

In elucidating how labeling others as extreme so that reactionary efforts can claim to be reasonable and common-sense and control the discursive and ideological terrain, this chapter examined the anti-CRT campaign and particularly the efforts of Cristopher Rufo and James Lindsay. But this instance is hardly unique. This chapter could have centered numerous examples: Anita Bryant's demonizing of LBGTQ folks as pedophiles, Rush Limbaugh's vilifying of feminists as gender-focused fascists, the taring of Civil Rights leaders like Martin Luther King Jr. and César Chávez as communists, or the assertion that environmental activists are merely antiprogress extremists. This rule of entrenchment is hardly new. Rather, it is a staple of the reactionary playbook that goes back well before the twentieth century. By highlighting these alternate routes of inquiry, I hope to indicate the pervasive nature of this rhetorical strategy and lay the groundwork for relational analyses of political discourse.

As noted earlier, the rhetorical strategy of labeling others as extreme in order to claim the position of the reasonable shares a similar dynamic to define and disavow. Because this rule successfully defines social justice efforts as extreme and dangerous, those aligned with social justice efforts are pushed to disavow their politics. However, in contrast to define and disavow, this rule does not require disavowing racism or sexism as some extreme, aberrant, and abhorrent Other. Rather, those committed to antiracism, feminism, and other efforts to build a more equitable world are cast as extreme, aberrant, abhorrent, and in need of disavowal. For those committed to publicly articulating a politics of justice, these moments come with the pressure to offer backstepping and (sometimes problematic) qualifying remarks and they are accompanied by the public and psychological taxation that comes with the fear of being rejected and vilified. Of course, when anti-CRT and "don't say gay" laws and policies are enacted, one need not only fear the pressures of social rejection—one may also fear losing one's job. As such, this vilification of social justice efforts transforms politics of equality, justice, and social transformation into the realm of the unspeakable. And when social transformation is unspeakable, the status quo maintains entrenchment.

Postscript:

While this manuscript is being prepared for publication in February 2025, the second Trump administration and its various governmental agencies have further mainstreamed its attack on social justice efforts, now under the banner of attacking DEI. The National Park Service removed references to "transgender" and "queer" from the Stonewall National Monument website. The National Endowment for the Humanities prohibited funding of projects that engaged gender or equity ideology, environmental justice, and DEI initiatives and activities. The National Science Foundation froze existing grants and prohibited future ones that would run afoul of the administration's executive orders attacking DEI and other justice efforts. On February 14, 2025, the Department of Education issued a Dear Colleague letter asserting that DEI initiatives—from training seminars and inclusive hiring plans to affinity-based housing and culturally inflected graduation ceremonies—are against the 1964 Civil Rights Act and the Equal Protection Clause of the constitution, ostensibly weaponizing the means of civil rights gains against aggrieved communities in the name of fairness. The terrain of discourse is changing, and with it, material and structural effects will follow.

RULE #5

Misdirect by Blaming a Convenient Cause

A problem in society is gaining widespread media and political attention. The issue may be one of persistent inequality, a pressing danger, or something different altogether. The issue is complex and multifaceted. The specific nature of the problem really does not matter. What's important is that some have identified a contributing cause of the problem and are calling for this cause to be addressed. And their plans for addressing this root of the problem will impact you. Perhaps you will lose social standing. Perhaps it will cost you financially. Perhaps it will cause you to alter the way you live your life or shift your worldview. Ultimately, addressing the cause they have identified poses a threat to you and the status quo. What do you do? Simple, use misdirection by blaming another, more convenient cause: "It's not x that has caused this issue. It's clearly y. Why are you focused on the wrong thing?" Such a move allows you not simply to redirect the discussion to a different cause and thus another potential solution. Rather, you can shift the focus from addressing the pressing issue to determining what the true cause really is. That is, instead of deliberating and acting on a prospective solution, you shift the discourse back to the problem and other potential causes, offering no solution and allowing the problem to continue unabated. After a short period of time, attention wanes, news analysis shifts, and the issue recedes from view. But the problem lurks, waits, metastasizes, because it has not been adequately addressed. When the problem gains renewed attention, simply misdirect again. Rinse. Repeat.

Tell me if you have heard this one before. A gunman shoots up a school, church, mosque, synagogue, or place of business. He murders and wounds children, worshippers, coworkers, customers, people. As outrage and media attention home in on the epidemic of mass shootings and the ease with which one can purchase an arsenal, politicians and gun rights proponents proclaim that *the guns are not to blame. The root of these killings is mental health.*[1]

Or an unarmed Black teenager is killed by police or an individual purporting to protect his community. As justice activists proclaim that "Black Lives Matter" and some in the news media ask how this keeps happening, reactionaries push back: *The murdered child was no angel. He smoked marijuana or shoplifted. The bigger problem, the real problem is fatherlessness or abortion in the Black community. These are the real causes of Black suffering.*[2]

Or a high-profile case involving the gender wage gap between men and women makes the news. Feminists and allied politicians call for new policies to ensure equal pay. In response, reactionary cultural workers argue that *the gender pay gap, to the degree that it exists, is the result of women's choices: women choose motherhood, women choose lower-paying jobs, women choose to work less, women choose not to negotiate for higher pay.*[3]

Or the climate crisis looms. Higher average temperatures and more volatile weather patterns demonstrate the need to address dependence on fossil fuels. The response: *Sure cars and plastics result in greenhouse gases, but do you realize how much methane is released every year because of cow farts? Why are we not addressing that cause?*[4]

Each of these examples illustrates a common rhetorical strategy deployed to halt calls for change. Reactionary rhetors use misdirection. As a problem, its cause, and a potential solution are deliberated, reactionaries shift the focus to another, more convenient cause. If they focus attention to a different cause, then they nullify the proposed solution. That is, if the real cause of mass shootings is not the proliferation of weaponry but mental health, then we need not propose new regulations regarding weaponry. If the real or greater cause of Black death and racial inequality is the breakdown of the Black family, then we don't need to hold police and neighborhood vigilantes accountable. Notably, in this rhetorical strategy, one does not simply blame a more convenient cause to offer another worthwhile policy change. When reactionary cultural workers blame mental health for gun violence, their allied politicians do not advance significant healthcare reform that would provide mental health services to those in the most need. Likewise, when cattle and their methane production are identified as a contributor to global climate change, reactionaries do not advocate an eco-friendly vegan lifestyle. Rather, these misdirections shift attention to another cause so that any prospective solution is dead in the water, change is forestalled, and the status quo remains.

In order to recognize, understand, and potentially contest the misdirection of blaming a convenient cause, this chapter explores the rhetorical foundation for why this strategy is effective. This type of misdirection is a means of changing the stasis (from the ancient Greek designating the taking of a position or stance, a "standstill" or "conflict") of an argument, the point of an argument that requires resolution in order to reach conclusion. This rhetorical strategy of changing the stasis is neither new nor unique to reactionary politics and shares common ground with other popular rhetorical strategies like whataboutism and bothsidesism.

With an understanding in how misdirection is grounded in rhetorical principles, this chapter examines this common rhetorical strategy as it is deployed regarding the gender pay gap. Through analysis of popular arguments diminishing the pay gap and countering proposed solutions, this chapter exposes how misdirection can appear like legitimate deliberation while it ultimately is an effort to forestall social change. Finally, the chapter explores how the misdirection of blaming another, more convenient cause reinforces the cultural logic of monocausality and how this rhetorical maneuver works to maintain the status quo.

Misdirection and the Art of Changing the Stasis

Blaming a different, convenient cause is but one of a number of misdirection strategies deployed to foment reactionary entrenchment. In recent years, other forms of misdirection have proliferated and gained traction in political and popular culture. With the political ascendancy of Donald Trump and the rise of Trumpism, political commentators and cultural critics have focused attention to the misdirection strategies of whataboutism and bothsidesism.

Whataboutism is when a rhetor responds to a claim by asking about a potentially similar claim that could be made about their interlocutor or someone else. In *The Washington Post*, Dan Zak described whataboutism as "the practice of short-circuiting an argument by asserting moral equivalency between two things that aren't necessarily comparable.... Whataboutism appears to broaden context, to offer a counterpoint, when really it's diverting blame, muddying the waters and confusing the hell out of rational listeners."[5] As noted by Alan Dykstra, this has been a common rhetorical maneuver by those engaged in human rights abuses— from authoritarian regimes to terrorist and paramilitary outfits.[6] For example, when pressed about the 2014 invasion of Ukraine, Russian president Vladimir Putin merely asked what about the US seizure of Mexican territory through the annexation of Texas.[7] As Dykstra and others have contended, whataboutism often involves what rhetoricians would call a tu quoque (i.e., and you), or even an ad hominem (i.e., to the person), fallacy wherein the misdirection places the other party and their credibility under scrutiny. For example, it would be a mistake to view Putin's misdirection as a concern for the respect for and sovereignty of Mexico's borders. Rather, his reference to the US conquest of Mexican territory underscores the hypocrisy of the US outrage at a similar invasion. By raising the issue of US colonial endeavors, Putin places focus on the United States' moral authority, thus shifting attention from the invasion at hand.

Rather than posing a question, bothsidesism asserts that a claim lacks significance because "both sides" are guilty. This form of misdirection works to achieve false balance. Writing for *The Washington Post*, Erik Wemple has explored how bothsidesism is particularly challenging for reporters and news media. While conservative news organizations like Fox News can use a desire to report both sides as a marketing strategy and a legal defense against defamation, journalists are trained to achieve objectivity which is often conflated with balance. Wemple warns that balance itself is not necessarily a good thing: "It depends on what you are balancing."[8] Balance can be "the enemy of truth" when one side is spreading disinformation or acting in bad faith.[9] For example, one may deploy bothsidesism to obscure the nature of the January 6, 2021, insurrection by invoking March 2023 gun violence protests wherein hundreds of protestors flooded the Tennessee statehouse. In both cases, US citizens protested by occupying government buildings. However, by focusing on this narrow similarity between both sides, a false balance would propel us to ignore that the January 6th protestors were spurred by lies and were violent in their insurrection.

In contrast, the Tennessee protestors were peacefully disruptive and motivated by gun violence that had actually rocked their community. The false balance of bothsidesism gives the appearance of revealing significant, new information connecting each side, yet it simultaneously obscures critical differences between them. While whataboutism and bothsidesism have been clearly identified and named, misdirection efforts that blame a convenient cause have flown below the critical radar, allowing them to appear as legitimate deliberation and not rhetorical entrenchment.

At their core, each of these rhetorical maneuvers is linked through its ability to change the stasis of an argument. In the field of rhetoric, stasis names the conflict within the terms of debate, marking the topic of conversation and the parameters of the discursive terrain. Patricia Roberts-Miller describes stasis as "the hinge of an argument—the place that two (or more) positions disagree."[10] A rhetor shifts the stasis when they alter the terrain of deliberation, disagree with their interlocutor's premises, and ostensibly change the subject. For example, Roberts-Miller illustrates how antebellum proslavery rhetors countered arguments that US slavery involved immoral practices including "failing to recognize slave marriages, breaking up of slave families, sexual exploitation of slaves, violence against and mutilation of slaves, kidnapping of free African Americans, [and] denying access to scripture."[11] Rather than taking on these specific anti-slavery arguments, proslavery rhetors moved "the discussion away from the specific practice of slavery to slavery in the abstract," underscoring that the Bible "did not condemn slavery in the most abstract form (one human owning another)."[12] As such, they shifted the basic premise and parameters of deliberation for specific forms of unchristian conduct to the more general acceptance of owning humans within the Bible.

In his examination of racist discursive strategies, Kenneth Ladenburg notes that reactionary rhetors can go beyond shifting the stasis to diffusing it. By offering a series of staccato-like, rapid-fire assertions tangentially related to a given topic, these rhetors create a discursive quagmire from which meaningful deliberation is impossible.[13] Ladenburg notes that each response has the potential of creating a new point of stress. Once the responding rhetor has concluded their series of assertions, their interlocutor faces a sprawling set of stress points and must decide which ones to respond to and how. Drawing on Roberts-Miller and Ladenburg, it is clear that altering the stasis is an essential strategy for obstructing deliberation on social transformation. If the two sides cannot come to an agreement on the parameters of deliberation, those sides can never decide what actions should be taken.

In their own ways, whataboutism, bothsidesism, and blaming a convenient cause are rhetorical maneuvers that obstruct deliberation by changing the subject, misdirecting participants by asking them to look elsewhere. Often offered in the guise of a question—*what about Black-on-Black crime? Where are the fathers? Why don't they just respect the police?*—whataboutism misdirects by seeming to open the aperture of argument, illustrating that there is a terrain with which the other rhetor has not grappled. As such, this move expands the terrain of deliberation to encompass more elements that may be largely irrelevant to the original stasis. Likewise, bothsidesism appears to broaden the deliberative terrain. Often offered as an assertion, bothsidesism foments a false balance by pointing to areas beyond the realm of debate to broaden the conversation and muddy deliberation. For example, as calls for police reforms grow due to violence toward communities of color, reactionaries will underscore the violence and danger faced by police: #bluelivesmatter. Similarly, blaming a convenient cause focuses attention on an issue outside or on the margins of the discursive terrain, centering the deliberation on an aspect that will not result in the called-for solution.

Consider figure 5.1; in this example, the problem is police violence toward communities of color and the cause is systemic racism. The solution would be to address racism in all its systemic manifestations. The stasis, the parameters of the discursive terrain, is marked by the clear lines of each rectangle. Each form of misdirection points to issues outside of this terrain. For the deliberation to go forward, the stasis must shift, obstructing calls for addressing the original cause.

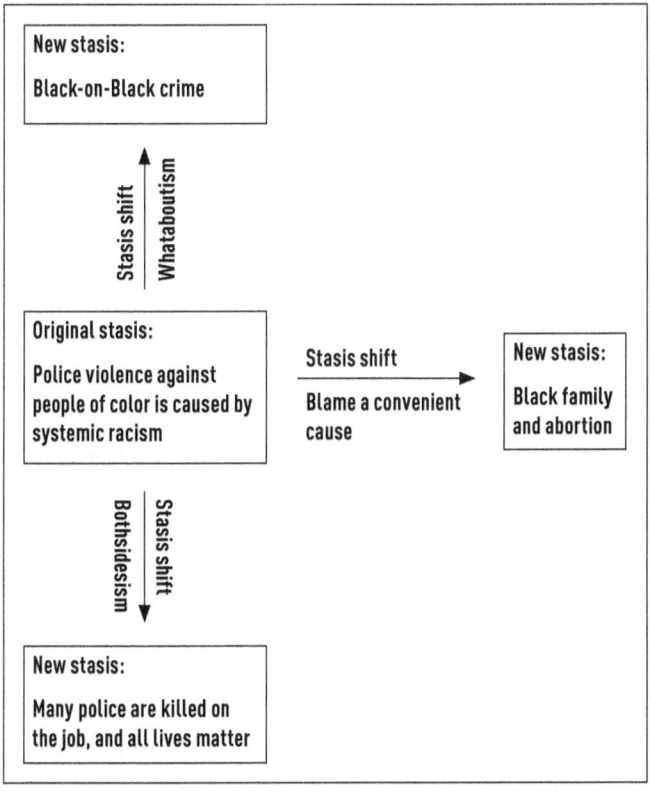

Figure 5.1: This diagram illustrates three distinct forms of misdirection or stasis shifting. When the stasis is shifted multiple times, either with the same form of misdirection or through a variety of them, the stasis is diffused by stretching the discursive terrain to a broader, more unwieldy territory.

Despite the shared dynamics of stasis shifting, these forms of misdirection bear significant differences. Whataboutism often implies that an argument is invalid or in bad faith because of a rhetor's hypocrisy. For example, in cases when Black-on-Black crime is articulated to nullify calls to address police violence toward Black people, one asserts that the lack of attention to Black-on-Black crime means that Black Lives Matter activists do not actually care about Black people. As such whataboutism is often manifested as a tu quoque fallacy that invokes elements of ad hominem attacks.[14] Bothsidesism places less emphasis on the credibility of the interlocutor and uses misdirection to foster notions of false balance between two issues. For example, when one asserts that Blue Lives Matter as a rejoinder to Black Lives Matter, this bothsidesism forges a false parallel wherein blue lives exist and are in danger and have been devalued due to their blueness akin to the devaluation and danger faced by Black lives.[15]

Blaming a convenient cause stands apart from whataboutism and bothsidesism because of how it shifts the stasis based on the cause structure of an argument. Social problems are complex and multifaceted. Even as social justice advocates may know this, calls for change are often rooted in identifying and addressing one cause, or at least one cause at a time. However, these causes, identified with simple phrases like systemic racism, may be broad, sprawling, and entangled social factors. The cause structure of these calls for action are linear. A policy, process, or collection thereof causes a problem. Enacting a solution will eliminate the cause and its resulting problem. For example, disproportionate police violence against communities of color is caused by a culture of racism in policing. Ergo, the solution would be to root out racism within police forces. Blaming a convenient cause highlights another potential cause, derailing the linear structure of the argument. Reactionaries may draw attention to the breakdown of Black family. For example, Bishop Willington Boone contends that if Black fathers were more present in their children's lives many aspects that lead to police violence would be reduced.[16] Drawing attention to this other, more convenient cause diverts the limited attention away from the one raised by activists, shifting the stasis and derailing deliberation. Notably these forms of stasis shifting are not mutually exclusive. Indeed, as indicated by Ladenburg's identification and mapping of stasis diffusion, these rhetorical maneuvers of misdirection are mutually reinforcing. That is, when Bishop Boone blames the absence of Black fathers as the reason behind violence and crime and police violence, he also engages in whataboutism through highlighting Black-on-Black crime and abortion as a form of self-genocide.

Unlike whataboutism and bothsidesism, blaming a convenient cause allows reactionary rhetors to go beyond nullifying arguments for social transformation. Critically, blaming a convenient cause allows these rhetors to advance solutions that more clearly align with reactionary politics. In the case of police violence, blaming a convenient cause allows reactionaries to further pathologize Black communities. Beyond pointing to a potential hypocrisy or creating a false equivalency, this rhetorical maneuver offloads the responsibility of oppression onto the oppressed. And because reactionary politics are rooted in ideology and discourse, not rigid forms of identity, blaming a convenient cause reaches its insidious potential as it allows those from aggrieved communities to pathologize the communities from which they come by embracing colorblind, genderblind tools to bolster inequality.

To better understand how this rhetorical maneuver works, this chapter turns to the debates surrounding the gender pay gap. I begin with the debate configured broadly across various professions, exploring how reactionary rhetors like Kay Hymowitz shift responsibility of unequal pay to women workers and naturalize inequality as an unquestionable outcome of personal choices and market forces. The chapter then examines a more specific case of unequal pay: the United States Women's National Soccer Team (USWNT) and their 2019 lawsuit against the United States Soccer Federation (USSF) and reactionary efforts to justify unequal pay.

The Gender Pay Gap, or How to Blame Women for and Naturalize Their Inequality

The gender pay gap names the phenomenon in the United States and globally wherein women workers are paid less on average than men. Often this gets discussed in generalized, aggregate statistics. For example, according to Payscale's *State of the Gender Pay Gap Report*, in 2022 women in the United States made 82 cents for every dollar earned by a man.[17] Today these discrepancies are largely due to type of career and time in profession. When these factors are controlled for, women still make less, but the gap shrinks dramatically to around 99 cents for each dollar earned by men.[18] Notably, the gender pay gap is not a singular phenomenon wherein bosses consciously conspire to pay women less. However, historically, women workers did face overt wage scales that offered them lower renumeration for their labor and men were paid more under the logic that they bore primary responsibility for supporting the family. But the gender pay gap has never been solely monocausal. The gender pay gap exists as an expression of social attitudes toward women, the disproportionate responsibilities women face in paid and unpaid work, and how those attitudes and responsibilities are valued.[19] In the United States, the gender pay gap is marked by Equal Pay Day, the day in each calendar year marking how long on average women would need to work in order to make as much as men earned the previous year. Over the last few decades, with the advances won by the women's movement of the 1960s and 1970s and key flashpoints like the Lilly Ledbetter Act, the presidential campaigns of Hillary Clinton, and the #MeToo movement, equal pay has become a core issue in progressive politics and thus reactionaries have sought ways of maintaining and advancing inequality by disrupting calls for equal pay.

One example of reactionary efforts to maintain the gender gap status quo can be found in the writing of Kay Hymowitz. Author of *Manning Up: How the Rise of Women Has Turned Men into Boys*, fellow at the Manhattan Institute, and a contributing editor at *City Journal*, Hymowitz has regularly published on shifting gender dynamics and their relationship to the economy. Unlike men's rights antifeminism discussed earlier, Hymowitz does not imagine men as victims of angry feminist wrath nor does she simply urge for a return to the status quo ante. The book *Manning Up* does argue, however, that technological advances from birth control pills to the information economy as well as social efforts to empower women have come at the expense of men, transforming them into child-men.[20] Drawing on analyses of popular culture texts like *Sex and the City* and studies focusing primarily on college-educated workers in business fields, Hymowitz's *Manning Up* focuses on white, middle- and upper-class women to the elision of working-class women and women of color. Published in *City Journal* and the *Wall Street Journal*, Hymowitz's 2011 "Why the Gender Gap Won't Go Away. Ever." questions the legitimacy of the gender wage gap. While recognizing that aggregate statistics indicate that income inequality exists along gender lines, Hymowitz asserts that these statistics are misleading. She contends that the pay disparity is not the result of discrimination but stems from a variety of factors. Hymowitz stresses that the real wage gap, at the time of her writing in 2011, is 7 percent when controlled for occupation and time in profession.

In arguing that the gender pay gap is not the result of discrimination, Hymowitz ignores that when scholars, feminist activists, governments and NGOs discuss the gender wage gap, they do so as a symptom caused by a constellation of structural issues. As such, Hymowitz winnows down a complex multicausal phenomenon into the monocause of employer discrimination. As a result, she frames discrimination as a purposeful, conscious act of employers aligning with the folk theory of sexism discussed earlier.

Thus, Hymowitz offers her readers a simplified model of gender inequality that both draws on and reinforces reactionary cultural logics of liberal individualism where if discrimination happens, it must be the result of a bad actor. From there, she pivots to blame a more convenient cause: women's choices. According to Hymowitz, women make choices that result in their lower average pay. Women take classes that prepare them for less lucrative career advancement, or they choose less lucrative careers altogether. Women become mothers. Women work fewer hours. Women have greater career interruptions, and so on.

If one wanted to contest Hymowitz's argument on her own grounds, one could point out that choices are never entirely free—individual choices are always constrained through the context of social structures. One must make choices about one's life in the context of other people and institutions. For example, if a woman chooses to take greater responsibility for her children, it may be well because a man has chosen not to. Or if a women chooses to interrupt her career, it may be in part due to the high cost of child care in the United States. But the importance of Hymowitz's writing is not simply its strawman understanding of discrimination or its logical blind spots. Rather, Hymowitz's argument about women "choosing" to be paid less is revealing for how it works to maintain the status quo.

By shifting the cause of the gender pay gap from a host of social factors to the result of women's choices, Hymowitz draws on and reinforces a popular investment in abstract liberal individualism. For those unfamiliar with the concept, abstract liberalism or liberal individualism names the belief that the individual is the social unit of primary importance. Emerging in the Enlightenment and revitalized by neoliberal thinkers like Friedrich Hayek, liberal individualism eschews structural considerations wherein social factors like the collective identifications of race and gender shape or constrain one's experiences.[21] Writing about how racism is maintained by colorblind language, Eduardo Bonilla-Silva identifies abstract liberalism as a key frame of colorblind racism: "By framing race-related issues in the language of liberalism, whites can appear 'reasonable' and even 'moral,' while opposing almost all practical approaches to deal with de facto racial inequality. For instance, the principle of equal opportunity . . . is invoked by whites today to oppose affirmative-action policies because they supposedly represent the 'preferential treatment' of certain groups."[22] Here we see another alignment between the ideological precepts of white supremacy and antifeminism. Hymowitz need not make essentialist arguments about women and their roles in society—indeed, she may well disagree with the arguments of men's rights antifeminists. Rather, by relying on the notion of choice, Hymowitz abstracts the very nature of equality. In her framework, equality does not mean equal pay for equal work. For Hymowitz, equality is bound to the ability to make choices within liberal individualism. As such, women can choose to become parents, and men can choose to take on less parenting responsibility. Women can choose to be paid less, and men can choose to be paid more. If women choose not to "stick around the office," so be it.[23]

This embrace of liberal individualism and choice plays a crucial role in this rhetorical strategy. By shifting the cause of pay inequality from multiple, intersecting social factors to women's individual choices, Hymowitz offloads the responsibility of addressing inequality. Within her logic, if women want to be paid more, then they should make better choices like pursuing more lucrative careers or deciding not to have children.[24] The extension of this logic is simple. Because unequal pay is due to women's choices, unequal pay is ultimately the fault of women. For Hymowitz, women have "bought tickets for what is commonly called the 'mommy track,'" and this choice absolves men of their social responsibility because they have their own individual choices.[25]

Beyond blaming women for not working enough or for not being paid equally, Hymowitz's rhetorical strategy also works to naturalize the gender pay gap. For Hymowitz, there is seemingly nothing that can be done. She notes that Nordic countries have increased support for parental leave and child-care programs, yet Sweden had only closed the gap to 15 percent. This leads Hymowitz to conclude that "feminists can object till the Singularity arrives that women are 'socialized' to think that they have to be the primary parent. But after decades of feminism and Nordic engineering, the continuing female tropism toward shorter work hours suggests that that view is either false or irrelevant."[26] Because she lays the blame on the individual choices of women and the "mommy track" in particular, Hymowitz does not need to put forward a potential solution. Any attempt to solve this problem—to the degree that unequal pay is even a problem—would result in limiting women's freedom via curtailing their choices or it would attack the central and sacred institution of the family. Since those options are anathema in US politics, Hymowitz's rhetorical strategy of blaming a convenient cause works to buttress the status quo. By shifting the stasis from the effects of a constellation of social attitudes and policies that devalue women to the abstract liberal individualism of choice, Hymowitz and others misdirect attention away from crucial points of deliberation. If we are focused on why women *choose* to rear children, we fail to address the social value of such work and why it is not adequately compensated. If we narrow our attention to why women *choose* lower paid professions, we are limited from understanding that "women's" professions (e.g., teaching, social work, nursing) pay poorly for the very reason that these professions have been historically occupied by women. When scholars, feminists, and others draw attention to the gender pay gap, they are highlighting the way in which inequality is infused in the very structures of society. When Hymowitz and others misdirect attention to women's choices, the possibility of a different world where men take greater responsibility for rearing children and "pink collar" work like teaching is compensated and valued similarly to engineering and finance is foreclosed. Reactionary entrenchment maintains the status quo.

While Hymowitz is a useful example of how blaming a convenient cause works to promote entrenchment of unequal pay generally, the case of the United States Women's National soccer Team (USWNT) demonstrates variations on this discursive maneuver. In 2019, twenty-eight current and former players for the USWNT sued the Unites States Soccer Federation (USSF) asserting that the organization's unequal pay of women and men soccer players violated the Equal Pay Act and Title VI of the Civil Rights Act: "According to the suit, a comparison of pay schedules for the teams shows that if each played 20 exhibition games in a year, members of the men's team could earn an average of $263,320 each, while women's team players could earn a maximum of $99,000."[27] In May 2020, the judge dismissed the equal pay claims of the case, finding "that the U.S. women had agreed to a different pay structure than the men in their previous collective bargaining agreement."[28] The judge did, however, rule that "claims of unequal treatment in terms of travel, medical staff and training equipment can go forward."[29] In April 2021, the players appealed the dismissal of the equal pay claims, arguing "that the judge had ignored evidence of 'direct discrimination'—including U.S. Soccer officials who themselves admitted that the women were paid unequally—and had improperly treated the women's collective bargaining agreement 'as somehow waiving their equal pay rights.'"[30] In a critical moment of solidarity, the United States Men's National Soccer Team filed an amicus brief supporting the women players. The brief argued that USSF had discriminated against the women players for decades, noting that the women's pay was not just due to the number of games played but also to their performance.[31] As litigation continued, the USWNT and USSF settled the case in February 2022. USSF agreed to pay the twenty-eight women players twenty-two million in damages and create a two-million-dollar fund to support women's and girls' soccer.[32] As part of the settlement, USSF also agreed to pay men's and women's players equally going forward.[33]

During the build up to and throughout the course of the lawsuit, the issue of US soccer's gender pay gap received widespread media attention, in part because of players like Megan Rapinoe were vocal and savvy in pushing the issue into the public sphere. Unsurprisingly, reactionary cultural workers aligned themselves with USSF and pushed back on the women athletes' claim, contending that claims of unequal pay were without merit. While the dynamics of the USWNT case differ from the more general gender pay gap, the arguments deployed to justify pay inequality share the same structure as those embraced by Hymowitz.

To understand this case and the rhetorical maneuvers at play, it is critical to recognize how player renumeration worked. Members of the women's team received a base salary, bonuses for winning, and paid medical leave and parental leave. The base salary was critical for women players because they could not rely on a robust women's professional soccer organization as the basis of their income. In contrast, men's team members often made most of their income through their play for professional teams. US soccer paid the men players on a per game basis with bonuses for success on the field. That is, in part because the men could rely on pay from professional club teams (i.e., a system of gender inequality outside of the Fédération Internationale de Football Association [FIFA]), USSF could offer the men a more flexible compensation model with higher pay per game.

Echoing Hymowitz's writing on the gender pay gap, editorialist Allysia Finely and Heritage Foundation research fellow Rachel Greszler both authored opinion pieces in the *Wall Street Journal* contending that the soccer gender pay gap was the result of choices. Writing in 2016, during the buildup to the lawsuit, Finely argued that the women's team does not simply receive lower pay than their men counterparts: "They're paid differently because the collective-bargaining agreements they have negotiated emphasize income- and job-security. Women players earn annual salaries of $72,000; the men get paid by how many games they play."[34] Likewise, when the lawsuit was filed in 2019, Greszler and USSF lawyers argued that this compensation package was agreed to as part of the USWNT's 2017 collective bargaining agreement (CBA) with USSF.

By highlighting that the different types of compensation are a result of the CBA, Greszler is able to achieve two argumentative objectives. First, she contends that the USSF has no choice but to agree to pay the women's team differently (i.e., less). Within her logic, US soccer and the women athletes had come to an agreement. This was the choice of both parties. For as long as the agreement was in place, there would be no room to make other choices, and the USSF would be locked in by the CBA. Second, blaming the

CBA offloads responsibility for unequal pay to the women. If women wanted to be paid like men, then they had their opportunity when negotiating the CBA in 2017 and they would have another opportunity in 2021. In other words, no backsies. By blaming the CBA and the choices of women, Greszler paints the players as bad faith actors and potentially renders the women players as irrational feminists who simply do not understand business, contracts, and compensation models. Using the unequal pay in US soccer as a foundation, Greszler then extends her argument about choice and the gender pay gap more broadly. Like Hymowitz, she contends "that choices—not discrimination—are the primary reason behind differences in pay. And a choice-based gap is cause for celebration."[35] Moreover, Greszler posits that policymakers who wish to end the gender wage gap are trying to take away the choices of women. That is, for Greszler, arguing for equal pay is ultimately antichoice and illiberal. Greszler, however, does not complete the logic of her argument by considering whether the women players' choice to sue is also an effort to counteract their own choice to be paid less.

Critically, however, women's choice embodied in the collective bargaining agreement was not the only convenient cause deployed to misdirect responsibility. Lawyers for USSF and reactionary rhetors asserted that the unequal pay was not due to discrimination on the part of USSF but due to the fact that FIFA, the international organization of which USSF is a member, paid different amounts for the men's and women's teams. Finely notes that "the U.S. women's team received $2 million from the Fédération Internationale de Football Association (FIFA) for winning the World Cup last year [2015], while the men's team landed $9 million merely for advancing to the round of 16 [in 2014]."[36] While the clear pay disparity underscores the women players' claim, Finely strategically locates the cause elsewhere. For her, USSF is not discriminating against women athletes. Rather, FIFA has chosen to renumerate women and men differently. According to Finley's logic, if the cause of the pay gap problem was not USSF's discriminatory actions but FIFA's, then the women's complaints about gender inequality within US soccer are misplaced and invalid. By redirecting the blame to FIFA, Finley, USSF lawyers, and other reactionary rhetors ostensibly contended that there was little that USSF could do. In this framework, USSF was just the middleman distributing FIFA's unequal pay.

Another manifestation of this rhetorical maneuver was to identify and blame market forces. The disparate funds FIFA distributes to USSF for the women's and men's world cups come from ticket sales and advertising revenue. Immediately after placing the blame of unequal pay on FIFA, Finely asks,

> How could that be? Simple: Men's soccer is much more popular than women's soccer world-wide. Historically, men's soccer has also been a bigger draw in the U.S. Between 2011 and 2015, men played in 53 home games with attendance averaging 35,536. During that period, women played 50 games in the U.S., drawing an average attendance of 16,559. In 2014, when the men's team was in the World Cup competition, their revenues were roughly four times that of the women's team. Last year, when the women's team was competing for the World Cup, their revenues ($23.5 million) beat the men's team's ($21 million) for the first time.[37]

This disparity in popularity results in FIFA's unequal support for women's and men's soccer. Likewise, Greszler also blames the convenient cause of market forces:

> There's also the fact that in soccer and across most sports, men's teams generate significantly more revenue than

women's teams. Pay-for-performance dictates that workers' pay should reflect what they produce.

The women's World Cup is expected to generate $131 million in revenues—just 2 percent as much as the $6.1 billion generated by the men's 2018 World Cup. Within the U.S., however, the success of the women's soccer team has turned the tables, and the women's team has generated slightly more revenue than the men over the past few years.[38]

By highlighting the difference in World Cup revenues, Finley and Greszler go a step beyond blaming FIFA. They locate the cause of the gender pay gap not on the decision of the parent organization but on the market forces, and in this framework, market forces are simply the cumulative result of billions of individual choices. As such, the market forces that shape the gender pay gap in soccer are naturalized. By blaming the cause of market forces, Finley, Greszler, and others shield USSF and even FIFA from culpability. Through this logic, the women's lawsuit against USSF makes no sense because the real blame lies elsewhere. However, one must also note that Finely and Greszler's blaming of market forces each end with a caveat that undermines their arguments: in the United States today, women's soccer is more popular and generates more revenue than men's soccer.

Blaming market forces is effective not just because it misdirects the cause elsewhere. Because of the centrality of free market ideology in the United States, blaming this convenient cause offers no immediately legible solution. One cannot impose an equal enthusiasm for women's and men's soccer. One cannot dictate taste through billions of choices. Thus, blaming market forces entrenches the problem, relying on the notion that it is simply natural for enthusiasts to prefer men's sports to women's.

While blaming market forces is incredibly effective, it is also deceptive. Despite their appearance, markets, opinions, and taste are not natural. They are socially constructed and cultivated. When Finely and Graszler point to market forces as the originating moment of gender pay inequality, they fail to account for the ways in which FIFA, its member organizations, and its athletes develop and nurture enthusiasm for soccer. Claire Poppelwell-Scevak notes that between 2015 and 2018, FIFA spent 211 million US dollars on marketing and television broadcasting. Of this expenditure, 55 percent (or 116 million USD) was invested in the 2018 men's World Cup: "When one looks at the different streams of prize money FIFA has created for the men's World Cup tournament and the investment placed on the sale of the men's television broadcasting rights, it is apparent that FIFA's expenditures reflect a prioritization in promoting men's football."[39] These factors reveal that the market is not some conglomeration of individual choice and naturalized taste. FIFA and its member organizations like USSF have historically invested lower amounts in women's soccer and cultivating a market for it.[40] Despite these lower rates of investment, women's soccer in the United States has become more popular and generated more revenue in recent years. But for reactionary rhetors like Finely, Greszler, and the USSF legal team, blaming the cause of unequal investment is far from convenient, for it would require an increase in investment in women's sports.

Taken together, these reactionary responses to the women athletes' case for equal pay go beyond the stasis shifting of Hymowitz's mommy track. Rather, Finley, Greszler, USSF lawyers, and others deployed a set of distinct yet interrelated efforts to blame a convenient cause. Their rhetorical maneuvering more accurately evidences a form of stasis diffusion, as depicted in figure 5.2. While each stasis shift is marked by the abstract liberalism of choice, the defense of USSF's

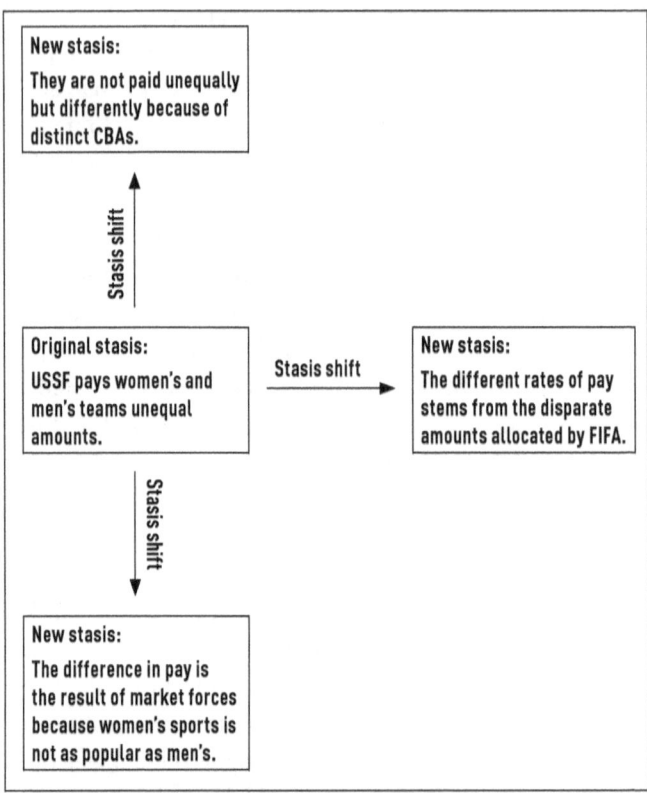

Figure 5.2: This diagram illustrates how multiple deployments of blaming a convenient cause work in tandem to diffuse the stasis and promote reactionary entrenchment by stretching the terrain of discourse.

unequal pay identifies a range of entities making this choice, deflecting from US soccer's responsibility.

Each iteration of blaming a convenient cause results in responsibility shifting and fostering a dynamic wherein no adequate solution can be advanced. Hymowitz blames the choices of women to become mothers, and the mommy track becomes the root cause of inequality. She does not need to ask if women should stop having children. Such a thought would be unthinkable. Yet she also fails to ask if men should take on more responsibility for rearing children. Simply put, there is no "daddy track" in Hymowitz's vision. The daddy track would be a choice, but it seems not only unmentionable but also unthinkable. Finley and Greszler underscore that women soccer players chose base salaries and medical leave, thus choosing to be paid differently than men. Finley also blames FIFA for the discrepancies in men's and women's pay. What can the USSF do about inequality if it is an international problem? Finley and Greszler stretch the blame even further by pointing to the market forces that shape and constrain the gender pay gap between women and men athletes. All these causes bear some responsibility, but the reactionary rhetors ultimately take complex social dynamics and distill them to a cause or a set of causes that seem impossible to address, resulting in reactionary entrenchment. In the cases of gender pay gap under study here, the convenient causes all result from choice and are entangled in the logic of abstract liberal individualism. Here, the goal is to make meaningful efforts at social transformation seem unwise, allowing for the status quo to stretch into the future.

Occam's Razor, Three Card Monte, and Structural Thinking

This chapter used writings on the gender pay gap to expose how reactionary rhetors deploy misdirection of blaming a convenient cause. The various examples demonstrate a reliance on the cultural logics of abstract liberal individualism. However, this cultural logic does not shape all manifestations of this form of misdirection. While blaming cattle for the production of greenhouse gases and mental health for mass shootings epitomize the strategy of blaming a convenient cause, they do not rely on abstract liberalism.[41] Another equally pernicious logic underwrites this discursive maneuver. The rhetorical strategy of blaming a convenient cause is undergirded by a societal embrace of oversimplified, monocausal explanations.

As humans, we embrace monocausal thinking because we are storytelling creatures, and all too often, we like our narratives simple, clear, and predictable. We follow Occam's Razor and the notion that the simplest explanation is often the correct one. Moreover, we desire stories that reaffirm our views of the world and do not implicate us in its problems. To believe that disproportionate police violence toward communities of color is the result of systemic white supremacy challenges the foundation of how white-aligned people view law, order, and justice in society. An easier, more adoptable narrative would blame a few bad actors or, better yet, the communities from which victims of police violence come. To believe that US gun culture is a primary cause of mass shootings and record numbers of gun deaths requires that narrative adherents not only question gun laws and the profitability of the industry but also our cultural investments in violence. Better to blame the failure of numerous individuals to seek mental health care. To believe that dependence on fossil fuels is a crucial component in the unfolding climate crisis requires that people question their reliance on cars and global trade. Better to blame cow farts, a natural, humorous, and seemingly unchallengeable contributor to climate change. To believe that 51 percent of the world's population earns less paid compensation for more work requires all people to ask how we rationalize and benefit from disparate and unequal gendered expectations. Better to deploy a folk theory model of discrimination and contend that inequality is really the result of choices, from individual women choosing the mommy track to international organizations deciding on distinct levels of compensation and the billions of choices congealing as market forces.

It is tempting to argue that right-oriented rhetors alone purposefully misrecognize complex social dynamics, distill them to a singular and convenient cause, and direct attention there. This is simply not the case. Consider, for example, how antiwar activists charged that the US-led wars in Iraq were driven by interests in oil. While oil revenues certainly factored into the reasoning behind these wars, oil was far from the only cause. Explaining away complex social issues through a singular cause evidences how reactionary impulses pervade the discursive and ideological terrain.

We should, however, distinguish between efforts to identify and address a significant cause and those that identify and often fail to address a convenient cause. When scholars, politicians, and activists identify a significant cause that they seek to address to solve a problem, they are often winnowing down complex, dynamic (i.e., multicausal) social issues to one cause out of a rhetorical and political necessity. For example, addressing gun violence may ultimately require significant changes to gun and tort laws, a shift in cultural production and values, and more robust budget for schools and mental health. When rhetors prioritize changing gun laws, it should not be seen as simply ignoring other factors. Rather it should be understood as a form of strategic essentialism wherein a significant cause is identified and treated as a pressure point wherein action on this issue will have the greatest impact. In this way, the significant causes of gun availability, carbon emissions, uneven gendered labor expectations, and so on are never truly monocauses. Rather, they are simply understood to be the most significant causes of multifaceted problems.

In contrast, reactionism blames convenient causes to foster sociopolitical entrenchment. Rather than identifying pressure points to propel social change, they direct attention to other causes in order to shift and diffuse the stasis. This is not to suggest that, for example, some people do not sincerely believe that mental health is a legitimate factor in gun violence and addressing mental health may not limit freedom in the same way as gun control. A key distinction between a significant cause and a convenient cause emerges from what actions people are called to take, if any. If a politician blames a lack of mental health care for gun violence and proposes legislation that will provide better support for those who need it, then this may be considered deploying a significant cause. However, if they blame a lack of mental health care for gun violence and then do nothing, we should recognize this for the effort to maintain the status quo that it is. In other words, the reactionary entrenchment of blaming a convenient cause emerges when the blame asks us to do nothing or at least nothing that challenges our vested interests.

In order to render blaming a convenient cause ineffective, we must foster an ability to both perceive the multiple factors contributing to social problems *and* simultaneously convey why addressing a single significant cause is exigent. In the case of pay in women's sports, we may say, sure US soccer has discriminated in terms of investment and compensation and this is tied to gender global popularity of sports. However, as US women working through the US legal system, USSF must be held accountable for its part in contributing to the gender pay gap.

Blaming a convenient cause provides simplified explanations that allow narrative adherents to escape culpability and defer addressing the problem. Here we would be wise to recall Patricia Williams's observation: "That life is complicated is a fact of great analytical importance."[42] For Avery Gordon, this seemingly "banal expression of the obvious" is "a profound theoretical statement . . . perhaps the most important theoretical statement of our time."[43] While Williams, Gordon, and others illustrate ways of exposing and exploring life's complexity, monocausal explanations resist the rich complexity of life and obscure more than they illuminate. If we are to grapple with the complexities of life and the social problems we face, we must eschew simple rhetorical games and foster an ability to recognize the multicausal, structural elements of the world we inhabit.

I conclude this chapter by offering two metaphors for how we may perceive sociopolitical challenges. First, blaming a convenient cause is a rhetorical game of three card monte wherein the rhetor shows her interlocutor one particular card, perhaps the ace of spades or the queen of hearts. As the rhetor moves the cards around the table, with a sleight of hand she slides the shown card behind another so that those playing the game will never be able to identify the card again without the rhetor allowing them to. It is a seemingly straight forward game, like the narrative explanation of these problems are seemingly simple. In truth, the game and the narrative explanation are all in the hands of the rhetor as she misdirects our attention elsewhere, pushing us to accept that we will not find the chosen card.

There are, however, other stories. And thus, there are other metaphors for thinking about complex social problems. We need to resist simple, comforting, obscuring stories in favor of multifaceted narratives that expose the messy complexity of life. Rather than the monocausal thinking of three card monte, we must discover hidden structures that underlie social problems. Here, I draw on a narrative strategy that my friend David Vázquez shared with me. When you walk into a room, you may see furniture, décor, and particular features like windows, doors, and so on. But behind the drywall exists a deeper structure: loadbearing and nonloadbearing beams, a foundation, electrical wiring, plumbing, insulation, and more. Each facet of this structure is put in place individually, yet they are all parts of the whole. When we discuss complex social challenges, from police violence and the gender pay gap to climate change and gun violence, we should be wary of reactionary rhetors showing one card only to slide it behind another and move the cards around so that we will never be able to locate the singular card and the cause it represents. Rather, we must think structurally, recognizing the multiple systems at play in any given problem. Thinking structurally means that when we remodel a room we must be aware of which beams are loadbearing and which are not. Likewise, we must plan our remodel or restructuring so that addressing the wiring does not interfere with changes to the plumbing. The metaphor of a room remodel elucidates the types of cognitive moves we must make to address structural problems within society. Ultimately creating a room large enough for all may require moving loadbearing beams as well as altering the wiring and plumbing. Or it may require us to gauge the limitations of our current dwelling and build something new.

CONCLUSION

On Faith in Dialogue: Cruel Optimism, World-Making, and Reimagining Conversation

Rules for Reactionaries has catalogued and analyzed a selection of rhetorical strategies used to foster reactionary entrenchment. Evading accountability by imagining racism, sexism, and other injustices as wholly Other. Claiming and weaponizing victimhood to develop and mobilize a political community based on aggrieved entitlement. Imagining a future built on a romanticized past when overt inequalities were seemingly unquestionable. Categorizing social justice advocates as un-American extremists so as to delegitimize their efforts and obscure the politics of reactionary entrenchment. Blaming a convenient cause so that conversations concerning addressing specific problems are derailed. These five rules are but a small sampling. Future cultural critics must continue a robust accounting and interrogation of the rhetorical strategies of reactionary entrenchment.

But a logical question naturally follows: How does one respond to or counter these maneuvers?

While I would be remiss if I did not briefly explore some ways to disrupt these discursive maneuvers and their impact, I must first return to something laid out in the introduction. *Rules for Reactionaries* is infused with a strong ambivalence about the notion that conversation about injustice will always lead to a better world. This is no apathetic ambivalence where broad social discourses have little impact on politics and lives. Rather, it is a forceful ambivalence where conversation can foster social transformation *and* it can be used to forestall change and make injustice endure. Indeed, romanticizing our national conversations positions them as a cruel optimism. Lauren Berlant describes cruel optimism as a relation that "exists when something you desire is actually an obstacle to your flourishing."[1] In this formula, the desired conversation may highlight areas of injustice, but through reactionary rhetorical strategies, the conversation simultaneously works to forestall social change. A politician is called to account for their racism, sexism, homophobia, but they deflect attention to a more easily agreed upon extremist Other. A solution is proposed to reduce disproportionate state violence against communities of color, and reactionary rhetors identify a more convenient cause, derailing the efforts to foment change. These examples and countless others signal the promise that conversation holds and the ease with which it can be subverted. But the affect of optimism is seductive. Even as the promise of national conversations yield few, often superficial results, with each new flashpoint—a moment of racist violence, a high-profile case of sexual harassment, another threshold of climate change reached—optimism springs anew that conversation will usher in a better world. It appears as a linear narrative that promises progress but in actuality bears a recursive structure, circling back to the promise without delivering the desired social transformation.

Here, a crucial question emerges: Why? Why do these conversations fail to deliver what so many hope for? Could it be that our conversation partners are simply bad faith actors who are struggling to protect inequality and forestall change at all costs? In some cases, the answer is clearly yes.

As Robert Proctor, Naomi Oreskes, and Erik Conway have demonstrated, the tobacco and oil industries purposefully deployed the same rhetorical strategies of calling for a false balance in order to undermine existing scientific consensus on the danger of smoking and the human causes of climate change.[2] Similarly, Christopher Rufo and James Lindsay egregiously manipulate intellectual history in order to demonize those committed to social justice and obstruct social transformation.

However, it would be a tremendous mistake to write off all who adopt these discursive maneuvers as operating in bad faith. Simply put, there is a difference between industry workers who promote ignorance about the effects of smoking and the causes of climate change and a friend who hears, adopts, and recirculates those reactionary perspectives. There is a difference between think tank sponsored media figures who decry diversity, equality, and inclusion initiatives and a relative who is interpellated by this reactionary discourse and then believes the world disadvantages him because he is a white male. While there are certainly people arguing in bad faith, it is a mistake to assume that all those who recirculate these reactionary positions do so with malicious purpose, for doing so relies on the good-bad binary thinking that hinders the ability to address investments in inequality.

Beyond blaming reactionism as inherently bad faith, a critical reason these national conversations function as cruel optimisms resides in facile and flawed understandings of conversation and its relation, persuasion. In my public talks and in my classes, I often get a question that goes like this: "How do you respond to people that say _____?" Perhaps the imagined speaker believes talking about racism only exacerbates the problem. Or maybe they advance the idea that women choose to earn less than men. The specific crux of disagreement does not matter. What is important is that the question itself reveals a too-common assumption that conversation begets persuasion. The barely unstated premise is that if one says the right words, in the right way, and at the right time, their conversation partner will change their mind, see the light, join the correct side. But this is not how conversation or persuasion works. It is a mistake to enter a dialogue with a steadfast belief in one's own rightness (or righteousness) and an equal commitment to the wrongheadedness of others. Moreover, people do not easily and quickly change their minds about thorny social issues by simply hearing the correct words. Yet this premise also underwrites the enduring faith in national conversations to rectify injustice and heal divisions. The cycle continues: An age-old problem has erupted to the surface, a crisis we cannot ignore; we will all come to the table, and we will move forward together. This optimistic attachment to national conversation as the means of solving injustice propels us to seek conversation with the false assumption that justice will follow.

While it is unwise to imagine a quick, linear progression from conversation to transformation, the study of rhetoric and a faith in dialogue underwrite the very notion of deliberative democracy. In *Talking to Strangers* Danielle Allen argues that rhetoric and dialogue are essential components to healing "interracial distrust" and fostering "political friendship" by "generating mutual benefit."[3] According to Allen, "Rhetoric, understood as the art of talking to strangers as equals and of proving that one has also their good at heart, inspires the trust that provides a consent-based regime with the flexibility needed to garner, from citizens of diverse backgrounds, consent to decisions made in uncertainty."[4] As a work of political theory invested in healing the racial wounds of the United States, Allen's treatise attempts to revivify the ancient Greek roots of both democracy and rhetoric in order to articulate a political friendship (i.e., citizenship) that can transcend racial divisions.

Shifting the emphasis from talking to listening, Krista Ratcliffe examines how the mutuality necessary for deliberative democracy can be cultivated through intentional, rhetorical listening. For Ratcliffe, "*rhetorical listening* signifies a stance of openness that a person may choose to assume in relation to any person, text, or culture," whereby listeners are positioned not to master the argument or best an opponent but to understand the cultural logics that inform their interlocutor.[5] Recognizing the cultural logics at play allows one to foster some form of "consubstantial identification" with the conversation partner and "to argue what we deem fair and just while questioning that which we deem fair and just."[6] For example, through Ratcliffe's logic, when engaging in a conversation about contemporary inequality, all parties must be willing to question their own perspectives and definitions. Placed along the social axes of race and gender, Ratcliffe envisions a world where intractable debate surrounding social experiences and inequality is remade with an understanding of where others come from and an interrogation of one's own beliefs. Critically, Ratcliffe's vision of rhetorical listening should not be confused with a romantic, hopeless idealism. Rather her approach to rhetorical listening is a painstaking practice that maps a potential route to deliberative democracy.

The faith in deliberative democracy grounded in rhetoric and conversation also propels the scholarship of those like Patricia Roberts-Miller who study demagoguery and propaganda.[7] Whether exploring the strategies of nineteenth-century proslavery rhetors or twentieth-century demagogues, Roberts-Miller exposes how rhetorical strategies may be used to subvert deliberative democracy. That is, while Allen and Ratcliffe explore the importance of rhetoric in forming the political friendship and identification necessary for democracy, Roberts-Miller examines how rhetorical strategies can be used to disrupt and undermine deliberative democracy. Yet a faith in the relationship between rhetoric and democracy propels Roberts-Miller, for she argues that the awareness of these strategies and how they work, the metacognition, allows individuals to be better prepared for when they encounter antidemocratic rhetorical efforts. Ultimately, this scholarship on the relationship between rhetoric and democracy underscores the need for enduring dialogue, but these scholars never make the fatal mistake in assuming that conversation surrounding justice will be quick, linear, or painless.

The Power and Function of Language

While I reject the cruel optimism that national conversations will automatically usher in an era of justice, I simultaneously acknowledge the power and function of language in shaping the sociopolitical landscape. To understand how discourse shapes politics beyond a facile notion of persuasion, two unstated aspects of language must be brought to the fore. First, as a rhetorical vehicle, language is not a solely external tool used to communicate ideas which people may find persuasive or insufficient. Popular embraces of conversation and persuasion often rely on the notion that people are fully aware of and in control of their faculties. Scholars would describe this as "autonomous subjectivity," but it is the idea that thought, being, and identity emerge from individuals, and those individuals wield language as they see fit. In truth, however, human subjectivity—what we may describe as our sense of Self, our consciousness, or our identity—does not exist outside of or apart from language. Rather, people and discourse share a dialogical relationship. Just as humans create and wield language, so too does language create subjectivity.[8] Yes, people use language to communicate their ideas but ideas communicated through language forge human consciousness. And through language, human subjectivity and the sociopolitical world continually evolve. As such, dialogue is not simply the use of language to consciously persuade another person. When people engage in dialogue, they open the possibility of changing the mind of their interlocutor as well as their own. Seeing language as constitutive of human subjectivity propels us to recognize that encountering new discourses does not merely mean that one may change the opinion or belief of someone but that those encounters actually change one's consciousness, Self, and the relationship to the world.

Second, because of this dialogic relationship between language and human subjectivity, we must also recognize the world-creating power of language. Michael Warner argues that language plays a significant role in forming publics and counterpublics. Here Warner is describing "the kind of public that comes into being only in relation to texts and their circulation—like the public of an essay."[9] Building on the idea that discourse shapes human consciousness, Warner explores how the circulation of language forges connections between people through shared and divergent perceptions of the world. Warner goes further to assert that "*a public is poetic world making.*"[10] That is, as discourse is addressed to an audience, that deployment of language constitutes the audience, and as that audience responds by accepting, rejecting, questioning, or some variation thereof, their relationship to the world is impacted. Examples of Warner's world-making power of language run throughout this book. When reactionaries assert their victimization, those who embrace the claim are imagined into a community, one that can be mobilized to act on the world. When a romanticized past is invoked as the foundation for a utopian future, the public it calls into being imagines that future world and acts to bring that world into fruition. These reactionary rhetorical strategies are not simply dangerous because they may hoodwink otherwise smart, good, rational people. Rather, their danger stems from the way these strategies shape human consciousness, craft social realities, forge identities, and mobilize communities, further entrenching systems of inequality.

Recognizing that language is essential to human consciousness and world creation provides a foundation for moving beyond the cruel optimism that national conversations will without question bring about justice and social transformation. We must reject the infantile notion that simply participating in the conversation will bring about change. However, undergirded by the work on rhetoric and deliberative democracy, we must also reject the cynical belief that talking to strangers, particularly those who disagree with us, is nothing but an exercise in futility and frustration.[11] So again, how do we move forward with ambivalence between the Scylla of naive hope and the Charybdis of cynicism?

My ambivalence about dialogue and the cruel optimism of conversations is rooted in a seeming contradiction: the recognition that conversation can be both a means of obstructing justice and it may also be a critical component to building a better world. How do we square these ideas? How do we move forward?

Nine Strategies to Counter Reactionary Entrenchment

One could read my assertion that national conversations function as cruel optimisms as a call to reject the project of talking to strangers. On the other hand, one could see my acknowledgment of the relationship between rhetoric and deliberative democracy as a call to engage those with whom one disagrees in hopes of swaying them and building a better world. Here I must make explicit three elements of the operative theory of social change that underwrites this book. First, despite the desire to see history as a linear progression where the present marks a sharp departure from and improvement on the past, social change is gradual, sporadic, uneven, and often tenuous. Second, changes to social structures cannot be enacted by policy alone. To reconfigure social structures requires talking to others: those we agree with, those we disagree with, and those who have no firm stance on a given issue. Finally, we must not confuse these conversations with facile, one-way routes of persuasion. Because language carries and imparts ideology, these conversations shape the world, our interlocutors, and ourselves, even when the impact is so small it is hard to see. Through these perspectives on social change and the role of language therein, I maintain a forceful ambivalence that requires more than one way forward, a strategy that shifts depending on the contextual needs of the moment.

In *Methodology of the Oppressed*, Chela Sandoval provides a model for navigating the tension between the possibilities and limitations of dialogue. Drawing on a metaphor of a standard transmission, Sandoval identifies "differential" consciousness and social movements as those that can shift between more fixed sociopolitical projects: "In this sense, the differential mode of consciousness functions like the clutch of an automobile, the mechanism that permits the driver to select, engage, and disengage gears in a system for the transmission of power. The differential represents the variant; its presence emerges out of correlations, intensities, junctures, crises."[12] This differential approach allows for activists and movements to occupy multiple ideological positions over time and deploy a varied range of tactics. Ultimately, there is no singular, unified strategy that will vanquish reactionary entrenchment. Rather, those committed to enacting social change must make use of a wide range of potentially contradictory tactics. Sandoval offers a model for using various strategies rather than investing solely in one way of engaging others. Echoing Sandoval's call to embrace multiple, contradictory tactics, the following approaches provide some ways to move with and through ambivalence in order to counter reactionary entrenchment.

One: *Determine whether it is worth engaging and potentially refuse.* Confronting these national conversations with a forceful ambivalence requires that we recognize that there are moments we should step back and strategically curtail our participation. Why might we refuse to engage others directly? There are a few reasons. As noted earlier, some participants in these conversations do operate in bad faith. If we know or sense that our interlocutor has little interest in truth and accuracy, what does anyone gain from dialogue with them? In truth engaging bad faith actors can simply recirculate and amplify their reactionary views. Consider how news media, working on a premise that objectivity requires airing "both sides" inadvertently gave legitimacy to and boosted the voices of the tobacco and oil industries. Similarly, when journalists uncritically platformed Christopher Rufo, James Lindsay, and activist groups like Moms of Liberty, they fostered a moral panic that lead to vicious harassment campaigns, curriculum bans, and reactionary legislation. This danger of amplification is not limited to traditional media. Social media platforms rely on algorithms to track engagement and promote content. When everyday people respond on X (formerly Twitter), Facebook, YouTube, or elsewhere, they feed the beast. Likes, dislikes, reposts, and responses—it doesn't matter. To the platform algorithm, it's all engagement that ultimately promotes the post to more viewers. Rather than responding directly, if one responds at all, it would be wise to take a screenshot of the post and include that in one's own post on their platform of choice. At least in that case, while the discourse may recirculate critically, it will not be amplified algorithmically.

Whether or not one's conversation partner is arguing in bad faith, participating in these conversations can be emotionally and psychologically taxing. Everyone has a different bandwidth for these dialogues, and that bandwidth changes depending on the individual and the context. Some may not want to engage others in these conversations. It's exhausting and fruitless, they may say. This may be particularly true of some who occupy multiple targeted identities. As Dylan Marron suggests, "Empathy across the divide is a luxury item that not everyone can afford."[13] As a middle-aged straight white guy committed to social justice, I view it as a significant responsibility to participate in these conversations, to push myself and others into moments of productive discomfort and ask thorny questions. But I also sometimes recognize my limits, those moments when the topic is so charged or the interlocutor so grating, or life so stressful that time and energy is best spent elsewhere. Refusing these conversations is not a permanent strategy. Rather, recognizing the world-building power of language, we may also rightly wish to surround ourselves with people and the discourses that nurture us against the harshness of a reactionary world. Conversations are not simply opportunities to change someone's mind. They are also the discursive nourishment that shapes identity and girds those who must face a hostile world.

Two: *Enter these conversations with a commitment to introspection and accountability.* We must be willing to pause, engage in self-reflection, and interrogate one's actions, beliefs, and impacts. In a TEDx Talk at Hampshire College, radio DJ, vlogger, and media personality Jay Smooth recognized the fraught nature of addressing the racism of someone else's actions. He suggested that perhaps we might be most effective if we focused introspectively. When someone calls our attention to our missteps, we should not treat these moments as an indictment of ourselves but as a critique of our actions. Smooth humorously asked the audience to consider when someone calls out one's moment of racism as akin to letting someone know that they have something stuck in their teeth.[14] Thinking about one's practices and investments as spinach in teeth fundamentally rejects the folk theory's reliance on fixed identities and the conception of racism as extreme and aberrant. To begin with one's self and one's own investments in inequality refuses the rejection of the racist, sexist, reactionary Other. There is no one and nothing to disavow. Rather, there is something to own, ruminate on, and address. Similarly, in writing about whiteness and antiracism, George Yancy has described calling out participation in racism as a gift:

> Seeing whiteness from the perspective of, in this case, Black people functions as an invitation *to see more*, to see things differently. It is a special call that reframes, that results in a form of unveiling, of seeing, and of recognizing a different side. It is a gift that invites an opening, perhaps having a Hubble telescope-like impact: "I had no idea there was so much more to see, and with such clarity!" I have had this experience while reading works by feminist theorists. I have dared to see the world and my identity through their critical analyses, from their experiences of male dominant culture, from their *mirror*. "Damn, what a sexist! I overlooked that one." Yet I am thankful for *their* gift.[15]

Recognizing the act of calling such moments to one's attention as a gift propels us to recognize both the vulnerability, trust, and generosity of those moments and that it is one's choice and responsibility to use the gift wisely. Everyone gets spinach in their teeth, toilet paper on their shoe, unexpected gas—choose your metaphor—the challenge Smooth and Yancy offer is to ask what we will do when these embarrassing moments are publicly or privately recognized. But it is truly a gift to have the spinach-in-teeth of inequality called to one's attention so that one can transform one's Self and the world. Ultimately Smooth asks us to pause, reflect, and act. Underwriting his approach is the recognition that we are not perfect, we will make mistakes, and, while we may not arrive, we can still approach.[16]

Critically, while Smooth and Yancy call for introspection when someone brings issues of injustice directly to our attention, this stance and practice can also be honed in other moments when one engages these conversations. When listening to talk radio, navigating social media, or talking with friends or strangers, if one recognizes an investment in inequality on the part of others, rather than simply correcting or rejecting those perspectives and the people who hold them, one should look inward. One should listen rhetorically, ask what cultural logics underwrite those perspectives, and explore whether one holds similar beliefs and investments. This stance of introspection allows for a more nuanced understanding of how reactionary politics pervade our lives and is a necessary tool for uprooting reactionary impulses.

Three: *Call attention to the words, logics, and practices of others and not their character.* The introspective stance just proposed does not erase the need to also hold others accountable. But too often we hold others accountable in ways that work against our goals. For example, if we are discussing structural racism and other forms of inequality, we must emphasize *the impact* of policy over the identities of those who design and implement the policy. Consider the danger of highlighting a fixed notion of identity. In 2016, Hillary Clinton declared that half of Donald Trump's supporters could be placed in a "basket of deplorables.... The racist, sexist, homophobic, xenophobic, Islamophobic—you name it."[17] This may have been an accurate description of how many felt about the constituent elements of the alt-right. This attack, however, personalized and overshadowed the more fundamental problem with white supremacy in US culture. By calling the alt-right portion of Trump's supporters those who could be placed in a "basket of deplorables," Clinton designated them as the racist, sexist, homophobic Other and asked voters including moderate Republicans to disavow Trump and the alt-right. This effort both demonized Trump's base and obscured how Clinton and other Democrats have actively benefited from and invested in white supremacy and other forms of inequality. In other words, Clinton lacked introspection and she further polarized the electorate by casting a group of voters as unredeemable Others.

Rather than calling out injustice as a flaw in the humanity of our neighbors, drawing careful attention to the effects of beliefs, words, and actions while simultaneously embracing the humanity of others opens the possibility for future relationships. In 2019, Kamala Harris offered a useful example of how one can address racist actions without condemning one's character. During the first Democratic primary debate, Harris held the frontrunner Joseph Biden accountable for both his chummy relationship with segregationists and for his opposition to federally imposed school busing. Harris stated,

> I'm going to now direct this at Vice President Biden, I do not believe you are a racist, and I agree with you when you commit yourself to the importance of finding common ground.
>
> But I also believe, and it's personal—and I was actually very—it was hurtful to hear you talk about the reputations of two United States senators who built their reputations and career on the segregation of race in this country. And it was not only that, but you also worked with them to oppose busing.
>
> And, you know, there was a little girl in California who was part of the second class to integrate her public schools, and she was bused to school every day. And that little girl was me.[18]

Notice how Harris began by assuaging Biden's, and presumably his white supporters', anxieties about being called a racist. For a moment she acknowledged the folk theory investment in fixed identity and white middle-class goodness. Then she pivoted to illustrate that Biden's policy position had a detrimental impact on people of color like her. In the words of Eduardo Bonilla-Silva, you can have "racism without racists."[19] Many pundits responded to the effectiveness of Harris's political attack. What they missed was the deft way that she set up her position; she began by shifting away from identity and then elucidating her opponent's policy position and his refusal to be introspective these many years later. Harris did not define Biden as an unredeemable racist Other and disown him. But she did expose how his policy positions hurt people of color. Here, Harris offered Biden a gift, to draw on Yancy, and from there, it was Biden's responsibility and that of the audience to use the gift wisely. Biden may have lacked the introspective dexterity, but in that moment, Harris did not only hold up a gift for Biden; she offered her gift to the audience and news media as well. It is their choice, our choice, as to whether we look inward and see our investments in inequality. Although some may not accept such a gift and may refuse to engage in self-reflection, emphasizing the deplorable inhumanity of others may make us feel better about ourselves, but it is unlikely to open hearts and minds.

Four: *Recognize rhetorical patterns, and call attention to them as a means of disruption.* This strategy has been a foundational precept of *Rules for Reactionaries*. There exists a set of reactionary rhetorical strategies. While pervasive, they too often fly below the critical radar allowing them to function with ease, shaping the grounds of what is considered normal or natural. Identifying these rhetorical strategies allows us to recognize that each manifestation is not a one-off historical moment, but a scripted routine, a social pattern, that follows and reinforces entrenched logics. Recognizing and calling attention to these patterns disrupts their natural flow, their hegemonic status, and allows moments of productive rupture to take place. This strategy both draws on and departs from the work of Clyde Miller and the Institute for Propaganda Analysis (IPA). In the 1930s, Miller and the IPA fought propaganda efforts by developing a set of ABCs for propaganda analysis and promoting media literacy curriculum in schools.[20] However, unlike the IPA's campaign against disinformation, reactionary rhetorics do not solely emerge from bad faith actors attempting to hoodwink people or from powerful cultural institutions. Thus, I advocate a sociopolitical and discursive literacy that allows people to recognize these reactionary patterns—a literacy Roberts-Miller would describe as metacognition. People are not autonomous, rationale subjects. Armed only with a set of analytical practices, they may not automatically reject disinformation and reactionary rhetorics. Like language generally, reactionary rhetorical strategies course through our world, carrying and imparting ideology, forging consciousness, and building our social worlds. Echoing the dictum in critical whiteness studies that countering normed and invisible social forces requires first making them "strange," I contend that recognizing these rhetorical maneuvers is crucial for disrupting their impact.[21]

But what does this disruption look like in action? Simply naming the rhetorical maneuver. For example, scholars and activists committed to social transformation need to call out the weaponization of victimhood, nostalgic renderings of pasts rooted in inequality, blaming convenient causes, and other rhetorical strategies when they see them. They must not let these rules for reactionaries course below the surface, maintaining privilege and aggrieved entitlement as the status quo. For example, simply drawing attention to weaponized victimhood—"Tucker Carlson just played victim so that he could. . . ."—functions as a discursive monkey wrench. By itself, calling attention to these strategies will not change minds, but it can disrupt the seemingly natural flow of reactionary rhetoric and ideology. This counterstrategy is not about changing minds of those deeply invested in reactionary entrenchment. Because reactionary rhetorical strategies pervade US culture, making these maneuvers legible and explicit fosters the grounds for those who may not consciously identify with reactionary efforts to develop the necessary metacognition to see how they inadvertently contribute to efforts they would otherwise reject.

Five: *Ask questions that allow people to unpack their thinking.* Frequently the temptation is to counter a position we disagree with by asserting our own perspective complete with facts, anecdotes, and opinions. The result rarely develops into something other than two sides deepening their entrenchment. Asking questions, on the other hand, does not respond to assertions with more assertions. Rather, opening lines of inquiry changes the stance of those involved, inviting each party to reflect on the foundation of their beliefs. Because reactionary entrenchment relies on recycled social narratives that have been repeated so often that their logic seems unassailable, asking thoughtful questions disrupts the flow of these narratives.

Allow me to offer an example. Years ago, I found myself in a conversation, a variation of which I have encountered numerous times. A person close to me, let's call her Janet, relayed that the son of a common acquaintance had not been admitted to the university of their choice because the school had to admit more Black students who were less qualified than the acquaintance's son. Have you heard this one before? In this common storyline, white people are deserving because of merit but victimized by people of color who receive unfair advantages and are not required to work hard by a system that privileges them.[22] It is the story of Allan Bakke, Abigail Fisher, and countless others. It is a story underwritten by numerous unspoken assumptions. So I questioned those assumptions: What do college admissions officers consider when making these decisions? If racial quotas in college admissions have been banned since 1978, how does this family know it was a Black student who was admitted instead of their son? Could it have been the child of an alum? A child of a Hollywood celebrity who paid to have their child admitted despite their less than stellar record? A student from out of state or from out of the country who would pay more in tuition? A student from an underrepresented region like a rural farming community? If they were certain it was a Black student, which I do not think they were, why are they so sure that the student was undeserving? Is it possible that this imagined student has an exceptional admissions profile?

I did not ask all these questions at once. To do so wouldn't really be asking questions, but simply making a series of assertions in question form. After each one, I waited for Janet to respond and think through her answers. Moreover, I asked each question with my most earnest and curious tone. I wanted Janet to know that I was listening. And while I have had many variations of this conversation, I was not going to simply dismiss her, telling her she's wrong or racist. But then I got to my final question: "You don't have to answer this. In fact I don't want you to. Just sit with it for a while. What does this family gain from imagining that they have been wronged by a Black college student and a faceless admissions system? Is it easier to imagine an undeserving Black student than to imagine their son may not be exceptional and deserving?" This question may not be much of a question. Maybe it's an argument. But framed with care and generosity, this question is also a sincere invitation to consider our social world and deeply entrenched narratives in a new light. And critically, we must be willing to sit in deep silence before moving to other topics.

Asking questions like these is not easy. It takes time. It takes emotional investment. And it requires willing introspection on the part of the interlocutor. These questions, however, are useful in scratching the surface to expose the cultural logics of aggrieved entitlement. By homing attention to cultural logics, I worked to not dismiss or demonize Janet or our mutual acquaintance. Rather, I sought to understand them while simultaneously asking Janet to reflect on the cultural logics that allowed her to so quickly believe in white victimization and Black undeservedness.

Six: *Shift the central question or terrain of debate to promote more fruitful conversation.* Although many people may consider their ideas entirely of their own making and each conversation a new, discrete event, in truth we are surrounded by and constituted by discourse that shapes our world and senses of self. Thus, each moment of dialogue is informed by and often recycles age-old questions and claims that lead to deadlock and entrenchment. We must actively devise new trajectories of dialogue.

As an educator, I have used this strategy to help students avoid conversational ruts that get us nowhere. For example, there is one question that I request students not ask: "Is X racist?" or "Is Y sexist?" For example, is *Adventures of Huckleberry Finn* a racist text? Or are the works of Ernest Hemingway and Oscar Zeta Acosta sexist? The answers to these questions are seldom interesting and often result in debates that spiral into nothing but judgement and mistrust. If a student named John declares *Huckleberry Finn* not racist or does not see sexism within Hemingway or Acosta, his peers may take his position as evidence of John's own investment in racism or sexism. If Rebecca, another student, views texts as racist or sexist, John and those who agree with him may write off Rebecca and those who agree with her as overreacting or politicizing the text. I have never found these conversations fruitful, just frustrating and dispiriting.

Hence, I circumvent this dynamic by saying that questions like these are not productive. I note that "Is X racist?" or "Is Y sexist?" are off-limit questions. Instead, I ask students to consider "How does race, gender, or sexuality function in this text or situation?" By shifting the conversation from one of character and identity, we are able to develop a collective inquiry and more nuanced understandings. For example, rather than declare *Huckleberry Finn* to be unredeemably racist or a paragon of antiracist virtue—answers that replicate the binary of the folk theory—we can discuss how a novel committed to the abolition of slavery reproduces the rhetorics of white supremacy. After all, it is in the moment where Huck realizes the full humanity of Jim that he reflects, "I knowed he was white inside."[23] Invariably some students will point to this epiphanic moment as central to Huck's and the novel's antiracism. To which I or another student will ask: What are the consequences of conflating whiteness with humanity? Does it follow that a nonwhiteness would mark something other than humanity? This textual conversation works as a model for how we may ask more nuanced, open-ended, and productive questions. While the answers of those we dialogue with may well differ from our own, these questions and answers offer greater opportunity for everyone to listen to how all involved come to their conclusion. And that listening is essential for introspection.

Seven: *Recognize secondary audiences and shift attention to them, even if indirectly.* Along with the facile belief in dialogue as a seamless persuasion, we too often imagine those we are responding to as the sole audience of our efforts. But this is not always the case. Unless we are speaking directly and only to one person, other audiences exist and should be taken into consideration. Broadening the potential audience allows us to change the impact of the conversation. For example, say you are at a family gathering and Uncle Harry espouses his opinion on LBGTQ issues by recycling reactionary talking points and conspiracy theories. This is likely not a productive moment to get Uncle Harry to question his perspectives. However, if you look around the room, you will see your younger cousins or perhaps some other relatives that are directly, but potentially silently, impacted by homophobia or relatives who are just unsure and unaware about the issue. In moments like these, we can recognize these other audiences as the grounds for responding. Perhaps we ask a strategic question not to get Uncle Harry to change his mind but to offer an invitation to others to ruminate on the issue in more complex and nuanced ways. Perhaps we offer a scripted retort so that others will have a model for responding to such perspectives in the future. Or perhaps we respond to Uncle Harry because we don't want Harry or others to think that homophobia will be met with silence and complicity.

This strategy goes beyond interpersonal conversations. Recognizing and speaking to secondary audiences can be a fruitful strategy in broader, national conversations as well. Consider the example of Rep. Steve King from the first chapter. What if instead of asking King if he regretted his stated nostalgia for days when "white nationalist, white supremacist, Western civilization" did not have such negative connotations (for white people), journalists and political figures recognized voters who are not attracted to white nationalism as the potential audience. Perhaps they could ask, "What is it, Representative King, that you mean by white nationalism and white supremacy? And why do you have such fondness for these concepts?" Or when King condemned white supremacy, stating that such ideas have never entered his mind, one might ask, "Do you think that racism is limited to conscious beliefs?" The thrust behind these questions is to draw the otherwise unstated premise of King's argument into the open. These questions make King's ideas legible to voters who have supported King and not fully considered his racial logics. The speaker may be reaching out to and galvanizing listeners who vociferously oppose inequality in all its forms, a type of subtle deictic rhetoric. Or they may be laying the foundation for future conversations and future ideological transformation.

Eight: *Develop and deploy counterframing, counternarratives, and scripted responses.* Reactionary rhetorical strategies are effective because they frame the conversation in ways that close off other modes of understanding the issues at hand. The "War on Christmas" frames Christians as victims who must fight back. The assertion that the wage gap is a result of women's choices highlights individual actions over societal structures and values. Decrying antiracism as a Marxist, Communist endeavor positions those advocating social justice as not simply antiracist or anticapitalist but also anti-American. George Lakoff warns against using the language of one's opponent in a political argument, for doing so may only reinforce the mental operations that the opponents' arguments elicit.[24] For example, arguing that there is no such thing as a War on Christmas inadvertently cedes the notion that the War is even a possibility. Lakoff's approach is to ignore the war frame and respond with a frame congruent with one's own values. In response to claims of the War on Christmas, one could state that the need to celebrate and respect numerous belief systems is a cornerstone of US democracy.

Lakoff's idea of counterframing finds resonance with those in critical race theory who have advocated counternarratives. According to Richard Delgado and Jean Stefancic, counternarratives or counterstories are used by those who wish to "challenge, displace, or mock" "the validity of accepted premises or myths, especially ones held by the majority."[25] Like counterframing, counternarratives reorient listeners on the discursive and ideological terrain, showing them possibilities that they may have never considered. Counternarratives exist in the histories we read, the literature and media we consume, and the stories we tell each other.

While counterframes and counternarratives are crucial to move broad, national conversations in productive directions, well-crafted scripted responses can be deployed similarly in interpersonal dialogues. For example, I often hear a variation of a question when giving public talks, teaching, or speaking with strangers or loved ones. The question goes like this: "Doesn't talking about racism bring more attention to tensions and make the situation worse?" I love this question because it is so common and those who ask it often consider it to be quite original. My scripted response: "That's a great question. Let's think about it for a moment. Imagine you are driving down the freeway and you notice the check engine light comes on. Maybe you smell smoke. The car is alerting you that things are awry. What do you do? Do you ignore it hoping that the car will fix itself? Or do you take it to a mechanic and get the car back in working order as soon as possible? Whatever you choose to do, I think it is safe to assume that the symptoms are not the cause of the problem—the check engine light has not caused your troubles, and ignoring it is likely just going to make things worse. Now the real question is why do we so often think that paying attention to a problem like racism will make it worse? What other problems do we solve by ignoring? And what do we gain by ignoring them?"

This is a scripted response to a recycled question. It allows me to explore the questioner's logic by reframing the question into a less thorny issue. Do I think that this scripted response will cause an epiphany? No. Probably not. It may raise questions and cause them to wrestle with them a bit. But the scripted response also allows me to take a repeated question and disrupt its natural flow. Moreover, if there are secondary audiences involved, using this response provides them with questions to ruminate on and a response that they can use as well.

Nine: *Foster humanities modes of inquiry and literacy.* The strategies I have explored thus far have focused on how one navigates a discursive situation. Fostering humanities modes of inquiry and literacy shifts attention to larger social and structural issues that shape the conditions for dialogue. For at least seventy years, the United States has disproportionately invested in STEM (science, technology, engineering, and mathematics) education, and for approximately half a century the United States has divested from public education, having a disproportionate impact on the humanities. Today, the arts and the humanities seem to be in a state of perpetual crisis as their skills and value are questioned, their enrollments dwindle, and their institutional support is reduced. This is clearly "a moment of danger" for the humanities, and this danger is not unrelated to the ongoing culture wars. However, focusing attention to humanistic forms of inquiry may also provide a moment of opportunity.[26]

The humanities prepare us to address reactionary rhetorical strategies on firm ground. For example, rather than accepting the utopian and dystopian visions and being interpellated into reactionary ideologies, the humanities offer practitioners a critical toolkit to better understand these narratives. Here are some routes of inquiry that particular fields within the humanities foster:

> *Rhetoric*: How does this discourse or narrative substantiate a worldview in the eyes of its adherents? How does it draw people into an imagined community and how does it mobilize them?
>
> *Literature*: What are the consequences, intentional and unintentional, that emerge from this narrative? What world does it imagine into existence and who is included or excluded from that world?

History: Why does this narrative emerge at this historical moment? How does this narrative reflect not just an ideology but the economic and social interests of its adherents?

Philosophy: What form of government and citizenly relations does this discourse or narrative seek to promote? How does language shape our understandings of ourselves and others? What are our ethical obligations to those we speak with and those we speak about?

Too often the humanities has found itself claiming that its fields teach critical thinking and rejecting narrowly defined learning outcomes as a tool of neoliberal rationalization. The first error both fails to define critical thinking and assumes that critical thinking is solely the purview of the humanities. The second forestalls the humanities from asserting its value, not as having a market value per se but as an answer to a collective intellectual and social need. The truth is that the humanities provides unique modes of critical thinking, the world needs these skills, and we should not be ashamed or afraid of the value of what we do.

Ultimately, these routes of humanistic inquiry are modes of metacognition: a deep consideration about how we think and how we come to understand the world. These modes of metacognition denaturalize reactionary rhetorics and cultural logics that people may live by, asking us to consider what makes these imaginings effective in spreading ideology, what their roots are, and what implications they may have. Here practitioners of metacognition are able to consider that these reactionary narratives, like all narratives, both emerge from and shape the sociopolitical terrain. Humanistic routes of inquiry will not end the culture wars by fostering a solitary, perfect narrative that unites everyone. But this metacognition does strip away power from these reactionary strategies, potentially offering a means for communication and human relations.

By suggesting the need to foster humanities modes of inquiry, I am not advocating that humanities education directly dismiss or contest reactionary politics. Rather, I contend that we more consciously place the various forms of humanities inquiry at the center of education. Moreover, we should argue for investing in the humanities not based on an abstract critical thinking or the promise that the humanities somehow builds good character or civic participation. Rather, we should advocate humanities education because these fields foster specific forms of inquiry that make deliberation possible.

Onward up the Hill

This list of strategies, of course, is both only partial and at times contradictory. Surely others could elucidate a broader array of methods for navigating thorny dialogues and challenging reactionary entrenchment. For instance, some may posit that ridicule is an effective means of shutting down reactionary discourse. Others may highlight the tension in this list of strategies. One cannot simultaneously refuse to engage a conversation partner and ask them questions that promote dialogue and self-reflection. There is a tension between depoying counterframes or scripted responses and engaging in careful introspection. Moreover, while I eschew the folk theory and an Enlightenment model of autonomous subjectivity, most of the strategies offered detail what individuals can do. These points of tension and seeming contradiction return us to Sandoval's model of differential consciousness. There is no singular, unified approach to countering reactionism and advocating social transformation. We must be able to shift between strategies, recognizing which ones are needed in the moment.

This differential approach is rooted in a rejection of the facile notion that a singular conversation will alone lead to persuasion. Rather than quickly changing the minds of others through correct logic and magic words, we must recognize that human subjectivity emerges from the wide terrain of discourse we inhabit. The goals of thorny conversations then shift. No longer should we aim to make someone see the light. Instead, we should seek to plant seeds and cultivate the garden, expand the discursive terrain and share in introspection and metacognition. Like geological changes of the Earth, transforming the terrain of inequality is often gradual and imperceptible.

Although I eschew the cruel optimism that conversation will lead seamlessly to social transformation—a singular dialogue about police brutality or rape culture cannot eradicate the effects of hundreds or thousands of years of inequality and injustice—I remain committed to participating in these conversations, whether between loved ones or strangers, over dinner or in news media. Sometimes it feels hopeless. Often it feels hopeless. Like Sisyphus, we continue to push the boulder up the hill only for it to roll down the other side. The error would be for us to be surprised when the boulder rolls down, shocked that there was no progress and we must start over again. While this Sisyphean task requires that we push the boulder day in and day out, we should also recognize that as we push, the weight of the boulder moved by our collective efforts gradually and imperceptibly alters the terrain. Moreover, like Albert Camus, we "must imagine Sisyphus happy" and seize what joy we can as we continue the task at hand, putting our "queer shoulder to the wheel."[27] In truth, we participate in these conversations as one form of struggle, and we struggle for a more just world because the other alternatives are simply not acceptable.

CODA

A Partial List of Additional Rules for Reactionaries

1. **Call for patience**—When people demand change, remind them that change takes time. Calls for patience can double as calls for passivity. As Martin Luther King Jr. noted, "'Wait' almost always [means . . .] 'Never.'"
2. **Highlight progress to obscure existing challenges**—Shifting the conversation to "how far we've come" undermines the urgency of calls for justice today. When someone laments the pervasive nature of sexism or the impending environmental collapse, you can point out that we now have a greater number of women in college and the workforce or that the Environmental Protection Agency regulates greenhouse gas emissions.
3. **Use one form of inequality to deny another**—Because society privileges single-axis frameworks for exploring inequality and injustice, you merely need to highlight another potential inequality to misdirect the conversation. For example, when discussing racism and unequal educational opportunities, you can bring up class.
4. **Misdirect through whataboutism**—When an issue of injustice is brought up, respond by changing the stasis with a "what about" question. For example, if someone calls attention to the dangers people of color face in

encounters with law enforcement, simply respond with "What about the dangers faced *by* police officers? It's a really dangerous job, you know."

5. **Misdirect through bothsidesism**—If a claim is made against a politician, party, or stance that you identify with, you can highlight a similar yet quite different claim to misdirect and nullify the critique. For example, if someone asserts that Fox News, Newsmax, or another media outlet is skewed toward reactionism, respond with an assertion that all news media has a slant (i.e., both sides do it) and NPR, CNN, and *The New York Times* are leftist outlets.

6. **Call for civility**—Sometimes calls for justice can become unruly or engage in practices that are disruptive or impolite. Focusing attention on the affect and tenor of protest distracts from the actual concerns and demands being brought to the fore.

7. **Call for free speech, the diversity of opinions, and the marketplace of ideas**—When you or others receive pushback for saying something untoward and embracing inequality, relying on liberal values of free speech, tolerance, and the marketplace of ideas allows you to invert the dynamic so that those calling for justice are put on their heels and made to defend their intolerance.

8. **Accept calls for justice and then delay action through emphasis on process**—If those calling for change have built enough popular support that they can no longer just be ignored or brushed aside, give them what they want but not how they want it. You can agree to (some of) their demands but require that they follow a specific process. Then you can draw more stakeholders into the conversation and pit them against each other. You can put them on committees and have endless meetings.

9. **Nullification by generalization or calls for nuance**—This strategy exists as two sides of the same coin. When

proponents of social justice call for change through highlighting the impact on one community, respond with a generalization (e.g., "Black Lives Matter" becomes nullified by "All Lives Matter"). Conversely when proponents of social change note the pervasiveness of a problem, respond with calls for nuance and specificity (e.g., "#NotAllMen" functions as a response to "MeToo").

10. **Inoculate by adopting and diffusing reactionary identities**—If someone calls you racist, sexist, or some other deplorable term, adopt it as a symbol of pride. You may do this proactively by saying "some might call me racist, but . . ." or you might don a shirt emblazoned with "Deplorables 2016." Either way, adopting this term limits the ability of others to effectively wield this term against you.

11. **Declare overcorrection**—Echoing the logic of building reactionary utopias, you can acknowledge injustice in the past but then claim that the justice struggles have gone too far. There has been an overcorrection and thus we must return to an earlier era. This is a key rhetorical strategy for the logic of backlash.

12. **Deploy a logic of possession**—If someone calls for changes in society that will impact you, argue that these changes will disadvantage you by taking away what is yours, as if it was earned through a meritocracy. For example, if the government promotes the use of energy efficient lightbulbs, decry that the government is coming for your incandescent bulbs, your right to choice, your freedom. When someone promotes diversity, equity, and inclusion initiatives in a company, you just need to claim that these efforts are aimed at taking away the opportunities and jobs of white people and men.

13. **Claim to be looking out for the aggrieved community**—When calls to address injustice impacting a community

are made, claim that you care about the community and focus the conversation on an element that pathologizes that community or maintains the status quo. For example, instead of simply decrying the influx of migrants at the US–Mexico border and how it is changing the cultural makeup of the United States, you may focus attention on the dangers faced by migrants. This is a concern shared by liberals, leftists, and migrants themselves, but you can deploy this concern as a reason to halt all undocumented migration as a means of removing migrants from danger.

14. **Label your opponents as irrational**—When you respond to calls for social transformation by declaring others irrational, you not only delegitimize their concerns, you also provide a reason to not bother understanding their concerns. If someone calls for the defunding of police departments, calling them irrational means that you never have to understand why they are making those demands and that you never have to find common ground to solve the issue at hand.

15. **Normalize inequality**—Inequality and other sociopolitical challenges have existed for a long time. A viable response to calls for change is to point out the long history of these issues and treat them as part of the human condition. For example, you can say something akin to "sure racial inequality exists today, but there has always been racism."

ACKNOWLEDGMENTS

This book emerges from a life of conversations with friends, family, students, and strangers, and I am indebted to many more than I can name here. Anthony Nadler and A. J. Bauer provided the initial opportunity to explore this project when they invited me to submit an early version of chapter 2 for their *News on the Right*. Their suggestions and editorial support helped me see the project as part of a larger genealogy. After that chapter was published, Meghan Conroy and Lauren Lassabe Shepherd reached out with enthusiastic support, helping me believe in this project as it began to grow unwieldy. Three anonymous reviewers for NYU Press provided detailed and substantive feedback that allowed me to clarify my analysis, elevate aspects of my argument, and hone the vision for the book. *Rules for Reactionaries* is much improved through their time and effort. Eric Zinner and Furqan Sayeed at NYU Press have been an amazing team to work with. Eric saw the potential in this project early on and often asked questions I had not considered. Eric and Furqan's feedback pushed me to be a stronger writer, and I am in their debt. Valerie Zaborski was tremendous heading up the production effort, and Ann Boisvert was the best copy editor that

I have ever worked with. And of course, any shortcomings in the book are mine alone.

I benefitted from presenting early portions of this book at various talks. At Purdue University, Susan Curtis, Chuck Cutter, Shannon McMullen, Nancy Peterson, and the folks in American studies were rich sounding boards for ideas in their early stages. At Jacksonville State University, Wes Bishop, Allegra Smith, and others welcomed me and provided for a robust and engaging exchange of ideas. Jennifer Ho, John-Michael Rivera, and Kirk Ambrose invited me to participate in University of Colorado Boulder's Racial Literacies group wherein we discussed a draft of chapter 1 and the need to foster racial literacies if we are to achieve the social transformation necessary for a just world. David Roediger, Kurt Braddock, Hannah Noel, Patricia Ventura, Jennifer Sdunzik, Wes Bishop, and others have offered support and shared insight at various conferences and in informal conversations. Arizona State University's Humanities Institute under the directorship of Ron Broglio provided funding to support the publication of this book.

I have also been blessed with great friends who helped me see this project completion. Conversations with Travis Franks, Alex Young, Drew Lopenzina, Jeff Crane, and Scott Kaukonen have often been a respite from a world on fire. My friends in Latina/o/x studies have been a source of strength for this book even as it has taken me on a detour away from the field I call home. Ylce Irizarry, David Vázquez, Anita Huizar-Hernández, Carmen Lamas, Rafael Pérez-Torres, Mike Innis-Jiménez, Ana Patricia Rodríguez, Frances Aparicio, Josie Saldaña, Julie Minich, Adriana Estill, Ben Chappell, Gilberto Rosas, and many I am failing to mention, our friendships and the work we have engaged in has been life sustaining. At ASU, Jeffrey Cohen, Krista Ratcliffe, Brad Ryner, Heather Maring, Jessica Early, Christina Saidy, Mark Hannah, Matt Bell, Tara Ison, Sally Ball, Jim Blasingame,

Matt Prior, Christian Ravela, Melissa Free, Brian Goodman, Mary Beth Rhydd, and others supported me in this endeavor and also helped me find purpose in directing ASU's literature program. My experience in academia has affirmed my understanding that many of the rhetorical strategies explored in this book are not isolated to some external world of politics but can be deployed within academia to forestall change as well.

I cannot express enough gratitude to my students, the students, our students. The reason why we do what we do.

My fascination with political culture and the need for meaningful dialogue has been forged through years of sometimes successful and sometimes counterproductive conversations with those closest to me. When I drafted the conclusion where I explore the need to keep talking and, more importantly, continue listening, I kept ruminating on my conversations with Mike Tucker, Tony Stampfl, William J. Link, Dave Dutton, and Kristine Frances Dutton.

My life and intellectual partner Sujey Vega is a model of how one can engage those she disagrees with. I wish I had her patience and appearance of tranquility. She has also been a consistent sounding board for the earliest thoughts that emerged into this book. For years, while spending hours in the car driving to various activities, our son Jayden Michael Bebout-Vega has helped me rediscover the need to have deep, meaningful, and messy conversations with those we love.

This book may not provide easy answers to forging a just and equitable world, but at its heart is the belief that language is commitment. Through language we commit to our values and through language we commit to those we love.

NOTES

Preface
1 Personal correspondence, May 7, 2024.

Introduction
1 Berlant, *Cruel Optimism*; Hughes, "Dream Deferred."
2 Bolick, "Clinton's Quota Queens."
3 Will, "Sympathy for Guinier."
4 Shepard, "Guinier Confronts Race Issue at Convention."
5 Brozan, "Chronicle"; Funderburg, "'Commonplace' Conversation with Lani Guinier." With the use of "tension" and "flashpoint," I am drawing on my work with collaborators Philathia Bolton and Cassander Smith. In *Teaching with Tension*, we explored how social, cultural, and political flashpoints in history caused or made visible preexisting tensions in the classroom. Bolton, Smith, Bebout, *Teaching with Tension*.
6 Clinton, "Executive Order 13050—President's Advisory Board on Race."
7 Lawson and Franklin, *One America in the 21st Century*, xxx.
8 Here "radical" signals the complete transformation or rebuilding of a social system. In contrast, the commission report recognized that there was a history of inequality and ongoing demographic changes and called for the country to address the situation without making fundamental changes to the United States itself.
9 Franklin, forward to *One America in the 21st Century*, xi.
10 Hartigan, *What Can You Say?*, 18.
11 Franklin, foreword to *One America in the 21st Century*, xi.

12 Ibid.
13 Clinton, *My Life*, 948.
14 Krauthammer, "Not Enough Conversation?"
15 Winant, *New Politics of Race*, xiii–xvi, 15–18.
16 Melamed, *Represent and Destroy*; Ferguson, *Reorder of Things*.
17 Ferguson, *Reorder of Things*.
18 Wise, *American Historical Explanations*, 131.
19 I use "multifocal" both to note the varied social justice struggles and to signal that these struggles often lacked an "intersectional" framework. Multifocal recognizes that the sociopolitical, discursive, and ideological terrain shifted along lines of race, gender, and sexuality, but that those changes did not align in ways that centered those at the intersections of systems of oppression.
20 Crenshaw, "Demarginalizing the Intersection of Race and Sex."
21 My conceptualization of these ideological systems converging in a terrain of inequality has been shaped by Jacques Rancière's conceptualization of the distribution of the sensible. Rancière, *Politics of Aesthetics*.
22 Jauss, *Toward an Aesthetic of Reception*. I draw on Hans Robert Jauss's concept of the "horizon of expectations" to indicate that inhabitants of the terrain of inequality will continue to discover new forms of inequality, but I am also drawn to Malcolm X's famous quotation that "racism is like a Cadillac. They bring out a new model every year." The structure of the terrain shifts over time and new forms of inequality are invented, but the inhabitants also continually make those new systems legible. Lipsitz, *The Possessive Investment in Whiteness*, 183.
23 My rejection of the fixed notions of identity echoes the work of Jasbir Puar. In *Terrorist Assemblages*, Puar critiques rigid notions of identity that she locates in intersectionality and advances the concept of assemblage where the act of being is continuously unfolding and dynamic. Drawing on Gilles Deleuze and Félix Guattari, Puar's reading of assemblage mirrors the way I imagine this terrain of inequality. According to Puar, "The assemblage, as a series of dispersed but mutually implicated and messy networks, draws together enunciation and dissolution, causality and effect, organic and nonorganic forces. . . . An assemblage is more attuned to interwoven forces that merge and dissipate time, space, and body against linearity, coherency, and permanency." Puar, *Terrorist Assemblages*, 211, 212. As a continuously unfolding as-

semblage where networks of white supremacy, heteropatriarchy, and other ideological and social systems grow and interconnect, the terrain of inequality is the social world we inhabit. As social, political beings, we do not remain still, located in fixed positions. Rather, we constantly navigate these interlocking systems, this assemblage, this unfolding terrain, as it too shifts and forms beneath us. The terrain and all those who inhabit it are not fixed into a state of being, but through an always ongoing dynamic of interaction, the terrain and its inhabitants are in a constant state of becoming. In this conceptualization of a terrain of inequality, there are no fixed locations of mainstream and extreme, and in this realm, we are constantly in flux.

24 Hirschman, *Rhetoric of Reaction*.
25 Shorten, "Reactionary Rhetoric Reconsidered," 179.
26 Ibid.
27 DuBois, *Black Reconstruction in America*; Roediger, *Wages of Whiteness*.
28 Just as DuBois's concept of wages becomes a useful metaphor for considering the dynamics of inequality, Cheryl Harris and George Lipsitz have offered the concepts of "property" and "investment," respectively. Harris, "Whiteness as Property;" Lipsitz, *Possessive Investment in Whiteness*.
29 *Rules for Reactionaries* builds on and contributes to a long and growing body of work on right-oriented political culture. Richard Hofstadter, Seymour Martin Lipset, and Daniel Bell paved critical ground in this effort during the 1950s and 1960s. More recently, Corey Robin explored the intellectual threads connecting reactionary thinkers from Edmund Burke to Donald Trump. Kathleen Belew has exposed the often-ignored rise of the white power movement. Geraldo Cadava has traced the history of Hispanic conservatism. Anthony Nadler, A. J. Bauer, Reece Peck, Khadijah Costley White, and others have examined the relationship between conservative media and populist development of right-wing politics. Lauren Lassabe Shepherd has exposed how college conservatives of the 1960s moved into and shaped higher education. I contend that we need to study the language strategies that allow for inequality to remain entrenched—these common strategies are found in the often-elided underside of our national conversation. Only by examining these discursive maneuvers can this dynamic

of entrenchment be addressed. See Hofstadter, "Pseudo-Conservative Revolt" and *Paranoid Style in American Politics*; Lipset, "Sources of the 'Radical Right'"; Bell, *New American Right*; Robin, *Reactionary Mind*; Belew, *Bring the War Home*; Cadava, *Hispanic Republican*; Nadler and Bauer, *News on the Right*; Peck, *Fox Populism*; Costley White, *Branding of Right-Wing Activism*; Lassabe Shepherd, *Resistance from the Right*.

30 Roediger, "On the Defensive."

31 Ibid.

32 Kendi, *How to Be an Antiracist*, see specifically 201–16. Notably, Kendi recognizes that white supremacy emerged from capitalism, yet unlike the more strident materialists Reed and Benn Michaels, Kendi does not treat racism as simply an identitarian concern.

33 *Harper's Magazine*, "Letter on Justice and Open Debate."

34 Ibid.

35 Ibid.

36 *The Objective*, "More Specific Letter on Justice and Open Debate"; Christopher, "More Than 150 Journalists and Academics"; Yang, "Problem with 'The Letter.'"

37 I am reminded of a student activist who, after having their demands for a multicultural student center rejected for years, was told that the university would open a center only to find themselves stuck in an endless process of administrators listening to them without taking action. She described this situation at the university as student-activists being "committeed to death."

38 King, "Letter from a Birmingham Jail."

39 Berlant, *Cruel Optimism*, 1.

40 DiAngelo, *White Fragility*; Kendi, *How to Be an Antiracist*; Oluo, *So You Want to Talk About Race*; Saad, *Me and White Supremacy*; Roberts-Miller, *Speaking of Race*.

41 One may also recognize that these works emerge after the popularization of antiracist terms and concepts on social media. Angela Nagle credits the rise of antiracism and other social justice content on Tumblr and other social media with laying the foundation for a conservative backlash on 4chan and other locations that would forge the alt-right. In some ways, these guidebooks introduce readers to the very concepts and terms in a book format that a younger, more progressive and digitally native audience was already familiar with. Nagle, *Kill All Normies*.

42 Coulter, *How to Talk to a Liberal*, 9.
43 Ibid., 9–15.
44 Roberts-Miller, *Rhetoric and Demagoguery*, 16, emphasis in original.
45 Coulter, *How to Talk to a Liberal*, 36–39, 86–94.
46 Ibid., 177.
47 Ibid., 1.
48 Shapiro, *How to Debate Leftists and Destroy Them*. For likely different reasons than Shapiro, I too believe that there is limited utility in calling someone "racist." This strategy ultimately allows for an easy countermove that I will discuss in a later chapter.
49 Roberts-Miller, *Rhetoric and Demagoguery*, 4, 16; Beltrán, *Cruelty as Citizenship*; Lipsitz, *Possessive Investment in Whiteness*, 50.
50 Hirschman, *Rhetoric of Reaction*; Roberts-Miller, *Rhetoric and Demagoguery*, 188.
51 A well-known, influential community organizer who was known for his battle against landlords, businesses, and local politicians, Saul Alinsky influenced key twentieth and twenty-first century activists and political figures of the US (center) left. In recent years, Alinsky has arisen as a boogeyman of the political right as they ascribe dirty tricks, scorched-earth politics, and class warfare to Alinsky and those of the (center) left, as if these elements of US politics were born via Alinsky and only exist in progressive and moderate circles. Alinsky's approach was morally agnostic about the means and ends of community organizing and social transformation. He recognized that strict adherence to ethical concerns can impede organizing when aggrieved communities are already at a structural disadvantage, yet he recognized that discourses of morality, ethics, and ideals can be powerful rhetorical tools. Alinsky advocated pragmatic tactics for effective mobilization. For example, "*Power is not only what you have but what the enemy thinks you have*," "*Ridicule is a man's most potent weapon*," and "*Pick the target, freeze it, personalize it, and polarize it*" (Alinsky, *Rules for Radicals*, 127, 128, 130; emphasis in original). As a guidebook, *Rules for Radicals* was not advocating completely novel ideas. Rather, Alinsky took common strategies that have been around throughout history but that he and others had shaped to the needs of community organizing, and *Rules for Radicals* articulated these concepts in a practical, digestible manner for those invested in social transformation. In his self-

published rejoinder to Alinsky, Jeff Hedgpeth both articulates a vision for Alinsky as a guru for contemporary leftist radicalism and draws on Alinsky's rules as a model for how the right must combat the left and win political power. Hedgpeth, *Rules for Radicals Defeated*.

52 A leading figure of the Chicano movement of the 1960s and 1970s, José Angel Gutiérrez founded the Raza Unida Party and advocated electoral organizing as a means for Chicanos to seize control of local systems of power. In 1974, he published *A Gringo Manual on How to Handle Mexicans*. Like Alinsky, Gutiérrez focused his attention on making the often-unrecognized tactics of power legible. From seeing "situations repeat themselves," Gutiérrez recognized that the tactics of power "are predictable." Gutiérrez, *Gringo Manual*, 73. Gutiérrez distilled and cataloged this array of situations and tactics into a list of 140 tricks used to maintain ethnoracial inequality. For example, Gutiérrez noted how diversifying law enforcement as a response to police brutality often led to a more diverse group of abusive police (Trick #8) and how when students protested educational inequality, they were threatened with not graduating (Trick #19). For Gutiérrez, recognizing these and numerous other "tricks"—or tactics—was essential to strategizing against these moves before they are made and developing countermeasures. Gutiérrez's *Gringo Manual* was revised and reprinted by Arte Público along with a second book, *A Chicano Manual on How to Handle Gringos*. Both offer a guidebook format for addressing racial injustice. Gutiérrez, *Chicano Manual*.

Rule #1

1 Gabriel, "Before Trump."
2 Ibid.
3 Beamon and Bachman, "Rep. Steve King Slams Norquist Over Attacks on Immigration."
4 Gabriel, "Before Trump."
5 Ian Haney López describes the use of race-neutral yet racially coded language as "dog whistle politics." Terms like "Western Civilization" and "American cultural values" are normed as white even as they appear to be unraced. Haney López, *Dog Whistle Politics*; Dyer, *White*; Chambers, "Unexamined."
6 Gabriel, "Before Trump."

7 Opsahl, "House Passes Resolution Rebuking Steve King."
8 Bixby and Bekiempis, "Steve King."
9 In referring to this "era," I am linking together the culture wars of the late twentieth century and its assertions of "political correctness" with the more recent culture wars and claims of a "cancel culture" run amok.
10 Dart, "Paula Deen Let Go by Food Network Over Use of Racially-Charged Language."
11 Ibid. This was Deen's second apology video. The initial apology offered more opportunity for meaningful engagement with the pernicious nature of white supremacy.
12 Koblin, "After Racist Tweet, Roseanne Barr's Show Is Canceled by ABC."
13 Hauser, "Roseanne Barr's Ambien Defense Is Disputed."
14 Karni, "Tlaib Accuses Meadows of Using 'a Black Woman as a Prop.'"
15 Ibid.
16 The examples of Lynne Patton and Elijah Cummings evidence a key variation of define and disavow. Their positioning as people of color undergirds the assertion that the person that they are speaking (or in Patton's case, silently standing) in support of cannot be racist because to be racist is definitionally mutually exclusive from having people of color willing to testify to one's "goodness."
17 One may find common ground between this pattern of define and disavow and Haney López's dog whistle politics. However, there are significant differences. Haney López's dog whistles need to be at least moderately subtle or explicitly race neutral. As the examples given illustrate, define and disavow works even for overtly racist statements. Moreover, Haney López advances that these rhetors are intentionally using racial code words to divide and mobilize an electorate. Define and disavow requires no such strategizing. Define and disavow is a reactive technique so engrained in US racial culture that it allows for an easy and reliable escape from accountability. Haney López, *Dog Whistle Politics*, 129–134; Hill, *Everyday Language of White Racism*, 88–118.
18 Drobnic Holan, "In Context."
19 Hill, *Everyday Language of White Racism*, 5–9. See also Goldberg, *Racist Culture*.
20 Hill, *Everyday Language of White Racism*, 88–118.

21 Hatch, "Beyond *Apologia*."
22 Holling, Moon, and Jackson Nevis, "Racist Violations and Racializing Apologia in the Post-Racism Era."
23 Here Derrick Bell's interest convergence theory may elucidate the dynamic. It is not within most white people's interest to identify as racist, which impedes white folks from recognizing, exploring, and counteracting their own investments in white supremacy. Bell, "Brown v. Board of Education and the Interest-Convergence Dilemma."
24 Even people committed to actively combatting white supremacy may deploy the limited and limiting definition of racism bound to a fixed, conscious identity. In his memoir, Arno Michaelis details his time within the violent, white supremacist skinhead movement of the 1980s and 1990s. The book focuses on the danger of racist ideology as well as explicit violence and hatred for people of color. Michaelis recalls how his warped view hindered him from finding humanity and common ground in the people he learned to hate. However, Michaelis's laser focus on the white power movement halts his ability to recognize other forms of racism. He could eventually see the common humanity with working-class Black folk he lived next to, but he is never able to address red-lining, deindustrialization, or other policies that had negative, disparate impact on communities of color. Michaelis, *My Life After Hate*.
25 Martinot, *Machinery of Whiteness*, 108, 111, 174.
26 Sullivan, *Good White People*; Feagin, *White Racial Frame*.
27 For just two examples of how people of color can contribute to and invest in white supremacy, see Lipsitz, *Possessive Investment in Whiteness*, 140–58, and Kendi, *How to Be an Antiracist*, 143, 153.
28 Jackson, "Enthymematic Hegemony of Whiteness"; Ratcliffe, "In Search of the Unstated."
29 Opsahl, "House Passes Resolution Rebuking Steve King."
30 Anderson, *Imagined Communities*.
31 Althusser, "Ideology and Ideological State Apparatuses"; Hall, *Reaction Formations*.
32 Noel, *Deflective Whiteness*.
33 Activists and scholars have challenged the identity label "ally" and offered more adequate terms like "accomplice" and "co-conspirator" to take its place. A foundational critique, "ally" and "allyship" misname and obscure the power dynamics between

communities because allies generally have similar stakes in achieving their goals. Feminista Jones argues that white folks and people of color may both occupy the terrain of white supremacy and seek to build a new, just world, but their stakes in such a struggle are markedly different. It's reminiscent of the old saying: "Question: What is the difference between the pig and the hen when it comes to breakfast? Answer: Commitment." Allyship discourse flattens out power differentials and allows for allies who occupy positions of relative privilege to take the lead, subordinating those with whom they claim allyship and reinforcing the ally's privileged standing. Feminista Jones, quoted in Hackman, "'We Need Co-Conspirators, Not Allies'"; Carlson et al., "What's in a Name?," 2.

34 Williams, *Alchemy of Race and Rights*, 10.
35 Gordon, *Ghostly Matters*, 4.
36 Sullivan, *Good White People*.
37 Ladenburg, "Everyday White Supremacy," 24, emphasis in original; Goldberg, *Racist Culture*; Ferber, *White Man Falling*.
38 Ladenburg, "Everyday White Supremacy," 29.
39 Despite the seeming distance and difference between the good, nonracist Self and the bad, racist Other, these are interdependent and mutually constructed categories. Scholars have examined rhetorical strategies that map the interconnected nature of ideological positions across the terrain. Dog whistle politics, information laundering, and the Overton Window are just three models for thinking about how clean, stable distinctions between mainstream and extreme are elusive and illusory. These strategies illustrate the danger in rigid, categorical thinking. Haney López, *Dog Whistle Politics*; Klein, "Slipping Racism into the Mainstream;" Amis, "Alt-Right's Long March."
40 We must reconceptualize allyship not as a fixed identity but a continually evolving reflective practice and orientation. Here, the model of the asymptote is useful. In analytic geometry, asymptote describes a line that increasingly approaches a point or other line without ever reaching or intersecting with it, the distance between the two ever diminishing and yet always existing. George Yancy advocates for this model of conceptualizing antiracist (and feminist) identity as he has suggested that those bound to positions of privilege may approach but never arrive at an identity outside of racism or sexism. Central to the dynamics of define

and disavow, this model recognizes that white supremacy and other forms of systemic inequality are never altogether Other. Moreover, the asymptote model emphasizes an identity based on practices, self-reflection, and purposeful transformation—the movement of the continued approach—over a fixed, static identity that either occupies the terrain of racism or sexism or is wrapped in claims of goodness and innocence. A personal example of asymptotic thinking may be useful. I am an expert in critical race theory, I teach courses in critical whiteness studies and Chicana/o/x studies, I am a member of a multiracial family, but I am also a white guy shaped by discourses, ideologies, and experiences within society. Despite my desire for achieving a more just and liberated world, I will never completely step outside of white supremacy and heteropatriarchy. I will never establish a pure feminist, antiracist identity, yet I still strive toward feminism and antiracism. Conceptualizing identity as processual with the asymptote as a visual representation may help people come to terms with their complicity in systems of domination. Karyn McKinney and Shannon Sullivan have advocated for a new white identity: one based on antiracist action and self-love. While these are laudable goals, I contend that these new identities must always be dynamic, identities not as an essence of being but as a constant unfolding. The moment they are imagined as fixed, static points, they calcify and reinforce the notion that the problems of the world exist out there, with those extreme or even mainstream Others. If fixed and stable, a new white identity based on antiracism and self-love runs the risk of misleading its adherents to believe that the work is over and that they have won the game of whiteness. An asymptotic model recognizes that antiracism, feminism, LBGTQ liberation, and social justice are commitments more than identities, even as they are commitments from which identities may emerge. Yancy, *Backlash*, 80; McKinney, *Being White*; Sullivan, *Good White People*.

41 Horton, "Tucker Carlson Suggested Immigrants Make the U.S. 'Dirtier.'"
42 Hill, *Everyday Language of White Racism*, 88–118.
43 Hatch, "Beyond *Apologia*."
44 Hatch, "Beyond *Apologia*"; Gordon and Crenshaw, "Racial Apologies"; Holling, Moon, and Jackson Nevis, "Racist Violations and

Racializing Apologia in the Post-Racism Era"; Spencer, "*National Geograhic*'s Racial Apology."
45 Carter and Sung, "Official."
46 "Paula Deen's First Apology Video."
47 "Paula Deen."
48 Gordon, *Ghostly Matters*, 17.
49 Boorstein, "Can Atheist Sam Harris Become a Spiritual Figure?"
50 Harris, "I'm Not the Sexist Pig You're Looking For."
51 Ibid.
52 While I recognize that these systems of inequality are intersecting, I have used single-axis (e.g., racism OR sexism) examples to flesh out how define and disavow operates. This is because entrenchment relies on framing issues along individual axes and obfuscating the interconnecting "matrix of domination." This is evident in Kimberlé Crenshaw's examination of intersectionality where she exposed how companies would *disavow* racism or sexism because of the *definitions* of who could speak for or represent a group constituted by race and/or gender. In this vein, single-axis thinking becomes another manifestation of define and disavow. Hill Collins, *Black Feminist Thought*; Crenshaw, "Demarginalizing the Intersection of Race and Sex."

Rule #2
1 Buchanan, *Death of the West* and *State of Emergency*; Beirich, "Lou Dobbs Citing Extremists, Again."
2 Taylor, "Rush Limbaugh."
3 Horowitz, *Professors*; Planas, "Fox News Raises Alarm Over College Course About Race."
4 O'Reilly, "War on Christmas Won by the Good Guys, but Insurgents Remain"; Wilson, "Texas ends 'The War on Christmas.'"
5 Brimelow promoted the War on his white supremacist and nativist site VDARE. When I noted this use of victimhood in an earlier publication, James Fulford responded on the VDARE website with the assertion that the "War on Christmas" started with conservative icon William F. Buckley Jr. in a 1957 issue of *The National Review*. I have been unable to locate any writing of Buckley's that ruminates on such a war. However, a 1959 Hubert Kregelow article titled "There Goes Christmas?!" in the John Birch Society's *American Opinion* argues that Christmas will lose its meaning as the United Nations' inclusion of Communist

countries and its sponsorship of global celebrations and campaigns geared around Christmas are an attack on the Christian and American celebration of Christmas. All this to say, the anxieties about Christmas may have existed prior to Brimelow and fearmongering was rooted in anti-communism. Gibson, *War on Christmas*; Cassino, "How Fox News Created the War on Christmas"; Fulford, "Whiteness Studies Educrat Says Trump Tapped Into 'White Victimhood'"; Kregelow, "There Goes Christmas?!"

6 Whitten, "Is Starbucks Waging 'War on Christmas'?"
7 Lakoff and Johnson, *Metaphors We Live By*.
8 News Hounds, "Bill O'Reilly."
9 While Paul Elliott Johnson also locates today's reactionary grievance politics as a response to the 1960s, Corey Robin notes that other manifestations of victimhood can be connected throughout the history of conservatism back at least until Edmund Burke. Johnson, *I The People*, 7; Robin, *Reactionary Mind*, 55.
10 Hannah Noel describes this adoption and adaptation of the rhetorical strategies of communities of color as a dynamic of "deflective whiteness." Noel, *Deflective Whiteness*.
11 I use the terms "relative power" and "relative privilege" to mark the ways in which the sociopolitical relationship to marginalization is always relational. As is often deployed as another strategy of entrenchment, bearing privilege does not mean that one will not struggle in life nor does it mean that one is exempt from forms of oppression. Rather, because all humans bear numerous social identities, they may also experience privilege and oppression across several axes of power.
12 Arizona's 2010 H.B. 2281 sought to ban ethnic studies curriculum under this logic.
13 Minnesota's *Booth v. Hvass* epitomizes this dynamic. *Booth v. Hvass*, 302 F.3d 849 (8th Cir. 2002).
14 Faludi, *Backlash*; Edsall, *Chain Reaction*; Nagle, *Kill All Normies*.
15 Lowndes, *From the New Deal to the New*; Zelizer, "Reflections."
16 Hofstadter, *Paranoid Style in American Politics*, 4.
17 Rogin, *Ronald Reagan, the Movie*, xiii, xiv.
18 Kimmel, *Angry White Men*, 24.
19 Echoing Cheryl Harris's formulation, in these moments, whiteness, masculinity, Christian identity, and other dominant social statuses function as a form of property that must be defended. Harris, "Whiteness as Property."

20 Roberts-Miller, *Fanatical Schemes*, 37, 39.
21 Hofstadter, "Pseudo-Conservative Revolt"; Lipset, "Sources of the 'Radical Right.'"
22 DuBois, *Black Reconstruction in America*.
23 Ibid., 21, 51–54.
24 While they do not require alignment, white supremacy and antifeminism may reinforce one another, as explored in Patricia Ventura and Edward Chan's *American Neoliberal Culture and White Power*.
25 Wiedeman, "Duke Lacrosse Scandal and the Birth of the Alt-Right."
26 Ibid.
27 Landsbaum, "Men's Rights Activists are Finding a New Home with the Alt-Right."
28 In contrast to men's rights, the men's liberation movement of the 1970s did argue that men were trapped by limited, hegemonic notions of masculinity. Interestingly, Warren Farrell was involved in men's liberation before becoming a leading men's rights activist. Kimmel, *Angry White Men*, 103–4.
29 Doyle, *Rape of the Male*.
30 Ibid., 1.
31 Ibid., 2.
32 Ibid., 8.
33 Ibid.
34 Ibid., 14.
35 Rendering oneself as an innocent victim is related to the logic of the "good white" or "good man" that underwrites the strategy of define and disavow discussed in the previous chapter.
36 Doyle, *Rape of the Male*, 15.
37 Ibid., 27, emphasis mine.
38 Ibid., 64, 69.
39 Ibid., 65.
40 Ibid., 71–72.
41 Ibid., 82.
42 Ibid., 91.
43 Ibid., 204.
44 Ibid., 235.
45 Ibid., 151, 224.
46 Ibid., 175.
47 Ibid., 178–180.
48 Ibid., 122, 176.

49 Ibid., 254–255.
50 Farrell, *Myth of Male Power*, 10.
51 Ironically, the images chosen for the bulletin board appear to be memes taken from online sites satirizing the concept of privilege.
52 Schallhorn, "App State Dorm Bulletin Board Shames 'Privileged' Students."
53 Fox News, "College Dorm's Bulletin Board Shames Christian, White 'Privileged' Students."
54 Ibid. Notably, when asked about the type of cyberbullying, Littler only states that she was told that because she was white and had not experienced oppression, she deserved the bullying.
55 Rukstuhl, "White Nationalist Group 'Defends' White Privilege."
56 Ibid.
57 Hutchison, "'Privilege Board' Gets Prominent Placement at App State."
58 Lott, "Boston University Prof Flunks 'White Masculinity' in Controversial Tweets."
59 Hoft, "Colorado Professor"; Jaschik, "Against Bullying"; Flaherty, "Furor Over Philosopher's Comments on Violence Against White People."
60 Schallhorn, "App State Dorm Bulletin Board Shames 'Privileged' Students."
61 Ibid.
62 Ibid.
63 Leonardo and Porter, "Pedagogy of Fear."
64 This framing of the privilege awareness campaign draws on not only the script of liberal elite college professors but also the extreme liberalism of San Francisco in the US conservative political imagination. Fox News, "College Dorm's Bulletin Board Shames Christian, White 'Privileged' Students"; Lit, "University Professors Attack White, Heterosexual, Christian Males for Being 'Privileged.'"
65 Beard, "Kaitlyn Schallhorn Joins TheBlaze's Dana Loesch to Discuss 'Christian Privilege' Bulletin Boards."
66 Thompson, "How the Great White Freakout Just Got Unleashed at Another University"; Oakes, "White Nationalists Target ASU."
67 Jacobson, *New Nativism*, 19, 40. Robin Dale Jacobson describes this maneuver as a "defensive bridge" that connects colorblind and race-realist discourses and ideologies.

68 Since the harassment campaigns of 2015, the NYF underwent a set of name changes and rebranding, becoming Identity Evropa in 2016 and American Identity Movement in 2019. In 2017, Identity Evropa joined with other white supremacist organizations for the "Unite the Right" rally in Charlottesville, Virginia, where they stoked fears of victimhood and expressed resistance by chanting "Jews will not replace us!"

69 Adam Klein demonstrates that white supremacist activists moderate their messages in order to make racism acceptable to mainstream media. Here, an inversion is also at play where mainstream rhetors give cover to white supremacy (and anti-feminism). Klein, "Slipping Racism into the Mainstream."

70 Smith, "Heteropatriarchy and the Three Pillars of White Supremacy."

71 Mills, *Racial Contract*, 18.

72 Kimmel, *Angry White Men*, 103–4.

73 Ibid., xiv, 24.

74 Ibid., xii–xiv.

75 DuBois, *Black Reconstruction in America*, 700; Roediger, *Wages of Whiteness*.

76 Olson, *Abolition of White Democracy*, 16–17.

77 For examples of and analyses of these racial scripts, see Bonilla-Silva's *Racism Without Racists*, 75–102.

78 Polletta and Callahan, "Deep Stories, Nostalgia Narratives, and Fake News," 403, 402.

79 Lipsitz, *Possessive Investment in Whiteness*, 50.

80 For example, see Minnesota's *Booth v. Hvass*.

81 Dragiewicz, *Equality with a Vengeance*, 3, 28.

82 Bacon, "'Ladies' Night' Lawsuits on the Rocks?"

83 Hoft, "Colorado Professor;" Jaschik, "Against Bullying;" Flaherty, "Furor Over Philosopher's Comments on Violence Against White People."

84 Rodger, "My Twisted World," 1.

85 *SPLC*, "Dylann Roof Murdered Nine People Because of a Lie About 'Black-on-White Crime'"; Ura, "Racist Manifesto and a Shooter Terrorize Hispanics in El Paso and Beyond."

86 As Roberts-Miller notes, it is the ubiquity of demagogic rhetoric that allows violence be enacted. Roberts-Miller, *Rhetoric and Demagoguery*, 3. While Rodger, Roof, Crusius, and other supposed lone wolves may be seen as isolated actors, as Kurt

Braddock demonstrates, we should see these violent actors as radicalized through persuasion. Braddock, *Weaponized Words*.

87 When these acts of violence are solely attributed to radicalized "extremists" and not connected to their supporting communities, we fall into the folk theory trap and leave "mainstream" reactionism free to radicalize others.

88 Nadler and Taussig, "Deep Story Beneath the Big Lie."

89 Bonilla-Silva, *Racism Without Racists*; McKinney, *Being White*; Cabrera, *White Guys on Campus*; Gonyea, "Majority of White Americans."

90 Anderson, "Monkeywrenching the Misogynists in Our Movements."

Rule #3

1 Hannah-Jones, "1619 Project"; Pulitzer Center, "1619 Project Curriculum." Two years after the initial publication, the project was expanded and published as a book: *The 1619 Project: A New Origin*. Hannah-Jones, *1619 Project*.

2 Washington, "Disturbing the Peace."

3 Bynum et al., "Re: The 1619 Project." "The 1619 Project" was far from unique in its argument of the centrality of slavery to the formation of the United States. As William Hogeland notes, scholars who approach the nation's founding and the field from a "bottom-up" perspective have long put pressure on the notion that apparent sociopolitical contradictions would be ameliorated by the nation's elite. Hogeland, "Historians Are Fighting." Indeed, political theorist Joel Olson contended that the enslavement of Black people was constitutive of American (white) citizenship. Olson, *Abolition of White Democracy*.

4 The entrenchment expressed by Bynum et al. (in "Re: The 1619 Project") is also worthy of exploration. One may examine specific scholarly fields, their methods, and their presuppositions to see how they engage in an entrenchment when facing new forms of knowledge.

5 Wise, "Trump Announces 'Patriotic Education' Commission."

6 The President's Advisory 1776 Commission, "1776 Report"; Crowley and Schuessler, "Trump's 1776 Commission Critiques Liberalism in Report Derided by Historians"; Brockell, "'A Hack Job,' 'Outright Lies'"; Nguyen, "Big Chunk of Trump's 1776 Report Ap-

pears Lifted from an Author's Prior Work"; *American Historical Association*, "AHA Condemns Report of Advisory 1776 Commission"; Association of University Presses, "AUPresses Responds to the 1776 Report."

7   Taviss Thompson, *Culture Wars and Enduring American Dilemmas*. Many would locate the culture wars as emerging in the 1980s and 1990s. However, Lauren Lassabe Shepherd offers a convincing case for dating the origins within the campus wars of the 1960s and 1970s. Lassabe Shepherd, *Resistance from the Right*.

8   Here "America" refers not simply to the United States but to the broader narratives and ideologies that forge meaning and are the site of contestation.

9   Machan, "Leo Strauss."

10 "The 1776 Report" contends that the nation was founded on a specific creed or set of beliefs. This distinguishes the report from other reactionary works that deploy "nation" as a stand-in for culture or ethnoracial identity. The President's Advisory 1776 Commission, "1776 Report," 1–4.

11 Ibid., 4.

12 Ibid.

13 Ibid., 11.

14 Jefferson, *Notes on the State of Virginia*.

15 This emphasis on individual rights versus group rights can be traced back to the logic found in F. A. Hayek's *Road to Serfdom*.

16 The President's Advisory 1776 Commission, "1776 Report," 12.

17 Ibid., 12–14.

18 Ibid., 16.

19 Ibid., 14.

20 Ibid., 20.

21 Bly, *Iron John*, 2, 35.

22 Johnston, "Why Iron John Is No Gift to Women."

23 Warren Farrell, mainstreamer of men's rights antifeminism, has noted the influence of Bly on his work. Farrell, *Myth of Male Power*, 360.

24 Bly, *Iron John*, ix.

25 Ibid., 2–3.

26 Ibid., 146–79.

27 Ibid., x, 19.

28 Ibid., 14–16.

29 Ibid., 179

30 Featured writers include Patrick J. Buchanan, Ann Coulter, Michelle Malkin, Jared Taylor, and Tom Tancredo, among numerous others.

31 Brimelow, *Alien Nation*, 49. The creation of a mythic white national origin story was replicated in the naming of Brimelow's VDARE site, which he considers an extension of his cultural and political work in *Alien Nation*. VDARE derives its name from Virginia Dare, "the first English child to be born in the New World. . . . And it is in the name of Virginia Dare herself that we defend the traditional American community and give it voice." Notably, VDARE's naming is rooted in white feminine childhood that serves as a locus of and analogy for white victimhood in the present. VDARE.com, "About".

32 Brimelow, *Alien Nation*, 49, 216.

33 Ibid., 46, 61, 75, 98, 219. Brimelow's racial nativism seeking to recuperate a lost past is not new. A similar logic underwrote the 1911 Dillingham Commission report that articulated the decline of US immigrant quality as the numbers of Southern and Eastern European immigrants rose. That report paved the way for racial immigration restrictions in 1917 and 1924.

34 Ibid., 28, emphasis mine.

35 For example, Brimelow contends that people of color in the United States are fostering a polarized and balkanized nation. Brimelow, *Alien Nation*, 28.

36 Ibid., 258–75.

37 These rhetorical and political renderings of time are not unique to Brimelow, for these dynamics can be found in the writings of Pat Buchanan, Samuel Huntington, Ben Shapiro, and numerous others. See Buchanan, *Death of the West* and *State of Emergency*; Huntington, *Clash of Civilizations and the Remaking of the World Order*; Shapiro, *True Allegiance*.

38 Khan, "Misandry Bubble." I first came across "The Misandry Bubble" on a seemingly now defunct site called TheManosphere.com.

39 Ibid.

40 Ibid.

41 In 2017, Donovan distanced himself from the alt-right. Lyons, *Insurgent Supremacists*, 172.

42 Ibid., 173.

43 Donovan, *Way of Men*, 60–64, 75, 104–5, 149.
44 Ibid., 5–16.
45 Ibid., 19–22.
46 Cernovich, *Danger & Play*, 21; Donovan, *Way of Men*, 1, 61, 109–28.
47 Donovan, *Way of Men*, 1.
48 When Donovan says globalism, he refers to the embrace free market global capitalism, the erasure of ethnic, racial, or national differences, so that all humans are interchangeable worker cogs in the machine. In some ways, "globalism" is a strategy for naming neoliberals, but it is difficult to ignore the way "globalism" as a nemesis works as a stand-in and dog whistle for "Jews." Donovan, *Way of Men*.
49 Ibid., 162, see also 153–66.
50 Ibid., 157. While each of these authors identify a crisis in the present and many view the threat of a civilizational collapse as imminent, Donovan seems to embrace this collapse as part of an accelerationist bent within white supremacy.
51 Donovan, *Becoming a Barbarian*.
52 Hayden White, Michel-Rolph Trouillot, and others explore how history (and the present and the future) is shaped by narrative conventions and rhetorical uses. White, *Metahistory*; Trouillot, *Silencing the Past*.
53 I capitalize More's Utopia as a specific fictionalized place and use lower case for general manifestations of utopia. More, *Utopia*.
54 Bloch, *Utopian Function of Art and Literature*, 3.
55 Utopian dreaming is in no way limited to reactionary politics. Rather, the collective imaginings of aggrieved communities working toward social transformation have long evidenced a future-oriented utopias. See Kelley, *Freedom Dreams*, 137; Burwell, *Notes on Nowhere*, 15; Chan, *Racial Horizon of Utopia*, 85–116; Bryant, *Kin of Ata Are Waiting for You*; Piercy, *Woman on the Edge of Time*; and Delany, *Triton*. Moreover, utopia's temporal dimension is not limited to the future. For examples of how aggrieved communities may imagine utopian pasts, see Moses, *Afrotopia*; "El Plan Espiritual de Aztlán"; Anaya, "Aztlán"; Muñoz, *Cruising Utopia*.
56 Bebout, *Whiteness on the Border*, 73–106.
57 Charles, "New York Times 1619 Project is Reshaping the Conversation on Slavery."
58 Chan, *Racial Horizon of Utopia*, 194.

59 Pierce, *Turner Diaries*; Arendt, *Reclaiming Aztlan*; Shapiro, *True Allegiance*.
60 Robin argues that a reactionary utopia is not one located in a feudal past but one where "power is demonstrated and privilege is earned." Robin, *Reactionary Mind*, 34. While I agree about reactionary views of power and privilege, my formulation of reactionary utopia highlights the use of the past to critique the present and imagine that reactionary future into being.
61 Bloch, Adorno, Krüger, "Something's Missing," 7.
62 I am drawing on and departing from Tom Moylan's concept of the "critical utopia." For Moylan, critical utopias are literary works that dream of a different world, focus on the conflict between the "zero world" and the utopia to expose how social change needs to take place, and emphasize the differences and imperfections in utopian society so as to make it realistic. Moylan's critical utopia is limited because it focuses on literary (i.e., narrativized) utopias and does not fully account for the often more gestural, political, and rhetorical utopias. Moylan, *Demand the Impossible*, 10–11.
63 Bloch, Adorno, Krüger, "Something's Missing," 12.
64 Ibid., 16.
65 Portolano, "Rhetorical Function of Utopia," 114. Like Karl Mannheim and Ernst Bloch, Portolano contends that utopia is an imaginative tool and strategy that can materially change the world (125). Critically, however, as a rhetorical force of social transformation, the rhetorical function of utopia does not rely on an objective goodness or improvement of society. Rather, it presumes and positions itself with an "ethical intention" but may actually work to produce and reinforce inequalities (116). Through this framework, the rhetor draws on an idealized notion of how the audience sees the world and themselves within it, forging a common ground between rhetor and audience, a collective identity, and a site of interpellation.
66 Portolano, "Rhetorical Function of Utopia," 114.
67 The culture/history wars may be seen as expressions of what Antonio Gramsci would call the war of position, the intellectual and cultural struggle that is foundational to establishing hegemony. Gramsci, *Prison Notebooks*, 3:109, 3:168–69.
68 Macintyre and Clark, *History Wars*.
69 For a critique of positivist conceptualizations of history that treat history as the study of fact divorced and isolated from sociopo-

litical contexts and meaning-making in the present, see Trouillot, *Silencing the Past*; Susman, "History and the American Intellectual"; Novick, *That Noble Dream*.

70 Regardless of grounding in historical research, both documents forge and advance narratives that are constitutive of sociopolitical communities. These narratives are forged in the process of remembering and forgetting (inclusion and exclusion) that are inherently limiting.

71 Padilla, *My History, Not Yours*, 16.

72 Mannheim, *Ideology and Utopia*, 55–108, 192–263.

73 In 1929, when *Ideology and Utopia* was initially published, Mannheim did not account for the wide range of freedom dreams that existed the world over to render a liberated world along the axes of race, gender, sexuality, and colonial status. However, after the global realignment of white supremacy, patriarchy, and heterosexism of the mid-twentieth century spurred by decolonial, civil rights, feminist, and queer struggles, the world is irreducible to Mannheim's framework of four Eurocentric utopian mentalities. Moreover, while it would be foolish to suggest that the world, or any country within it, has thrown off these systems of inequality, on this side of the global realignment, reactionary ideologies often position their adherents as social and political victims. This is a critical juncture where Mannheim's framework breaks down. While white supremacy and heteropatriarchy are still clearly in existence, the limited changes ushered in through what I earlier described as a multifocal break and realignment foment a sense of aggrieved entitlement. Imagineers of reactionary utopias do not align with the conservativism of Mannheim's model, for that form of conservatism sees utopia in the present and reactionaries see the present as nearly dystopian. Mannheim, *Ideology and Utopia*, 230.

74 Ibid., 203.

75 Portolano, "Rhetorical Function of Utopia," 114.

76 Althusser, "Ideology and Ideological State Apparatuses."

77 Ibid., 114; "The 1776 Report," 16.

78 This ethical intention forges what Benedict Anderson would call an imagined community. This is not just a dialogic connection between rhetor and audience but a connection between different members of the audience separated by space and time. More-

over, this ethical intention is rooted in a type of shared goodness, discussed in chapter 1. Anderson, *Imagined Communities*.
79 The President's Advisory 1776 Commission, "1776 Report," 18.
80 Ibid., 20.
81 Bly, *Iron John*, 179.
82 Baker, *Blues, Ideology, and Afro-American Literature*, 110.
83 As explored earlier, aggrieved communities have also looked to ancient pasts to contest oppression in the present and imagine a future of belonging. See note 55 of this chapter.
84 For example, see Muñoz, *Cruising Utopia*.
85 Kimmel, *Angry White Men*, 106. As noted earlier, Warren Farrell acknowledged Bly's influence on his own work. See note 23 of this chapter.
86 Benjamin, *Illuminations*, 265. Benedict Anderson deploys Walter Benjamin's concept of "homogenous empty time" in order to facilitate his understanding of "imagined communities." Anderson, *Imagined Communities*, 24.

Rule #4

1 Limbaugh, *Way Things Ought to Be*, 185–203.
2 For examples of this framing, see Rufo, "Cult Programming in Seattle," "'White Fragility' Comes to Washington," "Against Wokeness," and "Defending American Values, and History."
3 CS/CS/HB 1557, Parental Rights in Education, www.flsenate.gov/Session/Bill/2022/1557.
4 Rufo, "Disney is Interested in Your Kids," "Disney's Child Predator Problem."
5 Wallace-Wells, "How a Conservative Activist Invented the Conflict Over Critical Race Theory."
6 Notably, after the October 7, 2023, Hamas attack in Israel, Rufo offered a similar strategy, tweeting, "Conservatives need to create a strong association between Hamas, BLM, DSA, and academic 'decolonization' in the public mind. Connect the dots, then attack, delegitimize, and discredit. Make the center-left disavow them. Make them political untouchables." Christopher F. Rufo (@realchrisrufo), X, October 13, 2023, 5:10 p.m., https://x.com/realchrisrufo/status/1712938775834185891?lang=en. Quoted in Meckler and Dawset, "Republicans, Spurred by an Unlikely Figure."
7 Nericcio, *Tex[t]-Mex*, 16; Denis, *We Are Not You*, 178.
8 Rufo, "Cult Programming in Seattle."

9. Rufo, "Separate but Equal."
10. Wallace-Wells, "How a Conservative Activist Invented the Conflict Over Critical Race Theory."
11. Goldberg, "Meet Christopher Rufo."
12. Meckler and Dawset, "Republicans, Spurred by an Unlikely Figure."
13. Christopher F. Rufo (@realchrisrufo), "The Left will expect that, after passing so-called 'CRT bans' last year, we will overplay our hand [. . .]," X, January 7, 2022, 11:13 a.m., https://x.com/realchrisrufo/status/1479516522896781312?lang=ar.
14. Joyce, "Guy Who Brought Us CRT Panic Offers a New Far-Right Agenda."
15. Ibid.
16. Kafka, "'Sokal Squared.'"
17. Pluckrose and Lindsay, *Cynical Theories*.
18. Lindsay, *Race Marxism*, 5, 12.
19. Ibid., 146.
20. Ibid., 7, 19.
21. Ibid., 17.
22. Ibid., 161–66.
23. Ibid., 166, 165.
24. Kant is known for his critique of reason, and Plato and Aristotle for the dialectic.
25. Kuhn, *Structure of Scientific Revolutions*.
26. Lindsay, *Race Marxism*, 20, 42, 68–71, 139.
27. Ibid., 48–51.
28. Ibid., 2, 34, 60, 67, 72, 75, 95, 98, 100, 167, 169, 177, 179, 199.
29. Ibid., 169.
30. Ibid., 7, 19, 33, 34, 53, 57, 66, 117, 207, 233.
31. Ibid., 2.
32. Ibid., 5.
33. Ibid., 34.
34. Ibid., 15. Lindsay appears to be drawing on an interview of Horkheimer that has been published on YouTube. See "Max Horkheimer on Critical Theory."
35. Hill, *Everyday Language of White Racism*, 5–9.
36. Lindsay, *Race Marxism*, 7, 33.
37. Ibid., 68.
38. Ibid., 34.
39. Burden-Stelly, "Constructing Deportable Subjectivity."

40 Gardner, ¡Grito!, 16.
41 Pierce, *Turner Diaries*.
42 Lindsay, *Race Marxism*, 11.
43 Ibid., 101, 101–29.
44 Ibid., 50, 59.
45 In this way, Lindsay creates a spectrum of antiwhite racism and extremism. While critical whiteness studies is definitely antiwhite, according to Lindsay, there are elements of CRT that although Lindsay finds misguided, he also sees as well-intentioned. Ibid., 76–84.
46 Ibid., 214.
47 Ibid., 9.
48 Ibid., 238, emphasis mine.
49 Dyer, *White*; Chambers, "Unexamined."
50 Lindsay, *Race Marxism*, 254.
51 Ibid., 260.
52 Here, it must be noted that Lindsay fundamentally misunderstands Crenshaw's project in "Mapping the Margins." First, her vision of intersectionality is epistemological. It does not describe unchanging attributes of identity. Second, Crenshaw gestures toward a coalitional politics that can emerge if people are attuned to and focus their energies on combatting intersecting systems of oppression. When Lindsay is arguing that intersectionality hinders people from coming together around their shared humanity, he is offering a power-blind vision for identity, one that cannot account for systems of inequality and allows these systems to maintain the status quo (ante). Crenshaw, "Mapping the Margins"; Lindsay, *Race Marxism*.
53 Lindsay, *Race Marxism*, 279.
54 Ibid., 286.
55 Lindsay's use of "Americanism" tied to his vociferous rejection of the specters of Marxism and communism he imagines within social justice efforts echoes how traditionalist conservatives wielded "Americanism" as an identity in opposition to communism in the 1960s and 1970s. Lassabe Shepherd, *Resistance from the Right*, 139.
56 Quoted in Meckler and Dawset, "Republicans, Spurred by an Unlikely Figure."
57 There is a lovely irony in Lindsay deploying a motte and bailey rhetorical strategy when this is exactly what he accuses post-

modern and CRT thinkers of doing. While Lindsay is drawing on Shackel's polemic against postmodernists, Randy Harris's commentary on Shackel's initial paper eviscerates Shackel for not engaging in judicious research and good faith argumentation. This sourcing might suggest that Lindsay is also deploying poor research skills and bad faith arguments. Shackel, "Vacuity of Postmodernist Methodology"; Harris, "Commentary on Shackel."

58 Shackel, "Vacuity of Postmodernist Methodology."

59 Indeed, the desire to build and mobilize a reactionary coalition requires that one often not reject white supremacists. For example, Christopher Rufo and others have called for a practice that finds "no enemies on the right." Rufo, "No Enemies to the Right?"

60 Here, Lindsay seems to be invoking a horseshoe theory or model of political ideology wherein left and right politics exist along a continuum but the ends or extremes bend toward one another. This concept is attributed to Jean-Pierre Faye in his *Le Siècle des idéologies* (Century of ideologies).

61 Lindsay, *Race Marxism*, 14, 83.

62 Ibram X. Kendi typifies this antiracism-racism binary in his *How to Be an Antiracist*. In contrast, George Yancy offers a more philosophically rich take on this argument. Yancy contends that regardless of one's personal and political commitments, one's racialization in society will automatically make white people participate within and contribute to white supremacy. It is from Yancy's argument that white folk must approach without arriving at antiracism that I theorize the asymptote in chapter 1. Kendi, *How to Be an Antiracist*; Yancy, *Look, A White!, Backlash*.

63 For discussion of reactionary uses of the Overton Window, see Woods and Hahner, *Make America Meme Again*, 75, and Mercieca, *Demagogue for President*, 91.

64 Limbaugh, *Way Things Ought to Be*, 185–203.

65 Gramsci, *Prison Notebooks*, 1:173.

66 Hall and O'Shea, "Common-Sense Neoliberalism."

67 Rancière, *Politics of Aesthetics*, 7

68 Ibid., 8.

69 Moi, "'I am Not a Feminist But . . .'"; Elgin, "Feminist is What?"

Rule #5

1 "Texas Politicians Are Slow to Act on Both Guns and Mental Health"; Schreiner, "GOP Candidates Tread Cautiously on

Gun Issues in Kentucky." The italicized passages in this section are not direct quotations. Rather, they are common refrains that are regularly articulated and epitomize reactionary responses to a given issue using the rule of blaming a convenient cause.

2 Morrison, "George Zimmerman's Brother"; Schneider and Anderson, "Family of Slain Teen Goes on Defensive."

3 Hymowitz, "Why the Gender Gap Won't Go Away" and "Equal Pay Myths"; Finley, "Women's Soccer Plays a Phony Game"; Greszler, "Why the Big Pay Gap Between Women's and Men's Soccer?"

4 Brown and Fuhrman, "Commentary Cow Farts and Global Warming"; Woodward and Borenstein, "Cow Farts are Issue in Green New Deal"; Stevens, "Fear Cattle Not Wonderful Petroleum."

5 Zak, "Whataboutism."

6 Dykstra, "Rhetoric of 'Whataboutism' in American Journalism and Political Identity."

7 Zak, "Whataboutism."

8 Wemple, "Fox New Seeks Refuge in Bothsidesism."

9 Eshelman, "Danger of Fair and Balanced."

10 Roberts-Miller, *Fanatical Schemes*, 240. Originally conceptualized in antiquity by the Greek rhetoricians Hermagoras and Aristotle, stasis can be determined by asking and answering four types of questions: questions of fact and conjecture (e.g., Did something happen?), questions of definition (e.g., What is its nature?), questions of quality (e.g., How serious is it?), and questions of policy and procedure (e.g., What if any action should be taken?). Purdue Online Writing Lab, "Stasis Theory."

11 Roberts-Miller, *Fanatical Schemes*, 139.

12 Ibid., 139, 142.

13 Ladenburg, "Everyday White Supremacy," 101–41.

14 Dykstra, "Rhetoric of 'Whataboutism' in American Journalism and Political Identity."

15 Blue Lives Matter does not simply equate the dangers faced by unarmed people of color and armed police. It also constructs false equivalency between being racialized and choosing a career. This has been highlighted by those who have asserted that Blue lives do not exist as such. For example, Busch, "Blue Lives Don't Exist."

16 Boone, *Black Self-Genocide*.
17 Miller, "Gender Pay Gap Improvement Slowed During the Pandemic." When race and age are also taken into consideration, the gender pay gap increases. Ibid.
18 This narrower gap is also found when race is taken into consideration, illustrating that the causes of the gender pay gap are larger structural forces within society and not solely individual cases of purposeful discrimination. Miller, "Gender Pay Gap Improvement Slowed During the Pandemic."
19 Miller, "Gender Pay Gap Improvement Slowed During the Pandemic."; Hutt, "Do Women Work Longer Hours than Men?"
20 Hymowitz, *Manning Up*.
21 Hayek, *Road to Serfdom*.
22 Bonilla-Silva, *Racism Without Racists*, 28.
23 Hymowitz, "Why the Gender Pay Gap Won't Go Away."
24 One should note that this aspect of her logic invokes a pressure point within the reactionary coalition. While traditionalists hold fast to the heteronormative family, neoliberals (i.e., economic conservatives and libertarians) would likely emphasize the need for women to choose their futures. Because reactionary politics relies on obscuring potential tensions within the coalition, there is a rhetorical moment of opportunity here if one were to take up Hymowitz's argument and argue for women no longer bearing children.
25 Hymowitz, "Why the Gender Gap Won't Go Away."
26 Ibid.
27 Hobson, "Women's Soccer Players Sue U.S. Federation for Gender Discrimination."
28 Bonesteel, "Timeline of the U.S. Women's Soccer Team's Equal Pay Dispute with U.S. Soccer."
29 Ibid.
30 Hensley-Clancy, "In Equal-Pay Case, U.S. Women's Soccer Players Argue Judge 'Penalized' Them for Their Success."
31 Hensley-Clancy, "US Men's Soccer Team Backs Women in Equal-Pay Fight."
32 Bonesteel, "Timeline of the U.S. Women's Soccer Team's Equal Pay Dispute with U.S. Soccer."
33 Hensley-Clancy, "U.S. Soccer, Women's Team Members Settle Equal Pay Lawsuit for $24 Million."
34 Finley, "Women's Soccer Plays a Phony Game."

35 Greszler, "Why the Big Pay Gap Between Women's and Men's Soccer?"
36 Finley, "Women's Soccer Plays a Phony Game."
37 Ibid.
38 Greszler, "Why the Big Pay Gap Between Women's and Men's Soccer?"
39 Poppelwell-Scevak, "Gender Pay Gap."
40 Women's soccer in the United States is more successful and more popular than men's soccer in part because of the impact of Title IX of the 1972 education amendments, which prohibited sex discrimination in any educational setting or activity that receives federal funding. Among other things, this pushed educational institutions to fund and support women's sports. Masters, "Red Card on Wage Discrimination."
41 The convenient cause of cow farts can be tied to abstract liberal individualism when arguments are made that individuals should change their eating habits as a remedy for climate change instead of pushing for large-scale climate change.
42 Williams, *Alchemy of Race and Rights*, 10.
43 Gordon, *Ghostly Matters*, 3.

Conclusion

1 Berlant, *Cruel Optimism*, 1.
2 Proctor, "Agnotology"; Oreskes and Conway, "Challenging Knowledge."
3 Allen, *Talking to Strangers*, xix, xx, xxii.
4 Ibid., 156.
5 Ratcliffe, *Rhetorical Listening*, 1.
6 Ibid., 55, 25.
7 For other examples of scholarship that evidences a faith in deliberative democracy while also exploring propaganda and demagoguery, see Skinnell, *Faking the News*, and Mercieca, *Demagogue for President*.
8 Building on and departing from Althusser, Jonathan Hall explores how ideology and subject formation are dialogically entwined. Hall, *Reaction Formations*.
9 Warner, *Publics and Counterpublics*, 66.
10 Ibid., 114, emphasis in original.
11 Here I am troping on Berlant's concepts of infantile and dead citizenship. Berlant, *Queen of America*.

12 Sandoval, *Methodology of the Oppressed*, 58.
13 Marron, *Conversations with People Who Hate Me*, 157.
14 Smooth, "How I Learned to Stop Worrying and Love Discussing Race."
15 Yancy, *Look, A White!*, 10, emphasis in original.
16 Yancy, *Backlash*, 80.
17 Reilly, "Read Hillary Clinton's 'Basket of Deplorables' Remarks."
18 Jennings and Scott, "Full Kamala Harris-Joe Biden."
19 Bonilla-Silva, *Racism Without Racists*.
20 Schiffrin, "Fighting Disinformation in the 1930s." Notably, A. J. Bauer contends that "by using scientific language and claiming to be above the political fray," Miller and the IPA "conflated its progressive political ideals with democracy itself" and thus engaged in its own form of propaganda (1977). Bauer, "Glittering Generalities."
21 Dyer, *White*, 10; Yancy, *Look, a White!*
22 Bonilla-Silva, *Racism Without Racists*, 83.
23 Twain, *Adventures of Huckleberry Finn*, 290.
24 Lakoff, *All New Don't Think of an Elephant!*
25 Delgado and Stefancic, *Critical Race Theory*, 43, 144.
26 Lipsitz, *American Studies in a Moment of Danger*.
27 Camus, *Myth of Sisyphus*, 123; Ginsberg, "America," 34.

BIBLIOGRAPHY

Alinsky, Saul D. *Rules for Radicals: A Pragmatic Primer for Realistic Radicals*. New York: Vintage, [1971] 1989.

Allen, Danielle S. *Talking to Strangers: Anxieties of Citizenship Since Brown v. Board of Education*. Chicago: University of Chicago Press, 2004.

Althusser, Louis. "Ideology and Ideological State Apparatuses (Notes Towards an Investigation)." In *Lenin and Philosophy and Other Essays*, translated by Ben Brewster, 85–126. New York: Monthly Review Press, 1971.

American Historical Association. "AHA Condemns Report of Advisory 1776 Commission." January 20, 2021. https://www.historians.org.

Amis, Louis. "The Alt-Right's Long March: How the Overton Window Is Shifting." *New Statesman* 147 (2018): 13–14.

Anaya, Rudolfo. "Aztlán: A Homeland Without Boundaries." In *Aztlán: Essays of the Chicano Homeland*, edited by Rudolfo A. Anaya and Francisco A. Lomelí, 230–41. Albuquerque: University of New Mexico Press, 1989.

Anderson, Benedict. *Imagined Communities: Reflections on the Origins and Spread of Nationalism*. New York: Verso, 1991.

Anderson, Kiera Loki. "Monkeywrenching the Misogynists in Our Movements." *Earth First* 35, no. 4 (2015/2016): 57–61.

Arendt, Dave. *Reclaiming Aztlan*. Baltimore: Publish America, 2007.

Association of University Presses. "AUPresses Responds to the 1776 Report." January 19, 2021. https://aupresses.org.

Bacon, Brittany. "'Ladies' Night' Lawsuits on the Rocks?" *ABCNews*, July 25, 2007. http://abcnews.go.com.

Baker, Houston A. *Blues, Ideology, and Afro-American Literature: A Vernacular Theory*. Chicago: University of Chicago Press, 1987.

Bauer, A. J. "Glittering Generalities: Reconsidering the Institute for Propaganda Analysis." *International Journal of Communication* 18 (2024): 1976–94.

Beamon, Todd, and John Bachman. "Rep. Steve King Slams Norquist over Attacks on Immigration." *Newsmax*, July 18, 2013. www.newsmax.com.

Beard, Sterling. "Kaitlyn Schallhorn Joins TheBlaze's Dana Loesch to Discuss 'Christian Privilege' Bulletin Boards." *Campus Reform*, April 2, 2015. www.campusreform.org.

Bebout, Lee. *Whiteness on the Border: Mapping the US Racial Imagination in Brown and White*. New York: New York University Press, 2016.

Beirich, Heidi. "Lou Dobbs Citing Extremists, Again." *Southern Poverty Law Center*. July 31, 2008. www.splcenter.org.

Belew, Kathleen. *Bring the War Home: The White Power Movement and Paramilitary America*. Cambridge: Harvard University Press, 2018.

Bell, Daniel, ed. *The New American Right*. New York: Criterion Books, 1955.

Bell, Derrick A., Jr. "Brown v. Board of Education and the Interest-Convergence Dilemma." *Harvard Law Review* 93, no. 3 (January 1980): 518–33.

Beltrán, Cristina. *Cruelty as Citizenship: How Migrant Suffering Sustains White Democracy*. Minneapolis: University of Minnesota Press, 2020.

Benjamin, Walter. *Illuminations*. London: Fonatana, 1973.

Berlant, Lauren. *Cruel Optimism*. Durham, NC: Duke University Press, 2011.

Berlant, Lauren. *The Queen of America Goes to Washington City*. Durham, NC: Duke University Press, 1997.

Bixby, Scott, and Victoria Bekiempis. "Steve King: I'm Not a Racist & Americans Aren't Having Enough Babies." *Daily Beast*, January 26, 2019. www.thedailybeast.com.

Bloch, Ernst. *The Utopian Function of Art and Literature: Selected Essays*. Edited and translated by Jack Zipes and Frank Mecklenburg. Cambridge: MIT Press, 1988.

Bloch, Ernst, Theodor W. Adorno, and Horst Krüger. "Something's Missing: A Discussion Between Ernst Bloch and Theodor W. Adorno on the Contradictions of Utopian Longing." In *The Utopian Function of Art and Literature: Selected Essays*, by Ernst Bloch, edited and translated by Jack Zipes and Frank Mecklenburg, 1–17. Cambridge, MA: MIT Press, 1988.

Bly, Robert. *Iron John: A Book About Men*. Reading, MA: Addison-Wesley Publishing, 1990.

Bolick, Clint. "Clinton's Quota Queens." *Wall Street Journal*, April 30, 1993.

Bolton, Philiathia, Cassander Smith, Lee Bebout. *Teaching with Tension: Race, Resistance and Reality in the Classroom*. Chicago: Northwestern University Press, 2019.

Bonesteel, Matt. "A Timeline of the U.S. Women's Soccer Team's Equal Pay Dispute with U.S. Soccer." *Washington Post*, February 22, 2022. www.washingtonpost.com.

Bonilla-Silva, Eduardo. *Racism Without Racists: Colorblind-Racism and Racial Inequality in Contemporary America, Third Edition*. New York: Rowman and Littlefield, 2010.

Boone, Willington. *Black Self-Genocide: What Black Lives Matter Won't Say*. Duluth, GA: APPTE Publishing, 2016.

Boorstein, Michelle. "Can Atheist Sam Harris Become a Spiritual Figure?" *Washington Post*, September 12, 2014. www.washingtonpost.com.

Braddock, Kurt. *Weaponized Words: The Strategic Role of Persuasion in Violent Radicalization and Counter-Radicalization*. Cambridge: Cambridge University Press, 2020.

Brimelow, Peter. *Alien Nation: Common Sense About America's Immigration Disaster*. New York: Random House, 1995.

Brockell, Gillian. "'A Hack Job,' 'Outright Lies': Trump Commission's '1776 Report' Outrages Historians." *Washington Post*, January 19, 2021. www.washingtonpost.com.

Brown, Ian, and Olivia Fuhrman. "Commentary Cow Farts and Global Warming." *Salt Lake Tribune*, April 21, 2019. www.sltrib.com.

Brozan, Nadine. "Chronicle." *New York Times*, December 1, 1994.

Bryant, Dorothy. *The Kin of Ata Are Waiting for You*. New York: Random House, 1997.

Buchanan, Patrick J. *The Death of the West: How Dying Populations and Immigrant Invasions Imperil Our Country and Civilization*. New York: St. Martin's Griffin, 2002.

Buchanan, Patrick J. *State of Emergency: The Third World Invasion and Conquest of America*. New York: St. Martin's Press, 2006.

Burden-Stelly, Charisse. "Constructing Deportable Subjectivity: Antiforeignness, Antiradicalism, and Antiblackness during the McCarthyist Structure of Feeling." *Souls* 19, no. 3 (2017): 342–58.

Burwell, Jennifer. *Notes on Nowhere: Feminism, Utopian Logic, and Social Transformation*. Minneapolis: University of Minnesota Press, 1997.

Busch, Ethan. "Blue Lives Don't Exist." *Campus Times*, June 11, 2020. www.campustimes.org.

Bynum, Victoria, James M. McPherson, James Oakes, Sean Wilentz, Gordon S. Wood. "Re: The 1619 Project." *New York Times Magazine*, December 20, 2019. www.nytimes.com.

Cabrera, Nolan. *White Guys on Campus: Racism, White Immunity, and the Myth of "Post-Racial" Higher Education*. New Brunswick: Rutgers University Press, 2019.

Cadava, Geraldo. *The Hispanic Republican: The Shaping of an American Political Identity, from Nixon to Trump*. New York: Ecco, 2020.

Camus, Albert. *The Myth of Sisyphus and Other Essays*. Translated by Justin O'Brien. New York: Vintage, 1991.

Carlson, Juliana, Cliff Leek, Erin Casey, Rich Tolman, Christopher Allen. "What's in a Name? A Synthesis of 'Allyship' Elements from Academic and Activist Literature." *Journal of Family Violence* 35, no. 8 (2019): 889–98.

Carter, Chelsea J., and Carolyn Sung, "Official: Food Network Will Not Renew Paula Deen's Contract." CNN, June 23, 2013. www.cnn.com.

Cassino, Dan. "How Fox News Created the War on Christmas" *Harvard Business Review*, December 9, 2016. https://hbr.org.

Cernovich, Mike. *Danger & Play: Essays on Embracing Masculinity*. N.p.: CreateSpace Independent Publishing Platform, 2015.

Chambers, Ross. "The Unexamined." In *Whiteness: A Critical Reader*, edited by Mike Hill, 187–203. New York: New York University Press, 1997.

Chan, Edward K. *The Racial Horizon of Utopia: Unthinking the Future of Race in Late Twentieth-Century American Utopian Novels*. New York: Peter Lang, 2016.

Charles, J. Brian. "The New York Times 1619 Project Is Reshaping the Conversation on Slavery. Conservatives Hate It." *Vox*, Aug 20, 2019. www.vox.com.

Christopher, Tommy. "More Than 150 Journalists and Academics Sign Blistering Response to Harper's Cancel Culture Letter." *Mediaite*, July 10, 2020. www.mediaite.com.

Clinton, William J. "Executive Order 13050—President's Advisory Board on Race." *American Presidency Project*, June 13, 1997. www.presidency.ucsb.edu.

Clinton, William J. *My Life*. New York: Knopf, 2004.

Costley White, Khadijah. *The Branding of Right-Wing Activism: The News Media and the Tea Party*. Oxford: Oxford University Press, 2018.

Coulter, Ann. *How to Talk to a Liberal (If You Must): The World According to Ann Coulter*. New York: Crown Forum, 2004.

Crenshaw, Kimberlé. "Demarginalizing the Intersection of Race and Sex: A Black Feminist Critique of Antidiscrimination Doctrine, Feminist Theory and Antiracist Politics." *University of Chicago Legal Forum* 1, no. 8 (1989): 139–67.

Crenshaw, Kimberlé. "Mapping the Margins: Intersectionality, Identity Politics, and Violence against Women of Color." *Stanford Law Review* 43, no. 6 (1991): 1241–99.

Crowley, Michael, and Jennifer Schuessler. "Trump's 1776 Commission Critiques Liberalism in Report Derided by Historians." *New York Times*, January 19, 2021. www.nytimes.com.

Dart, Tom. "Paula Deen Let Go by Food Network Over Use of Racially-Charged Language." *The Guardian*, June 22, 2013. www.theguardian.com.

Delany, Samuel. *Triton*. New York: Bantam, 1976.

Delgado, Richard, and Jean Stefancic. *Critical Race Theory: An Introduction*. New York: New York University Press, 2001.

Denis, Claude. *We Are Not You: First Nations and Canadian Modernity*. Toronto: University of Toronto Press, 1997.

DiAngelo, Robin. *White Fragility: Why It's So Hard for White People to Talk about Racism*. Boston: Beacon Press, 2018.

Donovan, Jack. *Becoming a Barbarian*. Milwaukie, OR: Dissonant Hum, 2016.

Donovan, Jack. *The Way of Men*. Milwaukie, OR: Dissonant Hum, 2012.

Doyle, Richard F. *The Rape of the Male*. St. Paul, MN: Poor Richard's Press, 1976.

Dragiewicz, Molly. *Equality with a Vengeance: Men's Rights Groups, Battered Women, and Antifeminist Backlash*. Hanover: Northeastern University Press, 2011.

Drobnic Holan, Angie. "In Context: Donald Trump's 'Very Fine People on Both Sides' Remarks (Transcript)." *Politifact*, April 26, 2019. www.politifact.com.

DuBois, W. E. B. *Black Reconstruction in America, 1860–1880*. New York: Free Press, [1935] 1998.

Dyer, Richard. *White*. New York: Routledge, 1997.

Dykstra, Alan. "The Rhetoric of 'Whataboutism' in American Journalism and Political Identity." *Res Rhetorica* 7, no. 2 (2020): 2–16.

Edsall, Thomas B. *Chain Reaction: The Impact of Race, Rights, and Taxes on American Politics*. With Mary D. Edsall. New York: Norton, 1991.

"El Plan Espiritual de Aztlán." In *Aztlán: An Anthology of Mexican American Literature*, edited by Luis Valdez and Stan Steiner, 402–406. New York: Knopf, 1972.

Elgin, Suzette Haden. "A Feminist is What?" *Women and Language* 18, no. 2 (1995): 46.

Eshelman, Robert S. "The Danger of Fair and Balanced." *Columbia Journalism Review* 53, no. 1 (2014): 52.

Faludi, Susan. *Backlash: The Undeclared War Against American Women*. New York: Crown, 1991.

Farrell, Warren. *The Myth of Male Power: Why Men are the Disposable Sex*. New York: Simon and Schuster, 1993.

Faye, Jean-Pierre. *Le Siècle des idéologies*. Paris: Armand Colin, 2002.

Feagin, Joe R. *The White Racial Frame: Centuries of Racial Framing and Counter-Framing*. 3rd ed. New York: Routledge, 2020.

Ferber, Abby L. *White Man Falling: Race, Gender, and White Supremacy*. Lanham, MD: Rowman and Littlefield Publishers, 1998.

Ferguson, Roderick A. *The Reorder of Things: The University and Its Pedagogies of Minority Difference*. Minneapolis: University of Minnesota Press, 2011.

Finley, Allysia. "Women's Soccer Plays a Phony Game: Complaints about an Alleged Pay Gap Are a Public-Relations Ploy to Get a Sweetened Union Contract." *Wall Street Journal*, April 25, 2016. www.wsj.com.

Flaherty, Colleen. "Furor Over Philosopher's Comments on Violence Against White People." *InsideHigherEd*, May 11, 2017. www.insidehighered.com.

Fox News. "College Dorm's Bulletin Board Shames Christian, White 'Privileged' Students." April 2, 2015. http://insider.foxnews.com.

Franklin, John Hope. Forward to *One America in the 21st Century: The Report of President Bill Clinton's Initiative on Race*, edited by Steven F. Lawson and John Hope Franklin. New Haven: Yale University Press, 2008.

Fulford, James. "Whiteness Studies Educrat Says Trump Tapped Into 'White Victimhood,' Smears VDARE.com—As If Obama Didn't Do BLACK Victimhood For 8 Years." VDARE.com, January 8, 2021. https://vdare.com.

Funderburg, Lise. "A 'Commonplace' Conversation with Lani Guinier." *African American Review* 30, no. 2 (1996): 197–204.

Gabriel, Trip. "Before Trump, Steve King Set the Agenda for the Wall and Anti-Immigrant Politics." *New York Times*, January 10, 2019. www.nytimes.com.

Gardner, Richard. *¡Grito! Reies Tijerina and the New Mexico Land Grant War of 1967*. New York: Harper & Row, 1970.

Gibson, John. *The War on Christmas: How the Liberal Plot to Ban the Sacred Christian Holiday Is Worse Than You Thought*. New York: Sentinel Trade, 2005.

Ginsberg, Allen. "America." In *Howl and Other Poems*, 31–34. City Lights Books, 1959.

Goldberg, David Theo. "Meet Christopher Rufo—Leader of the Incoherent Right-Wing Attack on 'Critical Race Theory.'" *Salon*, August 1, 2021. www.salon.com.

Goldberg, David Theo. *Racist Culture: Philosophy and the Politics of Meaning*. Cambridge: Blackwell, 1993.

Gonyea, Don. "Majority of White Americans Say They Believe Whites Face Discrimination." NPR, October 24, 2017. www.npr.org.

Gordon, Avery. *Ghostly Matters: Haunting and the Sociological Imagination*. Minneapolis: University of Minnesota Press, 1997.

Gordon, Dexter B., and Carrie Crenshaw. "Racial Apologies." In *Approaches to Rhetoric*, edited by Patricia A. Sullivan and Steven R. Goldzwig, 245–66. New York: Sage Publications, 2003.

Gramsci, Antonio. *The Prison Notebooks*. Vol. 1. Edited by Joseph A. Buttigieg. New York: Columbia University Press, 2010.

Gramsci, Antonio. *The Prison Notebooks*. Vol. 3. Translated by Antonio Callari and Joseph A. Buttigieg. New York: Columbia University Press, 2011.

Greszler, Rachel. "Why the Big Pay Gap Between Women's and Men's Soccer? Another Viewpoint." *Wall Street Journal*, July 14, 2019.

Gutiérrez, José Angel. *A Chicano Manual on How to Handle Gringos*. Houston: Arte Público Press, 2003.

Gutiérrez, José Angel. *A Gringo Manual on How to Handle Mexicans*. Houston: Arte Público Press, 2001.

Hackman, Rose "'We Need Co-Conspirators, Not Allies': How White Americans Can Fight Racism." *The Guardian*, June 26, 2015. www.theguardian.com.

Hall, Jonathon. *Reaction Formations: Dialogism, Ideology, and Capitalist Culture*. Boston: Brill, 2020.

Hall, Stuart, and Alan O'Shea. "Common-Sense Neoliberalism: The Battle over Common Sense Is a Centra Part of Our Political Life." *Soundings* 55 (2013): 8–24.

Haney López, Ian. *Dog Whistle Politics: How Coded Racial Appeals Have Reinvented Racism and Wrecked the Middle Class*. Oxford: Oxford University Press, 2014.

Hannah-Jones, Nikole. *The 1619 Project: A New Origin*. New York: One World, 2021.

Hannah-Jones, Nikole, ed. "The 1619 Project." *New York Times Magazine*, August 14, 2019. www.nytimes.com.

Harper's Magazine. "A Letter on Justice and Open Debate." July 7, 2020. https://harpers.org.

Harris, Cheryl I. "Whiteness as Property." *Harvard Law Review* 106, no. 8 (1993): 1707–91.

Harris, Randy. "Commentary on Shackel." *OSSA Conference Archive*, May 17, 2003. https://scholar.uwindsor.ca.

Harris, Sam. "I'm Not the Sexist Pig You're Looking For." *SamHarris*, September 15, 2014. https://samharris.org.

Hartigan, John, Jr. *What Can You Say? America's National Conversation on Race*. Stanford: Stanford University Press, 2010.

Hatch, John B. "Beyond *Apologia*: Racial Reconciliation and Apologies for Slavery." *Western Journal of Communication* 70, no. 3 (2006): 186–211.

Hauser, Christine. "Roseanne Barr's Ambien Defense Is Disputed: 'Racism Is Not a Known Side Effect.'" *New York Times*, May 30, 2018. www.nytimes.com.

Hayek, F. A. *Road to Serfdom*. Edited by Bruce Caldwell. Chicago: University of Chicago Press, 2007.

Hedgpeth, Jeff. *Rules for Radicals Defeated*. CreateSpace Independent Publishing Platform, 2012.

Hensley-Clancy, Molly. "In Equal-Pay Case, U.S. Women's Soccer Players Argue Judge 'Penalized' Them for Their Success." *Washington Post*, July 23, 2021. www.washingtonpost.com.

Hensley-Clancy, Molly. "US Men's Soccer Team Backs Women in Equal-Pay Fight, Saying USWNT Should Have Been Paid More." *Washington Post*, July 30, 2021. www.washingtonpost.com.

Hensley-Clancy, Molly. "U.S. Soccer, Women's Team Members Settle Equal Pay Lawsuit for $24 Million." *Washington Post*, February 22, 2022. www.washingtonpost.com.

Hill Collins, Patricia. *Black Feminist Thought: Knowledge, Consciousness, and the Politics of Empowerment*. 2nd ed. New York: Routledge, 2000.

Hill, Jane. *The Everyday Language of White Racism*, West Sussex: Wiley-Blackwell, 2008.

Hirschman, Albert O. *The Rhetoric of Reaction: Perversity, Futility, Jeopardy*. Cambridge: Belknap Press, 1991.

Hobson, Will. "Women's Soccer Players Sue U.S. Federation for Gender Discrimination." *Washington Post*, March 8, 2019. www.washingtonpost.com.

Hofstadter, Richard. *The Paranoid Style in American Politics and Other Essays*. New York: Knopf, 1965.

Hofstadter, Richard. "The Pseudo-Conservative Revolt." In *The New American Right*, edited by Daniel Bell, 33–55. New York: Criterion Books, 1955.

Hoft, Jim. "Colorado Professor: 'Whiteness Is a Disease.'" *Gateway Pundit*, November 16, 2015. www.thegatewaypundit.com.

Hogeland, William. "The Historians Are Fighting." *Slate*, October 30, 2021. https://slate.com.

Holling, Michelle A., Dreama G. Moon, and Alexandra Jackson Nevis. "Racist Violations and Racializing Apologia in the Post-Racism Era." *Journal of International and Intercultural Communication* 7, no. 4 (2014): 260–86.

Horowitz, David. *The Professors: The 101 Most Dangerous Academics in America*. Washington, DC: Regenery Publishing, 2007.

Horton, Alex. "Tucker Carlson Suggested Immigrants Make the U.S. 'Dirtier'—and It Cost Fox News an Advertiser." *Washington Post*, December 15, 2018. www.washingtonpost.com.

Hughes, Langston. "Dream Deferred." In *The Collected Works of Langston Hughes*, vol. 3, *The Poems: 1951–1967*, edited by Arnold Rampersad, 145. Columbia: University of Missouri Press, 2001.

Huntington, Samuel P. *The Clash of Civilizations and the Remaking of the World Order*. New York: Simon and Schuster, 1996.

Hutchison, Sydney. "'Privilege Board' Gets Prominent Placement at App State." *Campus Reform*, August 18, 2016. www.campusreform.org.

Hutt, Rosamond. "Do Women Work Longer Hours than Men?" *World Economic Forum*, November 2, 2015.

Hymowitz, Kay S. *Manning Up: How the Rise of Women Has Turned Men into Boys*. New York: Basic Books, 2011.

Hymowitz, Kay S. "Why the Gender Gap Won't Go Away. Ever." *Wall Street Journal*, August 4, 2011. www.wsj.com.

Hymowitz, Kay S. "Equal Pay Myths." *City Journal*, April 9, 2018. www.city-journal.org.

Jackson, Matthew. "The Enthymematic Hegemony of Whiteness: The Enthymeme as Antiracist Rhetorical Strategy." *JAC: A Journal of Composition Theory* 26, no. 3–4 (2006): 601–41.

Jacobson, Robin Dale. *The New Nativism: Proposition 187 and the Debate over Immigration*. Minneapolis: University of Minnesota Press, 2008.

Jaschik, Scott. "Against Bullying." *InsideHigherEd*, February 15, 2016. www.insidehighered.com.

Jauss, Hans Robert. *Toward an Aesthetic of Reception*. Translated by Timothy Bahti. Minneapolis: University of Minnesota Press, 1982.

Jefferson, Thomas. *Notes on the State of Virginia*. New York: Penguin Books, 1999.

Jennings, Natalie, and Eugene Scott. "The Full Kamala Harris-Joe Biden Exchange Over Race and Busing, Annotated." *Washington Post*, June 27, 2019. www.washingtonpost.com.

Johnson, Paul Elliott. *I The People: The Rhetoric of Conservative Populism in the United States*. Tuscaloosa: University of Alabama Press, 2022.

Johnston, Jill. "Why Iron John Is No Gift to Women." *New York Times*, February 23, 1992. www.nytimes.com.

Joyce, Kathryn. "The Guy Who Brought Us CRT Panic Offers a New Far-Right Agenda: Destroy Public Education." *Salon*, April 8, 2022. www.salon.com.

Kafka, Alexander C. "'Sokal Squared': Is Huge Publishing Hoax 'Hilarious and Delightful' or an Ugly Example of Dishonesty and Bad Faith?" *Chronicle of Higher Education*, October 3, 2018. www-chronicle-com.

Karni, Annie. "Tlaib Accuses Meadows of Using 'a Black Woman as a Prop.'" *New York Times*, February 27, 2019. www.nytimes.com.

Kelley, Robin D. G. *Freedom Dreams: The Radical Black Imagination*. Boston: Beacon Press, 2002.

Kendi, Ibram X. *How to Be an Antiracist*. New York: One World, 2019.

Khan, Imran. "The Misandry Bubble." *TheFuturist*. www.singularity2050.com.

Kimmel, Michael. *Angry White Men: American Masculinity at the End of an Era*. New York: Nation Books, 2013.

King, Martin Luther, Jr. "Letter from a Birmingham Jail." April 16, 1963. https://letterfromjail.com.

Klein, Adam. "Slipping Racism into the Mainstream: A Theory of Information Laundering." *Communication Theory* 22, no. 4 (2012): 427–48.

Koblin, John. "After Racist Tweet, Roseanne Barr's Show Is Canceled by ABC." *New York Times*, May 28, 2018. www.nytimes.com.

Krauthammer, Charles. "Not Enough Conversation?" *Time*, December 22, 1997, 22.

Kregelow, Hubert. "There Goes Christmas?!" *American Opinion* (May 1959): 13–16.

Kuhn, Thomas S. *The Structure of Scientific Revolutions*. Chicago: University of Chicago Press, 2012.

Ladenburg, Kenneth James. "Everyday White Supremacy: Fundamental Rhetorical Strategies in Racist Discourse." PhD diss., Arizona State University, 2018.

Lakoff, George. *The All New Don't Think of an Elephant! Know Your Values and Frame the Debate*. White River Junction, VT: Chelsea Green, 2014.

Lakoff, George, and Mark Johnson. *Metaphors We Live By*. Chicago: University of Chicago Press, [1980] 2003.

Landsbaum, Claire. "Men's Rights Activists are Finding a New Home with the Alt-Right." *New York Magazine*, December 14, 2016. www.thecut.com.

Lassabe Shepherd, Lauren. *Resistance from the Right: Conservatives and the Campus Wars in Modern America*. Chapel Hill: University of North Carolina Press, 2023.

Lawson, Steven F., and John Hope Franklin. *One America in the 21st Century: The Report of President Bill Clinton's Initiative on Race*. New Haven: Yale University Press, 2008.

Leonardo, Zeus, and Ronald K. Porter. "Pedagogy of Fear: Toward a Fanonian Theory of 'Safety' in Race Dialogue." *Race, Ethnicity, and Education* 13, no. 2 (2010): 139–57.

Limbaugh, Rush H., III. *The Way Things Ought to Be*. New York: Pocket Books, 1992.

Lindsay, James. *Race Marxism: The Truth About Critical Race Theory and Praxis*. Orlando: New Discourses, 2022.

Lipset, Seymour Martin. "The Sources of the 'Radical Right'" In *The New American Right*, edited by Daniel Bell, 166–233. New York: Criterion Books, 1955.

Lipsitz, George. *American Studies in a Moment of Danger*. Minneapolis: University of Minnesota Press, 2001.

Lipsitz, George. *The Possessive Investment in Whiteness: How White People Profit from Identity Politics, Revised and Expanded Edition*. Philadelphia: Temple University Press, 2006.

Lit, Maggie. "University Professors Attack White, Heterosexual, Christian Males for Being 'Privileged.'" *Campus Reform*, November 7, 2014. www.campusreform.org.

Lott, Maxim. "Boston University Prof Flunks 'White Masculinity' in Controversial Tweets." *FoxNews*, May 8, 2015. www.foxnews.com.

Lowndes, Joseph E. *From the New Deal to the New Right: Race and the Southern Origins of Modern Conservatism*. New Haven: Yale University Press, 2008.

Lyons, Matthew N. *Insurgent Supremacists: The U.S. Far Right's Challenge to State and Empire*. Oakland, CA: PM Press, 2018.

Machan, Tibor R. "Leo Strauss: Neoconservative?" *Philosophy Now*, no. 59 (2007). https://philosophynow.org.

Macintyre, Stuart, and Anna Clark. *The History Wars*. Carlton, Australia: Melbourne University Press, 2004.

Mannheim, Karl. *Ideology and Utopia: An Introduction to the Sociology of Knowledge*. Translated by Louis Wirth and Edward Shills. New York: Harcourt, Brace, and World, 1968.

Marron, Dylan. *Conversations with People Who Hate Me: 12 Things I Learned from Talking to Internet Strangers*. New York: Atria Books, 2022.

Martinot, Steve. *The Machinery of Whiteness: Studies in the Structure of Racialization*. Philadelphia: Temple University Press, 2010.

Masters, Hannah L. E. "Red Card on Wage Discrimination: US Soccer Pay Disparity Highlights Inadequacy of the Equal Pay Act."

Vanderbilt Journal of Entertainment & Technology Law 22, no. 4 (2020): 895–922.

"Max Horkheimer on Critical Theory." YouTube video, 00:01:27, August 11, 2011. https://www.youtube.com/watch?v=OBaYo9Qi-wo.

McKinney, Karyn. *Being White: Stories of Race and Racism*. New York: Routledge, 2004.

Meckler, Laura, and Josh Dawset. "Republicans, Spurred by an Unlikely Figure, See Political Promise in Targeting Critical Race Theory." *Washington Post*, June 21, 2021. www.washingtonpost.com.

Melamed, Jodi. *Represent and Destroy: Rationalizing Violence in the New Racial Capitalism*. Minneapolis: University of Minnesota Press, 2011.

Mercieca, Jennifer. *Demagogue for President: The Rhetorical Genius of Donald Trump*. College Station: Texas A&M Press, 2020.

Michaelis, Arno. *My Life After Hate*. Chicago: Life After Hate, 2010.

Miller, Stephen. "Gender Pay Gap Improvement Slowed During the Pandemic: The Pay Gap is Worse for Minority Women and for Women Ages 45 and Older." *HRNews*, March 15, 2022.

Mills, Charles. *The Racial Contract*. Ithaca: Cornell University Press, 1997.

Moi, Toril. "'I Am Not a Feminist But . . .': How Feminism Became the F-Word." *PMLA* 121, no. 5 (2006): 1735–41.

Morrison, Sara. "George Zimmerman's Brother: Trayvon Martin Was 'Angry,' Possibly Growing Marijuana." *The Wrap*, July 16, 2013. www.thewrap.com.

More, Thomas. *Utopia*. Translated by Clarence Miller. New Haven: Yale University Press, 2014.

Moses, Wilson J. *Afrotopia: The Roots of African American Popular History*. Cambridge: Cambridge University Press, 1998.

Moylan, Tom. *Demand the Impossible: Science Fiction and the Utopian Imagination*. New York: Methuen, 1986.

Muñoz, José Esteban. *Cruising Utopia: The Then and There of Queer Futurity*. New York: New York University Press, 2009.

Nadler, Anthony, and A. J. Bauer, eds. *News on the Right: Studying Conservative News Culture*. Oxford: Oxford University Press, 2019.

Nadler, Anthony, and Doron Taussig. "The Deep Story Beneath the Big Lie." *Los Angeles Review of Books*, August 16, 2023. https://lareviewofbooks.org.

Nagle, Angela. *Kill All Normies: The Online Culture Wars from Tumblr and 4chan to the Alt-right and Trump*. Washington, DC: Zero Books, 2017.

Nericcio, William Anthony. *Tex[t]-Mex: Seductive Hallucinations of the "Mexican" in America*. Austin: University of Texas Press, 2007.

News Hounds. "Bill O'Reilly: Removing Christian Content From 'A Charlie Brown Christmas' Is Terrorism!" *CrooksAndLiars*, December 17, 2015. http://crooksandliars.com.

Nguyen, Tina. "A Big Chunk of Trump's 1776 Report Appears Lifted from an Author's Prior Work." *Politico*, January 19, 2021. www.politico.com.

Noel, Hannah. *Deflective Whiteness: Coopting Black and Latinx Identity Politics*. Columbus: Ohio State University Press, 2022.

Novick, Peter. *That Noble Dream: The "Objectivity Question" and the American Historical Profession*. Cambridge: Cambridge University Press, 1988.

Oakes, Anna. "White Nationalists Target ASU." *Watauga Democrat*, April 16, 2015. www.wataugademocrat.com.

The Objective. "A More Specific Letter on Justice and Open Debate." July 10, 2020. https://objectivejournalism.org.

Olson, Joel. *The Abolition of White Democracy*. Minneapolis: University of Minnesota Press, 2004.

Oluo, Ijeoma. *So You Want to Talk About Race*. New York: Seal Press, 2019.

Opsahl, Robin. "House Passes Resolution Rebuking Steve King after Comments on White Supremacy, Nationalism." *Des Moines Register*, January 15, 2019. www.desmoinesregister.com.

Oreskes, Naomi, and Erik M. Conway. "Challenging Knowledge: How Climate Science Became a Victim of the Cold War." In *Agnotology: The Making and Unmaking of Ignorance*, edited by Robert N. Proctor and Londa Schiebinger, 55–89. Stanford: Stanford University Press, 2008.

O'Reilly, Bill. "War on Christmas Won by the Good Guys, but Insurgents Remain." Fox News, December 15, 2016. www.foxnews.com.

Padilla, Genaro. *My History, Not Yours: The Formation of Mexican American Autobiography*. Madison: University of Wisconsin Press, 1993.

"Paula Deen's First Apology Video." YouTube video, 00:00:39, June 21, 2013. https://www.youtube.com/watch?v=yOsrrJdkp94.

"Paula Deen." YouTube video, 00:01:56, June 21, 2013. https://www.youtube.com/watch?v=jkwbyNKC9Kg&feature=emb_err_watch_on_yt.

Peck, Reece. *Fox Populism: Branding Conservatism as Working Class*. Cambridge: Cambridge University Press, 2019.

Pierce, William Luther [Andrew MacDonald]. *The Turner Diaries*. Hillsboro, WV: National Vanguard Books, 1978.

Piercy, Marge. *Woman on the Edge of Time*. New York: Ballantine Books, 1997.

Planas, Roque. "Fox News Raises Alarm Over College Course About Race." *Huffington Post*, January 24, 2015. www.huffpost.com.

Pluckrose, Helen, and James Lindsay. *Cynical Theories: How Activist Scholarship Made Everything About Race, Gender, and Identity— and Why This Harms Everybody*. Durham, NC: Pitchstone Publishing, 2020.

Polletta, Francesca, and Jessica Callahan. "Deep Stories, Nostalgia Narratives, and Fake News: Storytelling in the Trump Era." *American Journal of Cultural Sociology* 5 (2017): 392–408.

Poppelwell-Scevak, Claire. "The Gender Pay Gap: How FIFA Dropped the Ball." *International Journal of Constitutional Law* 20, no. 1 (2022): 325–50.

Portolano, Marlana. "The Rhetorical Function of Utopia: An Exploration of the Concept of Utopia in Rhetorical Theory." *Utopian Studies* 23, no, 2 (2012): 113–41.

The President's Advisory 1776 Commission. "The 1776 Report." trumpwhitehouse.archives.gov. January 18, 2021.

Proctor, Robert N. "Agnotology: A Missing Term to Describe the Cultural Production of Ignorance (and Its Study)." In *Agnotology: The Making and Unmaking of Ignorance*, edited by Robert N. Proctor and Londa Schiebinger, 1–33. Stanford: Stanford University Press, 2008.

Puar, Jasbir K. *Terrorist Assemblages: Homonationalism in Queer Times*. Durham, NC: Duke University Press, 2007.

Pulitzer Center. "The 1619 Project Curriculum." https://pulitzercenter.org.

Purdue Online Writing Lab. "Stasis Theory." https://owl.purdue.edu.

Rancière, Jacques. *The Politics of Aesthetics*. Edited and translated by Gabriel Rockhill. New York: Bloomsbury, 2013.

Ratcliffe, Krista. "In Search of the Unstated: The Enthymeme of/ and Whiteness." *JAC: A Journal of Composition Theory* 27, no. 1–2 (2007): 275–89.

Ratcliffe, Krista. *Rhetorical Listening: Identification, Gender, Whiteness*. Carbondale: Southern Illinois University, 2005.

Reilly, Katie. "Read Hillary Clinton's 'Basket of Deplorables' Remarks About Donald Trump Supporters." *Time*, September 10, 2016. https://time.com.

Roberts-Miller, Patricia. *Fanatical Schemes: Proslavery Rhetoric and the Tragedy of Consensus*. Tuscaloosa: University of Alabama Press, 2009.

Roberts-Miller, Patricia. *Rhetoric and Demagoguery*. Carbondale: Southern Illinois Press, 2019.

Roberts-Miller, Patricia. *Speaking of Race: How to Have Antiracist Conversations that Bring Us Together*. New York: The Experiment, 2021.

Robin, Corey. *The Reactionary Mind: Conservatism from Edmund Burke to Donald Trump*. 2nd ed. Oxford: Oxford University Press, 2018.

Rodger, Elliot. "My Twisted World: The Story of Elliot Rodger." https://archive.org/details/MyTwistedWorld.

Roediger, David R. "On the Defensive: Navigating White Advantage and White Fragility." *Los Angeles Review of Books*, September 6, 2018. https://lareviewofbooks.org.

Roediger, David R. *The Wages of Whiteness: Race and the Making of the American Working Class*. Rev. ed. Haymarket Series. New York: Verso, 2007.

Rogin, Michael Paul. *Ronald Reagan, the Movie: and Other Episodes in Political Demonology*. Berkeley: University of California Press, 1987.

Rufo, Christopher F. "Against Wokeness." *City Journal*, September 15, 2020. www.city-journal.org.

Rufo, Christopher F. "Cult Programming in Seattle." *City Journal*, July 8, 2020. www.city-journal.org.

Rufo, Christopher F. "Defending American Values, and History." *City Journal*, September 18, 2020. www.city-journal.org.

Rufo, Christopher F. "Disney is Interested in Your Kids." *City Journal*, March 29, 2022. www.city-journal.org.

Rufo, Christopher F. "Disney's Child Predator Problem." *City Journal*, March 30, 2022. www.city-journal.org.

Rufo, Christopher. "No Enemies to the Right?" *Christopher F. Rufo (blog)*, September 23, 2023. https://christopherrufo.com.

Rufo, Christopher F. "Separate but Equal." *Christopher F. Rufo (blog)*, July 29, 2020. https://christopherrufo.com.

Rufo, Christopher F. "'White Fragility' Comes to Washington." *City Journal*, July 17, 2020. www.city-journal.org.

Rukstuhl, Laney. "White Nationalist Group 'Defends' White Privilege." *The Appalachian*, April 15, 2015. https://theappalachianonline.com.

Saad, Layla. *Me and White Supremacy: Combat Racism, Change the World, and Become a Good Ancestor*. Naperville: Sourcebooks, 2020.

Sandoval, Chela. *Methodology of the Oppressed*. Minneapolis: University of Minnesota Press, 2000.

Schallhorn, Kaitlyn. "App State Dorm Bulletin Board Shames 'Privileged' Students." *Campus Reform*, March 16, 2015. www.campusreform.org.

Schiffrin, Anya. "Fighting Disinformation in the 1930s: Clyde Miller and the Institute for Propaganda Analysis." *International Journal of Communication* 16 (2022): 3715–41.

Schneider, Mike, and Curt Anderson. "Family of Slain Teen Goes on Defensive Victim was on Suspension for Marijuana at Time of Fatal Shooting by Neighborhood Watchman, Who Says He was the One Attacked. Trayvon Martin." *St. Louis Post-Dispatch* (Missouri), March 27, 2012. www.stltoday.com.

Schreiner, Bruce. "GOP Candidates Tread Cautiously on Gun Issues in Kentucky." *Associated Press International*, April 14, 2023. https://apnews.com.

Shackel, Nicholas. "The Vacuity of Postmodernist Methodology." *Metaphilosophy* 36, no. 3 (2005): 295–320.

Shapiro, Ben. *How to Debate Leftists and Destroy Them: 11 Rules for Winning the Argument*. Sherman Oaks: David Horowitz Freedom Center, 2014.

Shapiro, Ben. *True Allegiance*. Franklin, TN: Post Hill Press, 2016.

Shepard, Paul. "Guinier Confronts Race Issue at Convention." *Plain Dealer*, July 14, 1993: 7A.

Shorten, Richard. "Reactionary Rhetoric Reconsidered." *Journal of Political Ideologies* 20, no. 2 (2015): 179–200.

Skinnell, Ryan, ed. *Faking the News: What Rhetoric Can Teach Us About Donald J. Trump*. Exeter: Imprint Academic, 2018.

Smith, Andrea. "Heteropatriarchy and the Three Pillars of White Supremacy: Rethinking Women of Color Organizing." In *Color of Violence: The INCITE! Anthology*, by INCITE! Women of Color Against Violence, 66–73. Boston: South End Press, 2006.

Smooth, Jay. "How I Learned to Stop Worrying and Love Discussing Race." YouTube video, TEDx Talk given by Jay Smooth, 00:11:56, November 15, 2011, https://www.youtube.com/watch?v=MbdxeFcQtaU.

Spencer, Leland G. "*National Geograhic*'s Racial Apology: A Half-Performative." *Western Journal of Communication* 85, no. 5 (2021): 549–67.

SPLC. "Dylann Roof Murdered Nine People Because of a Lie About 'Black-on-White Crime.'" June 15, 2018. www.splcenter.org.

Stevens, Michael. "Fear Cattle Not Wonderful Petroleum." *Daily Gamecock*, March 21, 2007.

Sullivan, Shannon. *Good White People: The Problem with Middle-Class White Anti-Racism*, Albany: SUNY Press, 2014.

Susman, Warren I. "History and the American Intellectual: Uses of a Usable Past." In *Locating American Studies: The Evolution of a Discipline*, 17–42. Edited by Lucy Maddox. Baltimore: Johns Hopkins University Press, 1999.

Taviss Thompson, Irene. *Culture Wars and Enduring American Dilemmas*. Ann Arbor: University of Michigan Press, 2010.

Taylor, Sarah. "Rush Limbaugh: 'Feminazis' to Blame for Confusion of Traditional Gender Roles." *The Blaze*, July 17, 2017. https://www.theblaze.com.

"Texas Politicians Are Slow to Act on Both Guns and Mental Health." NPR, May 15, 2023. www.npr.org.

Thompson, Catherine. "How the Great White Freakout Just Got Unleashed at Another University." *Talking Points Memo*, April 24, 2015. https://talkingpointsmemo.com.

Trouillot, Michel-Rolph. *Silencing the Past: Power and the Production of History*. Boston: Beacon Press, 1995.

Twain, Mark. *Adventures of Huckleberry Finn*. London: Penguin, [1884] 2009.

Ura, Alexa. "A Racist Manifesto and a Shooter Terrorize Hispanics in El Paso and Beyond." *Texas Tribune*, August 5, 2019. https://www.texastribune.org.

VDARE.com. "About." https://vdare.com.

Ventura, Patricia, and Edward Chan. *American Neoliberal Culture and White Power*. Berkeley: University of California Press, 2023.

Wallace-Wells, Benjamin. "How a Conservative Activist Invented the Conflict Over Critical Race Theory." *New Yorker*, June 18, 2021. https://www.newyorker.com.

Washington, Mary Helen. "Disturbing the Peace: What Happens to American Studies If You Put African American Studies at the Center?" Presidential Address to the American Studies Association, October 29, 1997. *American Quarterly* 50, no. 1 (1998) 1–23.

Warner, Michael. *Publics and Counterpublics*. New York: Zone Books, 2002.

Wemple, Erik. "Fox New Seeks Refuge in Bothsidesism." *Washington Post*, May 21, 2021. www.washingtonpost.com.

White, Hayden. *Metahistory: The Historical Imagination in Nineteenth Century Europe*. Baltimore: Johns Hopkins University Press, 1973.

Whitten, Sarah. "Is Starbucks Waging 'War on Christmas'? Red Cup Stirs Controversy." *NBC News*, November 10, 2015. https://www.nbcnews.com.

Wiedeman, Reeves. "The Duke Lacrosse Scandal and the Birth of the Alt-Right." *New York Magazine*, April 14, 2017. http://nymag.com.

Will, George F. "Sympathy for Guinier." *Newsweek*, June 14, 1993. www.newsweek.com.

Williams, Patricia. *The Alchemy of Race and Rights: Diary of a Law Professor*. Cambridge, MA: Harvard University Press, 1991.

Wilson. "Texas Ends 'The War on Christmas.'" *Glenn Beck*, November 26, 2013. www.glennbeck.com.

Winant, Howard. *The New Politics of Race: Globalism, Difference, and Justice*. Minneapolis: University of Minnesota Press, 2004.

Wise, Alana. "Trump Announces 'Patriotic Education' Commission, A Largely Political Move." NPR, September 17, 2020. https://www.npr.org.

Wise, Gene. *American Historical Explanations: A Strategy for Grounded Inquiry*. Minneapolis: University of Minnesota Press, 1980.

Woods, Heather Suzanne, and Leslie A. Hahner. *Make America Meme Again: The Rhetoric of the Alt-Right*. New York: Peter Lang, 2019.

Woodward, Calvin, and Seth Borenstein. "Cow Farts are Issue in Green New Deal." *St. Louis Post-Dispatch*, April 29, 2019.

Yancy, George. *Backlash: What Happens When We Talk Honestly About Racism in America*. Lanham, MD: Rowman Littlefield Publishers, 2018.

Yancy, George. *Look, A White! Philosophical Essays on Whiteness*. Philadelphia: Temple University Press, 2012.

Yang, Jeff "The Problem with 'The Letter.'" *CNN*, July 10, 2020. www.cnn.com.

Zak, Dan. "Whataboutism: The Cold War Tactic, Thawed by Putin, is Brandished by Donald Trump: What About It?" *Washington Post*, August 17, 2017. www.washingtonpost.com.

Zelizer, Julian E. "Reflections: Rethinking the History of American Conservatism." *Reviews in American History* 38, no. 2 (June 2010): 367–92.

INDEX

"The 1619 Project." *See* Hannah-Jones, Nikole
The 1776 Commission, 89
"The 1776 Report," 89–92, 103, 105, 107–108, 111, 113, 131

Adorno, Theodor W., 103
Adventures of Huckleberry Finn, 191–192
Aggrieved entitlement, 26, 65–67, 80–81, 85–86, 93, 173, 188, 191
Algorithmic amplification, 182
Alien Nation. *See* Brimelow, Peter
All Lives Matter, 8, 10, 42, 151, 203
Allen, Danielle, 176–177
Ally and allyship, 44–46, 217–218n40
Alt-right, 41, 46, 67–68, 98, 185–186, 212n41
Althusser, Louis, 107
American Exceptionalism, 90, 105, 107
Americanism, 129–131,

Antifeminism, 14, 26, 57, 68, 72–73, 81–85, 94, 96–99, 103, 107, 109–114, 140–141, 155, 157
Antiracism, 15, 20–21, 38, 43, 45, 89, 121, 124, 130, 134–135, 142, 184, 217–218n40
Antiracist guidebooks, 20–22
Apologia, 37, 49. *See also* Apology
Apology, 37, 48–52, 57
Appalachian State University privilege controversy, 67, 73–77
Asymptote (as a model for justice), 217–218n40

Backlash, 64, 67
Bad faith argumentation, 44, 133, 148, 152, 162, 174–175, 182, 188
Bakke, Allan, 81, 83, 189
Barr, Roseanne, 33–34
Bauer, A.J., 205, 237n20
Belonging, 24, 40, 82, 105
Berlant, Lauren, 19
Biden, Joe, 89, 186–187
Binary model, 32, 42–44, 46–48, 52, 55, 175, 192

259

Black Lives Matter, 7–8, 21, 42, 44, 89, 145, 152, 203
Blaming a convenient cause, 146–147, 149–153
The Blaze, 60, 73
Bloch, Ernst, 101, 103–104
Blue Lives Matter, 42, 150, 152
Bly, Robert, 93–95, 99, 107, 109–111, 114
Boghossian, Peter, 120
Bolick, Clint, 2
Bonilla-Silva, Eduardo, 157, 187
Boone, Willington, 153
Boorstein, Michelle, 53, 55
Bothsidesism, 146–153, 202
Brimelow, Peter, 59, 95–98, 107–109, 111, 219–220n5, 226n31
Bryant, Anita, 116, 141
Buchanan, Patrick, 59
Burden-Stelley, Charisse, 126

Calhoun, John C., 91
Callahan, Jessica, 82
Campus Reform, 73–76, 81
Carlson, Tucker, 47, 188
Cernovich, Mike, 99
Chan, Edward, 102
Christian right, 12, 14, 53, 59–60, 63–64, 73, 74, 76, 78, 78, 85–86, 194
Civil Rights Act (1964), 77, 143, 159
Clinton, Bill, 2–6, 20
Clinton, Hillary, 137, 155, 185–86
Clinton's Advisory Board on Race: One America Commission, 2–5, 20
Cohen, Michael, 33
The College Fix, 73
Common sense (as a form of hegemony), 138–139, 141. *See also* Overton Window

Complex personhood, 45
Conversation (as persuasion), 175–176, 178, 181, 192, 199
Counternarratives, 194–195
Crenshaw, Kimberlé, 10, 126, 232n52
Critical Race Theory (CRT), 116–129, 131–135, 137–138, 140–142, 194
Critical whiteness studies, 128, 140, 188
Cruel Optimism, 2, 19–20, 174, 178, 180, 199
Crusius, Patrick Wood, 85
Culture wars, 76, 89–90, 104, 120–121, 141, 196–197, 225n7
Cummings, Elijah, 34, 39
Cunning projection, 65–66, 141
Cynical Theories (Pluckrose and Lindsay), 120–121

The Daily Caller, 73
Deen, Paula, 33–34, 45, 49–50
Define and disavow, 32–48
Delgado, Richard, 194
Deliberative democracy (civil dialogue), 18–20, 22, 176–178, 180. *See also* National
Demagoguery, 22, 177
DeSantis, Ron, 116
Discursive and ideological realm, 78–80, 85
Discursive terrain, 134, 149–151, 199
Dobbs, Lou, 59
Dog whistle, 215n17, 217n39, 227n48
Donovan, Jack, 98–100, 107, 109–111, 113
Doyle, Richard F., 67, 69–73, 77, 79, 81–83, 85

DuBois, W. E. B., 6, 12, 80, 128
Duke Lacrosse rape case, 68
Dykstra, Alan, 147–148
Dystopia, 82, 93, 95–97, 99, 102, 107, 110, 112. *See also* Utopia

Edsall, Thomas, 64
Enthymeme, 40, 47
Equal Pay Act, 159
Extreme and extremism, 37, 40–48, 55–56, 84, 86, 104, 117–142, 173–174, 184

Faludi, Susan, 64
Farrell, Warren, 69, 73, 85, 221n28, 225n23
Fédération Internationale de Football Association (FIFA), 161–167
Feminazi, 59, 86, 116, 137, 140–141
Feminism: Liberal, 137; Radical, 80, 86, 137
Finely, Allysia, 161–165
Fisher, Abigail, 81, 83, 189
Floyd, George, 1
Folk theory: of inequality, 32, 35, 52, 135, 168, 192, 198; of racism, 36–41, 43–48, 51, 125, 129, 184, 187; of sexism, 56–57, 156
Fox News, 47, 60, 73–74, 76–78, 81, 85, 148, 202
Frames and counterframes, 194–195
Frankfurt School, 119, 122, 124–125
Franklin, John Hope, 3–4, 20

Gage, John Angelo, 77
Gamergate, 84
Garner, Eric, 38–39

Gender pay gap, 145, 147, 153–167, 170–171
Gordon, Avery, 45, 170
Gramsci, Antonio, 120, 138, 228n67
Great Replacement Theory, 30–31
Greszler, Rachel, 161–167
Grooming, 116
Guinier, Lani, 2, 5–6

Hall, Stuart, 120, 138
Hannah-Jones, 88–90, 102, 105
Hannah-Jones, Nikole, 88, 102, 105
Harris, Kamala, 186–187
Harris, Sam, 53–57
Hasselbeck, Elisabeth, 59, 76
Hayek, Friedrich, 157
Hegel, Georg Wilhelm Friedrich, 122, 128
Herbert, Mike, 75–76
Heritage Foundation, 161
Hill, Jane, 36–37, 48
Hirschman, Albert, 11
Hofstadter, Richard, 64, 66
Horkheimer, Max, 124–125
Horowitz, David, 159
Humanities education, 196–198
Hymowitz, Kay, 153–162, 165–167

Identity Evropa, 223n68
Identity, fixed notions of 11, 32, 41, 44, 46, 48, 57, 184–185, 187 210–211n23, 216n24, 217–218n40
Ideology, 13, 16, 18–19, 47–48, 65, 106–107, 113, 153, 181, 188–189, 197
Imagined community, 40, 82, 196, 229–230n78
Information laundering, 217n39

Institute for Propaganda Analysis, 188
Interpellation, 40, 65, 82, 107, 113, 175, 196, 228n65
Intersectionality, 126, 130, 210n23, 219n52
Iron John. See Bly, Robert

January 6, 2021, Insurrection, 89, 148

Kendi, Ibram X., 16, 21
Khan, Imran, 69, 96–99, 107, 109–111, 113–114
Kimmel, Michael, 65, 80, 111
King, Jr., Martin Luther, xii, 16, 18, 89, 91, 127, 141, 201
King, Steve, 30–34, 40–41, 45, 51–52, 56, 134, 193
Krauthammer, Charles, 5

Label Opponents Extreme, 116–119
Ladenburg, Kenneth, 46, 149–150, 153
Lakoff, George, 194
"Letter from a Birmingham Jail." *See* King Jr., Martin Luther
"A Letter on Justice and Open Debate", 16–17
Liberal individualism, 156–158, 167
Lilly Ledbetter Act, 155
Limbaugh, Rush, 59, 116, 137, 141
Lindsay, James, 120–141, 175, 182
Lipset, Seymor Martin, 66
Lipsitz, George, 24, 82
Littler, Laurel, 73, 75–77
Lopenzina, Drew, xi, xiii, 206
Lowndes, Joseph, 64

Mainstream, 13–14, 26, 32, 42–43, 45–48, 59, 64, 68, 73, 77, 82, 85–86, 118, 121, 135–137, 142
Make America Great Again, 86
Mannheim, Karl, 106
Manning Up. See Hymowitz, Kay
Marcuse, Herbert, 103, 121, 124
Market forces, 154, 163–167
Martinot, Steve, 38
Marx, Karl, 122
Marxism, 118, 121, 123–130
Meadows, Mark, 33–34
#MeToo, 7–8, 155, 203
Men's Rights Antifeminism, 94, 96, 98, 103, 111–114, 155
Men's Rights Movement, 68–69, 97
Miller, Clyde, 188
Miller, Stephen, 68
"The Misandry Bubble." *See* Khan, Imran
Misdirection, 145–172
Misinformation and disinformation, 148, 188
Monocausal, 147, 154, 156, 168–171
Moral panic, 37, 48, 51, 73, 139–140, 182
More, Sir Thomas, 101, 103
Motte and bailey, 132–133, 232–233n57
Multicausal, 156, 169, 171
Multicultural dystopia, 102
Multifocal rupture, 9–10, 12, 63, 66

Nadler, Anthony, 85, 205
Nagle, Angela, 64, 212n41
National Conversation on Race, 1–7, 20–21, 23: National Conversations on justice

issues more broadly, 25, 27, 174–199; Underside of national conversations, 6, 21, 25. *See also* "Black Lives Matter;" #MeToo, "All Lives Matter;" and #NotAllMen
National Youth Front, 74, 76–77, 85
Nativism, 31, 41, 95–96
Negative thinking, 124–125
Neoconservatism, 90
Noel, Hannah, 42, 206
Normal and normalcy, 129–131, 135, 138, 187, 204
Nostalgia, 27, 105, 193
#NotAllMen, 8, 10, 203

O'Reilly, Bill, 59–60, 65
O'Shea, Alan, 138
One America Dialogue Guide, 20
"One America in the 21st Century," 4
Oppression Olympics, 45, 79
Other, 24, 36, 41–48, 51, 55–57, 125, 134, 142, 173–174, 184, 186–187
Outside agitators, xii–xiii
Overton Window, 120, 135–143, 217n39
Overton, Joseph, 138

Patton, Lynne, 33, 39, 215n16
People's Universities, xi
Pierce, William Luther (Andrew MacDonald), 102, 127
Pleasure, 24, 82
Pluckrose, Hellen, 120
Polletta, Francesca, 82
Portolano, Marlana, 103–104, 107
Privilege, 12, 59, 65, 67, 73–77, 80–81, 83, 85, 86, 188, 217n33, 217–218n40, 220n11

Pro-Palestinian/Anti-Genocide/ Anti-Zionism Protests, xi–xii
Psychoaffective realm, 80–82, 84
Putin, Vladimir, 148

Quinn, Zoë, 84

Race Marxism. See Lindsay, James
Racial break, 9. *See also* multifocal rupture
Racism, Critical theory of 37–39. *See also* folk theory
Rancière, Jacques, 10, 120, 139
The Rape of the Male. See Doyle, Richard F.
Rapinoe, Megan, 160
Ratcliffe, Krista, 177, 206
Reactionary, 11–12
Reactionary alignment and coalitions, 13–14, 61, 64, 68, 98, 110, 112, 114, 157
Reactionary entrenchment, 5, 8, 159
Reactionary guidebooks, 21–24
Reactionary utopia, 105, 108, 228n60
Reasonability and moderation (claims to), 117–119, 121, 127–129, 131–142
Reconquista (Hispanic Invasion), 59, 85
Roberts-Miller, Patricia, 21–22, 24, 65–66, 149–150, 177–178, 188
Rodger, Elliot, 84–85
Roediger, David, 15, 18, 206
Rogin, Michael, 64
Roof, Dylann, 84–85
Rousseau, Jean-Jacques, 122
Rufo, Christopher, 116–121, 132, 140–141, 175, 182

Sandoval, Chela, 181, 198
Sarkeesian, Anita, 84
Schallhorn, Kaitlyn, 76
Shackel, Nicholas, 132
Shapiro, Ben, 22–24, 102,
Shorten, Richard, 11
Smooth, Jay, 183–184
Sociopolitical realm, 83–84
Spencer, Richard, 68
Starbucks, 60, 78
Stasis: shifting 151–153, 165–166; definition of, 146, 149; diffusion, 153, 165
Status anxiety, 66
Stefancic, Jean, 194
Sullivan, Shannon, 38

Taussig, Doron, 85
Terrain of inequality, 10–11, 48, 52, 57, 199
Tlaib, Rashida, 33–34
Triad model, 43–44, 46–48, 55, 129, 136
Trump, Donald, 17, 21, 33, 37, 89, 92–93, 142, 147, 185–186
Tu Quoque fallacy, 148, 152
The Turner Diaries, 102, 127
Turning Point USA (TPUSA), 59

Unite the Right Rally, 37, 223n68
United States Men's National Soccer Team (USMNT), 160
United States Soccer Federation (USSF), 154, 159–167, 170

United States Women's National Soccer Team (USWNT), 154, 159–161
Usable past, 90, 95, 100, 104–105, 111
Utopia. *See* More, Thomas
Utopia: critical function of, 103; rhetorical function of, 103–104; as a place, 101; as a temporal dimension, 101

V-Dare, 95
Vázquez, David, 171, 206

Wages (public and psychological), 12, 66, 80–81
War of position, 104
War on Christmas, 59–61, 79, 194
Warner, Michael, 179
The Way of Men. *See* Donovan, Jack
Weaponized victimhood, 59–66. *See also* aggrieved entitlement
Wemple, Erik, 148
Western Civilization, 30, 122, 124–125, 130, 138, 193
Whataboutism, 146–153, 201
White genocide, 59, 76, 81, 137
Will, George, 2
Williams, Patricia, 45, 170
Winant, Howard, 9–10
Wu, Brianna, 84

Yancy, George, 74, 184–185, 187, 217–218n40, 233n62

Zak, Dan, 147
Zelizer, Julian, 64

ABOUT THE AUTHOR

LEE BEBOUT is Professor of English at Arizona State University. Bebout teaches about and researches the areas of race, social justice, and political culture. He is also the author of *Whiteness on the Border: Mapping the US Racial Imagination in Brown and White* and *Mythohistorical Interventions: The Chicano Movement and Its Legacies* as well as coeditor of *Teaching with Tension: Race, Resistance, and Reality in the Classroom.*

www.ingramcontent.com/pod-product-compliance
Lightning Source LLC
Chambersburg PA
CBHW020400080526
44584CB00014B/1099